Philosophy in World Perspective

David A. Dilworth

Philosophy in World Perspective

A Comparative Hermeneutic of the Major Theories

YALE UNIVERSITY PRESS *New Haven and London*

To Walter Watson

Published with assistance from the Kingsley Trust Association Publication Fund established by the Scroll and Key Society of Yale College.

Set in Palatino type
by The Composing Room of Michigan, Inc.
Printed in the United States of America
by Vail-Ballou Press, Binghamton, New York.

Library of Congress Cataloging-in-Publication Data
Dilworth, David A., 1934–
Philosophy in world perspective.
Bibliography: p.
Includes index.
1. Philosophy, Comparative. 2. Hermeneutics.
3. Religions. I. Title.
B799.D54 1989 109 88–28035
ISBN 0–300–04357–0 (cloth)
0–300–05126–3 (pbk.)

The paper in this book meets the guidelines for permanence and durability of the Committee on Production Guidelines for Book Longevity of the Council on Library Resources.

10 9 8 7 6 5 4 3 2

Contents

Acknowledgments

This book is the result of an intellectual odyssey over many years, and through several of the world's cultures, in pursuit of the principles of the philosophical and religious classics. I like to think that I began this journey in my college years when, as a classics major under excellent teachers, I read the Iliad and the Odyssey, the works of Aeschylus, Sophocles, and Euripides, and half of the Platonic corpus. The study of Plato naturally led me back to the Pre-Socratics, and forward to Aristotle and Plotinus, and drew me to philosophy. At a later point I was essentially to repeat this experience by embarking on years of study of Chinese and Japanese and the originary paradigms of Asian thought.

Among my most influential teachers were Herbert Musurillo and Edmund Cuffe, who imparted to me something of their appreciation of the classics of Greek and Roman antiquity and of the European literary traditions, and Gerald McCool and Robert Johann in philosophy. From the former I gained, I think, a better appreciation of Plato, Aristotle, the Stoics, and Plotinus, and from the latter a certain fondness for systematic speculation.

Now, years later, the process of putting this book into its final form has afforded me an opportunity to reminisce further on the stages of my education. Indeed, over the past several years I have sought consciously to recall the classes and conversations of some of my graduate school teachers; and I continue to do so. Although these are composite memories, I think I have succeeded to some extent in revisiting those pedagogical settings, while rethinking their substantive lessons.

Prominent among my graduate school memories are the classes of Dietrich von Hildebrand, Quentin Lauer, Robert Pollack, and John McDermott from my Fordham University days, and of Loretta Pan, Charles Lo, Wing-tsit Chan, William Theodore de Bary, Donald Keene, Arthur Tiedemann, Yoshito Hakeda, and Philip Yampolsky from my years at Columbia University.

I have profited enormously from my twenty years' participation in the Columbia faculty seminars on Oriental thought and religion and on Neo-Confucian studies. In my judgment, the intellectual and moral leadership of William Theodore de Bary in these circles has been very significant. Over as many years, the diverse intellectual styles in the philosophy and religious studies departments at the State University of New York at Stony Brook have provided a continuous context of collegial exchange. I was twice visiting professor in the philosophy department at the University of Hawaii at Manoa, Honolulu. My book is an attempt to rethink these experiences, too.

Limiting myself to those Stony Brook colleagues who have directly stimulated the systematic reflections of this book, I must cite Justus Buchler, Harold Zyskind, Robert Sternfeld, Robert Neville, Thomas Altizer, and Edward Marcotte. In immediate retrospect, I owe the largest debt of gratitude to Walter Watson, whose pioneering work in the architectonics of meaning provided the springboard for my comparative hermeneutic of the world's philosophical and religious classics. I have sought to extend his thoughts in my own way, but my conclusions have grown out of a constant dialogue with Walter Watson on the principles of the major philosophers, artists, writers, and musical composers. In all the phases of envisioning and completing this work I have had the special resources of his sagacious judgment and generous encouragement.

In the wider orbit of my professional career I owe thanks to a number of colleagues in the field of modern Japanese philosophy. Prominent among these are the distinguished Kyoto School philosophers Nishitani Keiji, Takeuchi Yoshinori, and Abe Masao, and such scholarly comrades as Robert Wargo, V. H. Viglielmo, Jan Van Bragt, and Stuart Kiang. I have sought to continue our conversations in the pages that follow.

My associations with other circles of colleagues are also directly represented in the hermeneutical judgments of this book. These include, among others, long-standing informational and critical exchanges with Julia Ching, John Berthrong, and Mary Evelyn Tucker in Chinese and Japanese intellectual history; with Edith Wyschograd, Robert Magliola, and Dorothea Olkowski in Continental philosophy; with George Pepper in Jaspers studies; and with Angus Kerr-Lawson in Santayana studies. I have attempted to preserve many of these influences intact in the pages that follow.

Finally, let me thank Jeanne Ferris, my editor at Yale University Press, Emily Boochever, my manuscript editor, and Caroline Murphy, my production editor, for the considerable competence they contributed in bringing this book to press. I also appreciate my daughter Theresa's critical comments on the final drafts of the manuscript.

1

Introduction: Resources for an Intellectual Renaissance Today

Multiple Heritages of World Philosophy

Consummate, perfect perceptions of the world and of human life have been realized in history. Great works of civilization—Aristotle's *Ethics*, Newton's *Principia*, Mozart's *Don Giovanni*, for example—embody these insights. A distinctive feature of such works is their recombinant powers. They are still alive today, providing inspiration for contemporary thought, action, and expression.

The great works of civilization are clearly the products of greater minds, and require greater proficiency in interpretation. Acquiring this proficiency, we can continue to learn from Homer or Sophocles; Plato or Aristotle; Confucius, Lao Tzu, or the Buddha; Murasaki Shikibu or Sei Shōnagon; Dante or Michelangelo; Shakespeare or Goethe; Bach, Mozart, or Beethoven; and other creative geniuses. Nourished by them, we may also be inspired to produce comparable works of achievement that will serve as new resources for our own times and for all times.

I would venture to add that it is such universally esteemed works that really count. These immortal works transcend the vicissitudes of time and circumstance. In the continuity of their influence they form the real bonds of our common humanity.

Mozart, for example, has been called the musical genius of a millennium. Such a statement goes well beyond personal preference; it purports to define human accomplishment according to several historical criteria. The author of this judgment, Wolfgang Hildesheimer, has this to say about genius itself:

> The concept originated in the eighteenth century and has become a questionable one. Indeed, we cannot call any of our contemporaries by this term. Not only do we lack the necessary distance from the

> individual, but we also cannot adequately define the concept in terms of works that are created as we look on. We are dependent on models. . . . But let us retain the concept. The reader knows who is meant: the rare executor of enduring high achievement, independent of social conditions, uncomprehended by sociology and anthropology, recognized but apparently insufficiently comprehended by psychology; the executor of works that have contributed to our own formation and without which we cannot conceive our own existence. I speak of the creative genius of the past.[1]

It is well worth pondering the pedagogical implications of this passage. A list of such geniuses of higher civilization would include, among others, Homer, Confucius, Plato, Aristotle, Shakespeare, Newton, Mozart, and Van Gogh. Any set of such judgments will confirm the proposition that it is the great works of recognized geniuses that form our vital resources.

I will enlarge on this theme in various ways. A distinctive feature of our own times is that we command unprecedented access to various cultural heritages, as these are becoming available to us through solid advances in learning, translations of foreign texts, the technologies of travel, and other innovations. We are as much at home today with the aesthetic sensibilities of Chinese landscape paintings or Zen gardens as with the musical masterpieces of Bach or Mozart. We meet Asians everyday who are Christians or Marxists, and Westerners who live their lives according to the codes of Confucius or the Buddha. Indeed, we know more today about the Taoist paintings or Zen gardens, and the compositions of Bach and Mozart, than the people who lived at the time these works were created. Similarly, we have a more sophisticated understanding of the works of Homer, Plato, Aristotle, Confucius, Lao Tzu, Chu Hsi, Dōgen, and many others than all previous ages combined.

Extrapolating from this evidence, we can forecast that future ages of mankind will achieve even greater insight into our many cultural traditions. Here I am making two points. First, the generations to come will undoubtedly develop even more sophisticated approaches to past works of human genius. Second, they will produce other geniuses, whose own works will stand the test of time in company with the great accomplishments of the past. The work of contemporary hermeneutics should therefore gather our present resources and stimulate new possibilities of thought, action, and expression.

The program of this book flows from this consideration of the enduring worth of the immortal works, their interrelationships, and the possibilities of the future. I limit myself in the main to the observation of philosophical forms. I hold, on the one hand, that there is nothing sacred in any of the past philosophical (or religious) systems in themselves—nothing that renders them impervious to reinterpretation. On the other hand, I maintain that it is foolish to think one can refute or even deconstruct any of the great philosophical texts. That would undermine the ground on which we now stand. Rather, the task must be to repossess—to remember and to re-appreciate—past philosophical accomplishments as they relate to present and future developments in philosophy.

Academic philosophy, I trust, will make a contribution to such an instauration in our own times. The emergence of a sense of world history and world philosophy among professional scholars is already a trend of considerable importance. The number of international conferences under such a rubric in recent decades and the increasing number of scholarly publications in such fields as comparative politics and religion give us some indication of the growing interest in this phenomenon. At the grass roots level, innumerable smaller conferences and colloquia have been focusing on similar themes.

Such scholarly currents reflect the convergence of modern and premodern, Eastern and Western civilizations in our times. Philosophy has become global, just as human life has been transformed by worldwide political, economic, and cultural forces. Philosophers have already begun reflecting upon the intercultural transformations that are shaping their lives. Conversely, philosophical definitions elucidate and sometimes determine the transformation of civilization that is taking place.

The history of ideas is replete with precedents of cultural cross-fertilization and attendant reconstruction of philosophical traditions. We need only think of the reclamation of the pre-Socratic schools of thought in the Athenian, Hellenistic, and Roman worldviews; or of the restoration of the latter by the Neoplatonists of the third and fourth centuries A.D.; or again of the confluence of Aristotelian, Arabic, and Neoplatonic traditions in the thirteenth century. The translation of Indian Buddhist sutras into Chinese in the fourth century A.D. presents a case of West-East philosophical interaction, with far-reaching effects for Korea and Japan as well. Japanese culture is itself a showcase of global philosophical interchanges, first in its assimilation of Indian and Chinese traditions and later in its broadly based syncretism of Western ideas and institutions.

Although harder to estimate at close quarters, the reenactive character of philosophical activity is evident in this century as well. Santayana, for example, was a remarkably cosmopolitan, supranational, and supracultural thinker. Freud was another. What is valuable about Santayana's or Freud's writings is that they convey a sense of civilization that takes us back to the worldviews of the Greek tragedians and pre-Socratic philosophers and yet range even more widely among the forms of ancient and modern life.

Before Freud, Nietzsche and Schopenhauer also produced texts that bring Hinduism, Buddhism, and other Eastern religions into a common purview of discussion with classical Greek, Christian, and other Western philosophies and religions. Hegel traces the movement of philosophy from East to West, for reasons connected with the dialectical movement of his thought. Controversial though this may be in the perspective of other systems, his writings also reflect the kind of reconstructive classicism to which I am alluding here.

Precedents for Hegel's enlarged vision derive from the sense of "world" that emerged with the eighteenth-century philosophers, if not from the Renaissance, which introduced a generic sense of "new worlds" in geographical explorations, scientific discoveries, and artistic and philosophical pursuits. But in broader perspective, the Renaissance and Enlightenment mapped new worlds while repossessing the old worlds of classical antiquity and the Far East.

Leibniz's search for a "universal characteristic," for example, was a feature of his comprehensive cast of mind. He pursued this theme in his quest for what he called "the principle of all principles," which would reconcile the paradigms of the ancient, medieval, and modern philosophers, scientists, alchemists, and cabalists. His text covers a multidimensioned world, including that of the Chinese, interpreted by claims of universally valid principles of philosophy.

This sense of the recurrence and connectedness of foundational ideas is again conspicuous in the "principles of nature" celebrated during the Enlightenment. Its background can be traced to the physics of Newton and the political theory of Locke, both of whom looked to the Bible and the ancient Greek philosophers (notably the Epicureans) for first principles. In the eighteenth century Hume also turned to the ancients for the precedents of modern life.[2]

Kant's work provides us with other dimensions of the concepts of worlds and worldviews I am exploring here. In response to the developments of post-Renaissance science and philosophy, Kant's first *Critique* purported to map universal forms of sensibility, of intellectual judgment, and of the ideas of pure reason. His second *Critique* extended the concept of universality to a realm of ends as a moral universe shared by all rational beings. His third *Critique* took as its theme the transcendental subjective validity of our aesthetic and teleological judgments.

Thus Kant contributed another, explicitly theoretical focus to the subject of this work. This was his conception of philosophy itself—a definition that echoed the formulations of Aristotle and other classical Greek thinkers. Only philosophers, Kant argued, formulate "cosmical concepts," as distinguished from the merely "technical concepts" of the logicians, mathematicians, and students of nature, for philosophers concern themselves with foundational questions of human knowing, acting, and making.[3] Therefore philosophical, or "cosmical," concepts are to Kant the only concepts having universal human significance and validity.

On the basis of Kant's definition we can assert that each philosopher produces a universal Weltanschauung—literally intuits the world—in his or her legislative act. A philosophy is a world-perceptual—that is, world-theoretical or world-formative—act that frames the possibilities of every subordinate species of perception of the world.

Kant's definition overshadows all the merely relativistic, culture-bound strains of Weltanschauung generated by subsequent thinkers. It confirms the perennial vocation of philosophy, which is to provide the theoretical framework for the sciences and the humanities. It resists the subversion of its essential function by every kind of "sociology of knowledge."

At the end of his *Critique of Pure Reason* Kant even muses about a "history of pure reason"—a work that would coordinate the formal and material aspects of the history of the "cosmical concepts" of mankind. Kant's writings in fact reflect the influence of his philosophical and religious predecessors: the British empiricists, the Continental rationalists, the Epicureans and Stoics, the philosophers of ancient Athens, and biblical exegetes. But he finally sees them as "merely scholastic" and, with the mordant passage of time, "in ruins only."[4] Kant never followed up on his own suggestion, though; he left it to us to write the history of pure reason.

Such considerations as these have the salutary effect of "relativizing" the concepts of East and West, ancient and modern, while placing claims of historical novelty in a broad perspective. They also return us to one of the themes of this work, which is the fundamental question of what philosophy is or can be. If philosophy is the unique act of world-formation, what are its essential forms and possibilities? How does the abundance of worldviews in our emerging world-culture contribute to this inquiry?

The increasingly global interconnections of twentieth-century political, economic, and cultural life generate the same kinds of questions. Institutions of higher learning, no less than the seats of political power and the marketplace, reflect a new, more abundant pluralism, as East meets West and old meets new. On all these fronts, we require systematic concepts adequate to the forces and materials at hand.

This reconsideration of a universalistic perspective—global both in its transcultural reference and in conceptual form—may fly in the face of some current trends that are narrow in focus and technocratic in character, or again merely relativistic and culture-bound. Many specialists seem to feel more secure in merely exhibiting some regional style, usually to fellow stylists, even taking a kind of perverse pride in being ignorant of other styles, not to mention the grand traditions of East and West. Every large tradition, however, subsumes such localized forms within itself. The narrow-gauge styles of contemporary philosophy seem particularly in need of a framework that can relate them to the many currents of world philosophy in which they have their sources. They have not themselves provided such a picture.[5]

I suggest, then, that the time is ripe for constructing a theoretical framework that repossesses our premodern and modern, Eastern and Western philosophical heritages. If authentically theoretical, such a framework may serve to stimulate discussions within a variety of disciplines, each of which can contribute further to unified cultural configurations—the pedagogical configuration of the current university, for example, and in particular the structure and function of philosophy departments within the university.[6]

We need a new and essentially comparative hermeneutical expertise to be able to understand and appreciate the major texts of world philosophy, and to coordinate their lessons into a single intertextual picture. Such a philosophy would not merely reorient us in the world history of thought, but would also nurture a philosophical culture that permits us to combine the texts into a single purview.

Probably the best ancient or modern precedent for this intertextual hermeneutic can be found in writings of Aristotle, who investigated the teachings of his predecessors and contemporaries in pursuit of the first principles of all of the sciences and arts. Kant's text, we shall see, is a variant of Aristotle's. However, we need to update Aristotle's works and all the other philosophical projects alluded to above, in the light of our vastly more complex picture of world philosophy today.

Such a project will amount to a transcultural hermeneutic. It will be transcultural not only because it will map the various historically formed worldviews, but also because it will compare the several contemporary styles of philosophy—each style consisting of "cultures" of texts too. Questions concerning the character and significance of various regional styles of philosophy—American, Anglo-American, Continental, Asian, and so on—will fall into place when set into this perspective. We can of course imagine any number of new philosophical systems in the future of humanity. But even the best of these must finally take their places among the great systems of the past and the present. In short, since this transcultural approach calls for a study of all the possible forms and functions of philosophical texts, it requires a comparative hermeneutic.

An Architectonic, or Governing, Theory

The point of departure for this work is an inquiry into the resources of our higher philosophical cultures. At the same time, this project requires a definition of the kind of method our global hermeneutic of the first principles of philosophy must have.

I have advanced the claim that the great books of world philosophy provide the indispensable materials for this endeavor. But the peculiarity of the world classics is that they flourish only when repossessed in some contemporary hermeneutical act. Therefore, our pedagogical method must be both interpretive and encompassing. Such a reading of the philosophical classics must resolve each one into its essential form and reach its own internal completion in the form of a ruling, or architectonic, theory.

It will be proper, therefore, to speak of the conceptual form with which we measure the theoretical potentialities of other such works. Once again, the great texts recall us to the perennial vocation of philosophy itself, which is to enunciate foundational truths about the world and our relations to it. Individual philosophical methods, however specialized they become, still form part of a set of historical claims as to true philosophical method. Even the sophistical, skeptical, and deconstructive methods reenacted in the academy today are philosophically legislative.

Our preliminary consideration of the proper methodology of a comparative hermeneutic must accordingly define its own rule of conceptual organization. For reasons elaborated below, a method that compares the material and formal parameters of world philosophy will be called synoptic.

In this work I will sketch the outline of the architecture of theories, East and West, by examining the implications of a series of comparative judgments. In essence, I will show that all the major theory-formations fall under four generic types, themselves systematically related—Sophistic, Democritean, Platonic, and Aristotelian.[7] (This nomenclature refers to and is drawn from historical paradigms, for the principles of philosophy come to light in exemplary texts and can be known in their essential variety from no other source. But I will demonstrate that, while they are associated with classical Athenian philosophers, the four pure types transcend their historical models.)

All the other possible theory-formations are contractions of these four types. In a current economic idiom, the mixed types of philosophical texts are subsidiaries. While they seem to function independently, they still presuppose and ultimately rely on their parent companies. In this sense each of the four pure modalities of theory-formation has its own synoptic character.

I will show that Aristotle's instantiation of the "Aristotelian" type determines the relation of his own theory to that of the other pure types, as distinguished from the subsidiary types. (One of the four pure types, the Sophistic, embodies principles of historical relativism that the proposed architectonic theory will overcome.) I will show, in brief, that the Aristotelian type, whether fully realized or not by Aristotle himself, is the ruling theory.

The Aristotelian theory will be shown to function by virtue of its normative principle of moderation. In its architectonic, or ruling, capacity it moderates the truth claims of the other theories. In adjudicating the varied truth claims it also displays the required reflexivity in philosophical method. In its discursive practice this book must inevitably enact, or reenact, one of the possible forms of philosophical thought. Searching through great works of world philosophy, I find that the synoptic form of discourse required for this book has its own precedents in the works of such philosophers as Aristotle, Kant, and Peirce.

I propose to employ a synoptic method of architectonic analysis to coordinate the essential principles of thought that inform the great books of world philosophy. Such a method must proceed on two levels of textual operation. First, it requires a holistic orientation to the reading of individual classics. Second, it requires a resolution of the points of convergence and divergence of these works.

As to the first methodological obligation, a great book will be seen to have its own semantic integrity. It is the function of genius to produce paradigmatic representations of the world, as the great authors themselves insist. Whatever the aims of contemporary criticism, therefore, let it be clear that it is no longer its proper function to tell Mozart that his work has too many notes—or to deconstruct the text of Confucius, Plato, or Aristotle. (The ethics of intertextuality suggests that such deconstructive criticism be limited to debates among living authors.)[8]

To cite only one illustration of this point here, Descartes in his *Second Replies to Objections* writes as follows: "But I know how difficult it will be, even for those who pay attention and seriously seek the truth, to perceive in one intuition the whole body of my *Meditations*, and at the same time to have distinct knowledge of each of its parts. Yet I think that both of these things should be done at once, if the whole fruit of the work is to be captured."[9] Doctrinally, Descartes advances a logistic method in formal epistemic procedure in his *Meditations* and other writings. But he asks us to read his own work synoptically. Generalizing from this interesting case, I submit that we must treat every great book as a semantic whole, having its own beginning, middle, and end. The reason for this is that texts are noetic products, unities of mind. They are like James's beads of water falling from the edge of the table: they drop all at once or not at all. Moreover, the great works have achieved a special status because they have stood, and continue to stand, the test of time.

The second level of methodological obligation derives from the juxtapositions of such great books in our philosophical heritage and in contemporary texts. Their synoptic resolution into one theory generates precisely the legislative, and therefore architectonic, project I envisage here.

The employment of a synoptic method in architectonic theory is both a general possibility of method and a historically validated technique of inquiry. This axiom proves to be of immediate value, for it allows us to capitalize on the fact that different versions of the synoptic method were used in the past, and continue to function in the present.

Methodological Precedent in Kant

In its strategic position in the history of modern Western philosophy, Kant's career-text looks back upon the methodological revolution initiated by Bacon and Descartes and comments explicitly on the empiricist and rationalist forms of inquiry promoted by his seventeenth- and eighteenth-century predecessors. Kant's self-styled Copernican revolution in critical philosophy, however, actually completes the turn of a methodological circle that goes back to Aristotle.

A differential analysis of these two exemplary exponents of synoptic method provides a significant lesson in the continuity of philosophical strains, while keying our comparative hermeneutic to major examples. In archaeological fashion, I will here trace this intertextual relationship from Kant to Aristotle, that is, from a modern to a classical version.

Kant's core doctrine of synthetic a priori forms—forms of sensibility, of the discursive concepts of the understanding, and of moral, aesthetic, and teleological judgments—amounts to a repudiation of the methodological form advocated by logicists from Descartes to Hume. Kant, moreover, was a keen student of the scientific revolution, which was successfully employing the logistic method along a broad front.

As Kant saw it, his method was different in kind. He characterized the forms of our cognitive faculties as combining the apparently diverse elements of experience in holistically constitutive ways. Thus, while the logistic method adopts the formal epistemic rule of parts outside of parts, which is a mechanical rule, Kant's synoptic method discriminates among parts according to an organic model of organization. The mechanical model is epitomized in Newton's physics, or in Hume's dictum that whatever is distinguishable is separable. In the Kantian model, on the other hand, epistemic parts have no status outside of the holistic functionings of the mind of which they are parts. Mental life proceeds from germs of organization of the materials of life to construct sophisticated edifices of scientific knowledge. In analogous fashion, moral life proceeds from germs of moral sensibility and training to legislate the rational grounds of our actions.

For Kant, this constructive activity of the cognitive sciences and moral life ultimately requires a critique of the faculties of reason. Reason must establish its inventory of possible forms by distinguishing in the first instance between its own legitimately employed antecedent and consequent concepts, and in the second instance between the essential and accidental concepts in the subjects of its investigations. Thus reason discovers that its processes of organization are divisible. But what is epistemically distinguishable is not necessarily separable. Noetic distinction is, rather, a function of the mind's own discursive activity.[10]

Kant employs this discursive presupposition in the organization of his own critical project, namely, the architectonic distribution of transcendental philosophy into three synoptically organized *Critiques*, corresponding to the three faculties of knowing, willing, and aesthetic judgment. Each of the *Critiques* asserts and exhibits a doctrine of methodological procedure in the same form.

The fundamental assumption underlying Kant's critical writings is that procedural validity resides in the reciprocity of the parts and the whole. A theoretic concept (*Begriff*) grasps a set of facts, while the facts simultaneously inform the theory. In Kant's often quoted dictum: Intuitions without concepts are blind, while conversely concepts without intuitions are empty. The mind's discursive operation, then, consists of analyzing a subject into its component parts so as to reconstitute them in their essential order.

A scientific problem is addressed; one works methodically toward its solution. What is at first indeterminate and problematic is resolved through analytical inquiry. Kant argues that this procedure applies primordially to the problem of pure reason. It is pure reason that must take up this problem and bring it to its essential resolution by reconstituting its own essential faculties in a complete set.[11] It is instructive to note that Kant did not write a fourth critique; the distribution of the three *Critiques* comprises the complete synopsis of Kant's architectonic project.

Kant proceeds to specify all the problems and solutions of his critique of pure reason with respect to this kind of holistically differential model. He therefore regards each of the sciences, transcendental or empirical, as proceeding from its own principle. His writings also emphasize the architectonic character of philosophical science, which views the speculative and practical parts of its own activity as a complete set. He envisions his critical project as laying the groundwork for all the sciences within the master-text of his own transcendental "metaphysics as science."[12]

For our comparative hermeneutic, Kant is an exemplary model of the synoptic philosopher at work. His text recapitulates the prevailing concern among his philosophical predecessors for fundamental concepts and particularly for laying the groundwork of the sciences, both cognitive and moral.

In regard to a critical grounding of the cognitive sciences one can see that the crux of Kant's analysis of the speculative use of reason must be his doctrine of a transcendental unity of apperception.[13] Kant explicitly intended that form or function as "unifying act," both in definition and in textual organization, transcends the logicist form of rationality that combines putative atoms of sense-perception or of intellectual intuition.[14] The very meaning of Kant's own doctrine is configured in the synoptic form of conceptual organization. In his second *Critique,* he applies the same methodological obligation to the definition of the moral person, who legislates his or her own moral maxims by a universal rule of rational conduct.

Kant's *Critique of Judgment,* which is designed to interrelate the first two *Critiques,* is also noteworthy in the context of this work. Kant's doctrine of the a priori teleological judgment becomes a paradigm of the form of judgment I will employ to establish certain principles of discourse as the infrastructural variables of all philosophical texts.

My comparative hermeneutic seeks to organize the variety of texts in the history of philosophy and contemporary interpretive practices into networks of internally consistent theoretical formations. In order to do so, what I am calling the career-text of an author—although it may amount to many separate volumes and many thousands of pages—must be assumed to constitute a single, internally coherent train of thought. Every great book, representing its author's mental life, presents itself as a semantic whole, with its own exemplary sensibility and configuration of the world. That philosophical authors construct and elaborate such meaning-formations across the mature phases of their careers is, in Kantian language, an indispensable supposition of a reading of such texts. The same presupposition underlies one's active participation—one's various acts of reenactment—in the transmission of such texts.

Of course, some alleged philosophical texts or traditions may fall short of internal coherence. One is always free to find internal contradictions in another's text or its tradition, so long as one's own text remains internally coherent.

My comparative hermeneutic therefore sees fundamental philosophical concepts as being expressed in a variety of major texts. But at the same time, because of the recombinant forces that form the larger history of ideas, I strive to analyze the relationships of those texts. Of relevance to this present hermeneutical project, therefore, is Kant's argument for the concept of "natural purpose" in his third *Critique.*[15] He argues that for a thing to have a natural purpose, its parts must be conceivable only through their reference to a whole.[16] An analogous concept of natural purpose informs the hermeneutical function of this book. Each of the great philosophical books forms its own natural (that is, theoretical) synopsis of the world and of itself. Quite naturally, the historically related philosophical works tend to refer to one another, forming various strains of agreement and disagreement. My comparative hermeneutic studies the semantic (sense-legislating) configurations of the major philosophical texts and does so precisely in regard to their interrelationships. It can only do so by progressively unfolding its own theory of theories.

Certain philosophical texts address the subject of intertextuality more directly than others. Aristotle's text, with its orientation to the historical realization of principles of thought, exemplifies this methodological orientation.

Methodological Precedent in Aristotle

Although a precedent can be traced to the teachings of the school of Hippocrates, Aristotle's text displays the most developed model of a synoptic method among the classical Greek philosophers. In the subsequent traditions of Western intellectual history, the contour of Aristotelian thought functioned as the methodological precedent for such pivotal figures as Aquinas and Kant. But in the final analysis, Aristotle's career-text has the advantage for the present project of exhibiting a reflexive orientation to historical examples of the first principles of thought.

In certain postmodern styles of philosophy practiced today one encounters a self-serving strategy of declaring the end of metaphysics—that is, its closure and demise. The phrase and the strategy can be traced to Heidegger, although it now enjoys a wider currency. Heidegger's claim is in fact an old one—at least as old as the text of some of Aristotle's Athenian contemporaries, with parallels in ancient Hebrew and Asian texts. The reverse side of this coin is that Aristotle's text is also perfectly contemporary. One of the theses of this book will be that the passage of time in no way diminishes the relevance of the major works of philosophy. Indeed, Croce's dictum that all history is contemporary history has its full application with regard to the major worldviews.

In studying the history of philosophy, it is hard to avoid the conclusion that Aristotle did in fact correctly view the purpose of metaphysics as an architectonic inquiry into the first principles of thought. He correctly saw an opening for a metaphysics of philosophical texts, so to speak—a metaphysics of the historical manifestations of worldviews organized into their various interconnections. In this sense his text demonstrates its own cardinal doctrine of thought thinking itself.

Aristotle brought this perennially contemporary project to one completion in his own career-text (which, of course, includes his *Metaphysics* in a wider set). Every philosopher who debates Aristotle over the first principles of philosophy reopens, rather than closes, the same discussion. Indeed, the very pedagogy of philosophy keeps reestablishing certain points of contact among major philosophical texts.

Aristotle's own analyses of the problems of philosophical inquiry always proceed by factoring out a covariable set of material and formal causes. He sometimes works with the matter-form variable as a generic hermeneutical set; his fuller doctrine is to devise a set of material, structural, efficient, and final factors, as constituting the essential features of natural processes and activities. The intellectual activity of metaphysical definition falls under the same rubrics of analysis in Aristotle's text, which is markedly self-reflective in character.

Aristotle reasons from a rationally legislative principle, which he defines as guiding the discursive operations of the scientific mind in general, thereby establishing the precedent for Kant, among others. Characteristically, he writes:

> Once the mind has become each set of its possible objects, as a man of science has, when this phrase is used of one who is actually a man of science (this happens when he is now able to exercise the power on his own initiative), its condition is still one of potentiality, but in a different sense from the potentiality which preceded the acquisition of knowledge by learning or discovery; the mind too is then able to think *itself*.[17]

This description applies preeminently to the hologrammatic series of writings that comprise Aristotle's career-text. But it applies as well to the career-text of any philosopher, each of whom claims final jurisdiction over the domain of scientific discourse.

It is not irrelevant here to recall that intellectual historians of all epochs have considered Aristotle the philosopher's philosopher. One of the arguments of this book is that nothing has happened within Western intellectual history to diminish that status. However, this perception of Aristotle can now be brought up to date through a new survey of the major traditions of philosophy, East and West.

For present purposes, what is instructive in Aristotle's depiction of "the man of science" is his possession of the holistic form of a subject, which then allows him to think at once of all its essential parts. The scientist, as well as the artist, sees and forms the parts and the whole together in some significant perception of the real world.

Thus a scientific view of a topic does not spring up ex nihilo. Framed in a historical and social matrix of inquiry, action, and expression, a topic is at first indeterminate, obscure, recalcitrant. The hard facts only reluctantly yield their true forms. But once realized, this scientific view can produce a complex network of essential configurations.

Aristotle's sense of intellectual penetration entails precisely this kind of active inquiry and accomplishment. He formulates this general theory of scientific ordering in his *Posterior Analytics,* then reformulates and exemplifies it in each of the speculative, practical, and productive sciences.[18]

In the case of a living body, for example, the psychologist must define its animating form, which is the first principle of a body having the potential for life.[19] In the case of a human life, various goods are pursued, but some are subordinate and some are final.[20] *Ethics* inquires into the consummatory and enduring good of a human life, which is happiness; *Politics* inquires into the good of a community of citizens. *Ethics* is a subdivision of *Politics,* even though it also retains its status as a legitimate science in its own right.[21]

Surveying its own possible forms, the human mind distinguishes between its essentially cognitive and essentially practical functions. This philosophical distinction is itself synoptically exhaustive, converting the genus of science, which sees the universal, into two specific forms. The cognitive sciences then naturally subdivide into the three distinguishable forms of physical, mathematical, and metaphysical sciences, with possible further subdivisions. The practical function is divisible into sciences of human acting, as in politics and ethics, and of human making, as in the greater variety of productive or technical sciences. In all these discriminations, Aristotle remains true to the doctrinal assertions of his method.

The gist of Aristotle's doctrine is that we must continue to work, however laboriously, from the interpretations of our sense experiences and the perceptions of reasonable men to a knowledge of principles and causes, thereby achieving a rational analysis of the world. But things that are first in the order of experience are distinguished from those which are first in the order of nature and of knowing. The intuition of what is first in the order of nature (or being) finally transforms experience into art and science—the domains of the truly universal in the practical and theoretical spheres, respectively. In both art and science, the particular is reconstituted in the light of the universal. Indeed, the particular achieves its epistemic and ontological status only through this reconstitutive process.[22]

The significant variable one encounters here in the text of Aristotle is the methodological one—namely, that of the reciprocity of form and matter in the mind's act of thinking. As both Aristotle and Kant aver, this is the methodological sense in which the mind forms universals.

Aristotle's universalizing method can be found in every segment of his works. It culminates in his discussion of the "man of wisdom" in the first book of the *Metaphysics*. Wisdom is knowledge of principles and causes at the most fundamental level. That is why, Aristotle says, we suppose that the wise man knows all things, as far as possible, although he does not have knowledge of each of them in detail; knowing the universal, he knows in a sense all the instances that fall under the universal. Moreover, the most exact sciences are those that deal most directly with first principles.[23]

On this basis Aristotle proceeds inductively through a consideration of the theories of his philosophical predecessors, from Thales to Plato, only to reconstitute their views in the light of his intuition of the most universal and irreducible first premises, or principles. In Aristotle's final analysis, the "four causes" are the "first," primordial meanings—the basis of all philosophical thinking as exhibited in the views of his predecessors.

It is crucial to observe, then, that Aristotle's *Metaphysics* takes its point of departure from a conjugation of a material (historically formed) variety of philosophical views into their paradigmatic forms. It proceeds synoptically to reconstitute these views into a theory of the essential number and character of such first principles. By contrast, the contending speculations of his pre-Socratic predecessors as to the number and character of first principles and causes reminded him of the way untrained men behave in fights. "For they go round their opponents and often strike fine blows, but they do not fight on scientific principles, and so too these thinkers do not seem to know what they say."[24]

For both Aristotle and Kant, a true grounding of the sciences cannot take the form of either a merely dialectical gathering of opinions—in a postmodernistic "conversation among the humanities," for example—or any other relativistic, politicized discourse. A nonsophistical grounding of human wisdom must establish the primary principles of cognitive, practical, and productive human activity in functionally complete sets. The philosopher engaged in this enterprise must therefore reflect on the very possibilities of thinking, doing, and making as he can gain access to these through their best exemplifications. Doing so, the philosopher must also reflect on his own essential forms of conceptual analysis, while establishing their historical relationships and relevance.

To complete the circle of this Aristotelian paradigm, any aspiring architectonic project of this sort must situate itself in relation to already established views on the first principles of thought. In the present epoch, the same project suggests itself anew. It does so in view of the multiple heritages of world philosophies, whose abundance in contemporary life calls for a modernized theory of their relationships. To deal responsibly with these great works in their variety and to focus responsively on their inexhaustible potential as texts for all ages, such a theory of their intertextuality must itself be synoptic.

I insist that such theoretical work can be done, and this book represents my own attempt at it. Such a system of recursive interpretation will require future fine-tuning, but even at this juncture certain prolegomena to any future hermeneutic can be established.

2

Prolegomena to Any Future Hermeneutic

The great works of philosophy generate a common realm of discourse. We enter this realm each time we describe these texts or connect them in any new interpretive act. The many different interpretations of the great works already indicate the formal nature of their interrelationships.

Philosophies share in common with all texts the property of conceiving of, or interpreting, the world. Their special function is to interpret the world fundamentally. Philosophies conceive of the world comprehensively. But while each worldview does this individually, on its own terms, they still belong to a common realm of discourse.

Our fundamental concepts are those dealing with the world itself, which is not a text or any possible sum total of texts, and with philosophies as ultimate theories of the world. The world is always both pretextual and posttextual in the sense that it gives rise to and yet transcends all actual or possible theories. The two concepts combine in what I call the world-texts of philosophies to account for the final ontological, or worldly, reference that such theories always achieve. Religious texts are not different from philosophical texts; both address the nature of being.

The interrelationships of philosophical and religious texts suggest other categories of expression and of their semantic transferences in the transmission (reinterpretations) of their doctrines. For the sake of a nomenclature, I will identify these transcendental forms of philosophical expression as *assertive, active,* and *exhibitive* and will further characterize their semantic transference as *homoarchic* or *heteroarchic*. The question of transferences introduces the more complex topic of the actual contact points and differential vectors of philosophical texts. I address this topic under the heading of the *archic variables* of philosophical texts and go on from there to chart the *archic profiles* of several taken from the great traditions of philosophy and religion.

Transcendental Forms of Expression or Judgment

A musical composition, painting, sculpture, scripture, novel, poem, play, mathematical system, and scientific or technological treatise are all texts. Individually and jointly they present themselves to us as intellectual products and processes. We learn to understand, to live by, and to make more and more complicated texts in the course of our lives.

We become involved in increasingly complex interpretive acts, entailing various kinds of readings—that is, of intertextual transferences. We judge our youthful readings and utterances by adult standards. We judge adult utterances according to established standards of competence and excellence. In all these cases, we measure intellectual capacities.

Every reading entails an interpretation, or a way of conceiving of the world. Although not entirely in Derrida's sense, our readings are often writings, especially in those categories of texts I call active and exhibitive. Thus we continually reinterpret our own or others' concepts of the world.

All texts convey meaning in assertive (propositional), active (morally and politically agential), and exhibitive (aesthetic, performative) modes of expression or judgment.[1] We translate feelings into actions and thoughts, thoughts into actions and feelings, and actions into thoughts and feelings, at various levels of mental activity. These modes are the human vectors of expression, so to speak. They often function simultaneously in complex combinations.[2]

So true is this of philosophical texts that we cannot imagine them otherwise. Hegel's writings propose a doctrine of dialectical method and exemplify it in literary style. Leibniz's and Hume's texts illustrate their own logistic doctrines, just as Kierkegaard and Nietzsche give rhetorical expression to their own agonistic methods. And all such philosophical texts have practical consequences—that is, they can be applied to problems of human life.[3]

A good text is always internally consistent, revealing some unified grasp of life in its various forms of expression. For example, the Zen master shouts "Ho!" in a simultaneous assertion, enactment, and aesthetic exhibition of the ego-shattering truth of the Buddhist teaching. In the case of the sages, saints, and soldiers of all ages and cultures, we honor their lived commitments to their own principles. By contrast, we regard as a bad text one whose semantic forms are not conceptually consistent or sincerely lived; we consider characters who change their identities in midscript to be bad.

But in the realm of philosophy we are well beyond all that. We expect and find a high degree of internal consistency in the semantic forms of the great texts. Indeed, these texts have achieved such consummate unions of form and content that it is impossible to imagine them otherwise.

The burden of disproof clearly falls upon those who practice a hermeneutic of ambiguation. Granted, for instance, that it is possible to play the deconstructionist game—to put play back into play, in Derrida's phrase.[4] The danger is that this kind of disingenuous interpretive practice may distort more important philosophical goals. In particular, it may impair the greater interpretive sensibilities that civilization requires of us.

Archaeologists, psychoanalysts, and many other kinds of interpreters produce texts whose express purpose is to restore fragments of other texts to their pristine forms. Performing artists—musicians, for example—devote their lives to authentic renditions of immortal works, which do not truly lend themselves to indefinite supplementations. By the same token, the great clarity of such works positively resists erasure.

My point here is that the immortal texts command attention in a special way. They shape our attitudes toward them and become ingrained as standards of excellence for our own contemporary interpretations. It is the great texts themselves that inspire our habits of faithful translation or representation.

But at the same time, interpretation may involve inconsistency in semantic transference in another, quite different sense. Some texts, in any of the three modes, adapt the content of other texts in a way that departs from their original meaning. The reinterpreting text usually manages to make good sense in its own fashion, even though this may require a radical break with the interpreted text's original intentions. Philosophical texts furnish abundant evidence of what I have called heteroarchic semantic transference.

Texts that faithfully represent, reproduce, and restore the essential meaning of another text are homoarchic in semantic transference, a definition philosophers need not find problematical. As every good text translates its own phases of significant expression, it inevitably demonstrates the property of homoarchic semantic transference. As a matter of course (as well as of scholarly practice), we excerpt passages within an individual text, to which we also assign a place within the unfolding career-text of an author, agent, and performer.

It thus takes a disingenuously heteroarchic text—and still one with an internally consistent form—to reduce a good text to a discontinuous series of semantic displacements. Intuitively, there is good reason to extend the homoarchic property to semantic transference between or among certain texts, as well. We settle this question every time we deal with traditions and cultures. Certain traditions and cultures of texts engender heterogenous elements, but others do not. These are adjudicable factual questions and cannot be prejudged by an epistemological theory. Christian, Pure Land Buddhist, Jewish, and Muslim parents, for example, surely pass down the faiths of their parents and ancestors to their children. Thomists faithfully reproduce the text of Saint Thomas; Wittgensteinians, the text of Wittgenstein; Derrideans, of Derrida.

The hermeneutical insight we gain from these observations is that even such a radical deconstructionist as Derrida must presuppose some concepts of consistency and identity. While Derrida may deconstruct other texts, he cannot deconstruct his own.[5] Derrideans then faithfully repeat his exact meaning in various ways. In so doing they run afoul of the homoarchicity of their own school or professional affiliation, which collides with their official doctrines.

At any rate, let us call those reinterpreting texts that are genuinely sense-altering heteroarchic in their semantic transferences. Many philosophical texts are deliberately heteroarchic: they change the rules of the game, subordinating the interpretive principles of other philosophical texts to their own. This is a characteristic feature of nomothetic texts, which establish the validity of certain assumptions at the expense of others.

Heteroarchic transference, therefore, is another transcendental property of texts in general. But neither modality, the homoarchic or the heteroarchic, can take precedence within a comparative hermeneutic. Philosophical texts function in one or the other of these modes because of their substance or method of discourse. However, we can still distinguish between homoarchic and heteroarchic semantic transferences.

We turn now to another concept of our comparative hermeneutic—that of the career-text of a philosophical author. This is something that applies preeminently to the texts of the major figures of the world traditions. The great philosophical texts can be described as well-wrought mental products. Set within the career-text of an author, his or her text expresses fundamental feelings and perceptions of the world. The pleasures and sorrows of an individual historical life are only gradually transformed into discursively unified thoughts and thereby communicated to other individuals with comparable mental habits.

Thus philosophical texts are achieved unities of mind. They enter into the intertextual domain as certain grades of active interpretation of the world. As a rule, we tend to identify one or several works as the representative—in the sense of consummate—expressions of a person's career. But again, we locate and critically evaluate such individual and career-texts within a wider set of civilizational products.

Teaching philosophy requires indeed a whole series of interpretive acts. I assert that if philosophies are world-interpretive in purpose, then the way they are taught must be essentially comparative as well. Despite this fundamental consideration, the contemporary schools promote narrow, technical expertise in the field of philosophy. We will be true to the grand traditions of philosophy if we take these threads of pedagogy in hand and weave them into a unified pattern of their actual and potential achievements.

What, then, are the conditions under which a philosophical text functions comparatively, that is, participates in the wider intertextual realm of philosophical discourse? This question raises another: What are the essential points of contact among philosophical texts in general?

The Archic Variables of Philosophical Meaning

World-texts are nomothetic because each such philosophical work orders a real world in the assertive, active, and exhibitive modes of expression. Therefore such world-texts function differently from the ordinary pragmatical texts of daily life. Such ordinary texts presuppose one another indefinitely; many dissolve (in the cinematic sense) into one another. But they are not world-texts; they tend, however, to presuppose world-texts of certain kinds. The world-texts provide the justification for the ordinary texts.

The world-texts, too, generally presuppose one another; but they do not dissolve into one another. World-texts tend to exclude and to displace one another instead. Each makes an essential judgment on the world.

The political philosophies of Locke and Marx, for example, are mutually exclusive. So too are the epistemologies of Hume and Kant, or the grammatologies of Wittgenstein and Derrida. Taoists have ridiculed Confucians, Confucians have denounced Taoists and Buddhists, and Buddhists have been intent on refuting all false views for centuries. This is easier to see at a distance, but it remains true at close range, in the ways schools of theory and practice divide in our contemporary philosophical culture.

Present philosophical culture may be described in terms of a vigorous heterogeneity. The situation reminds us of Darwin's concept of the "polity of nature," in which all available spaces tend to get filled up by the profusion of different species, which still interact symbiotically in a common ecosystem. The rule here is that the denser the occupancy of the same area (the profession of philosophy, in this case), the greater the divergence in structure, habits, and constitution. The historical evidence suggests that we can extrapolate from our own experience of such heterogeneous philosophical activity to any previous culture of civilized thought and verify the same phenomenon of an interacting ecosystem of worldviews.

Pace Dewey and others who describe the progressive career of philosophy, however, the concomitant Darwinian rule that there must be competition leading to extinction among some of the types, with a resultant development of new types, does not seem to apply to the case of philosophical differences. Darwin's and Dewey's concepts already presuppose certain kinds of philosophical assumptions as to natural or human progress.[6] But in our comparative hermeneutic, the analogy between philosophical texts and evolutionary phenomena must eventually break down. For in their capacity as world-texts, philosophies define evolutionary phenomena.

In other words, philosophies are intellectual products and processes of their own kind. The principle here seems to be that there are certain fundamental world views, occupying specific niches in the broader realm of discourse, that are reenacted in various philosophical configurations. This realm of discourse may develop historically along certain lines, but it is not necessarily historically generated. The forms of thought, rather, appear to represent eternal intellectual possibilities of the world.

The point to bear in mind is that each of the worldviews realizes some final form of this realm of intellectual discourse. Unlike ordinary texts with their indefinite intertextuality, world-texts concern themselves with the nature and relations of being and seek to discover universal principles.[7] The history of philosophy, no less than of religion, is a book of orthodoxies and heterodoxies. This also accounts for the tendency of contemporary philosophers to divide into clear-cut schools.

Let us now analyze the reasons why a philosophical text, in any of its modes, functions as a nomothetic judgment on the real world and thus on real human life, including its own intellectual life. First, as I have just indicated, a philosophical text entails an ontological, or world, orientation. Conversely, texts that do not form some sense of the reality of the world are not philosophical. This is true even of certain ostensibly disontological philosophical texts.

The texts of the Greek Sophists and the Mahayana Buddhists, for example, are actually world-referring (or ontological). Like the texts of Berkeley, Hume, James, Nishida, or Wittgenstein, they affirm an existential sense of the reality of appearances. These, of course, are the human appearances—the acts of human perception, volition, or concrete linguistic transactions and their contingent contents—which for existential philosophers form the real basis of the abstractions of the sciences, whether natural, philosophical, or theological.

The texts of such philosophers as Lao Tzu and Chuang Tzu, or of Democritus, Locke, Marx, or Nietzsche, deny that such existential forms of life are truly real. To these philosophers, the surface life of human consciousness is only an epiphenomenal play of illusory appearances—what Santayana calls "the trooping essences" on parade.

According to them, it is the material forces and energies underlying this surface of human consciousness that are causative. Some philosophers, like Freud, devise methods to decipher the surface text of consciousness in terms of its substrative causes.

My point here is that these philosophers of the hidden substrate make ontological commitments, too, however much they differ from the existential philosophers. Other philosophers reject both the existential and the material senses of reality and advance some special views of their own.

Thus, the world itself, which is not a text, appears in a philosophical text only in a particular ontological focus. Moreover, the world's worldhood is always caught in the meshes of a philosophical text's discursive, or methodological, form of expression. This is as true of the dis-ontological texts that purport to negatively grasp the real properties of language (about the world) as it is of pro-ontological texts that claim to address directly what is or what can be known.

Philosophers have fought fiercely over both these questions—namely, (1) what is real, really real, or ultimately real, and (2) what are concepts and how are they legitimately associated or disassociated in true concept-formations.

Philosophers also ask (3) what are the grounding principles of theoretical assertion, political and moral practice, and aesthetic enjoyment. In doing so, they give precedence to their own views, for they automatically put into play their own goals and motives.

Moreover, they always approach these questions from (4) some valid perspective, or standpoint. Presuppositionally, they challenge the authority of other standpoints as they advance their own.

Even when philosophers do not consciously make use of these four archic variables, they invoke them at an infrastructural and presuppositional level. A sense of reality and its formal order, together with an authorizing perspective and grounding principle, function as the transcendental conditions of every worldview.

Therefore, there is always a point of contact among the foundational world-texts.

Plato's text, for example, represents the perspective of a higher wisdom, an illumination of the soul from on high, so to speak, which simultaneously repudiates the personal perspective advocated by Protagoras and the other Sophists. From this authorizing perspective, Plato's text refers simultaneously to a truly real realm of immortal soul or souls and one of immutable forms or essences, in which the apparent world of our senses participates in varying degrees. Contrary to the teachings of the Sophists, Plato's concept of the form of true reality encompasses ever higher orders of being, culminating in a supersensuous, or noumenal, realm, which is experienced only through dialectical assimilation of the lower forms into the higher. The final form of true reality—the goal of the dialectical method—is the governing principle of all encompassment, the form of the good, which is the form of the whole and its hierarchical distribution in an ideal set.[8]

We can say that Plato's text postulates a noumenal sense of true reality; a dialectical sense of order; a higher, illuminative perspective; and a hierarchically comprehensive principle.[9] In all these respects Plato consciously repudiates the positions of his contemporary adversaries, the Sophists. Conversely, Plato's text makes contact with the Sophists' texts along the same four dimensions of philosophical expression.

Democritus, in contrast to his near-contemporary Plato, postulates a material sense of reality, reduced to two ultimate ontological concepts, atoms and the void. The authorial attitude of his text is that of an objective observer; its grounding principle presupposes the eternal necessity of the material particles that underlie the cosmic and human processes. Although they may dovetail in certain conclusions, the texts of Plato and Democritus differ radically in their first premises.

Artistotle, among many others, noted that the texts of Plato and Democritus were incompatible in various fundamental respects, although he sided with neither but tended to steer a middle course between them. Other philosophers, of East and West, steer courses between and around them, as well.

Many philosophical positions share some semantic assumptions while diverging in others. They partially overlap in fundamental presuppositions. Newton consciously reinterpreted the physical atomism of Democritus, even though he replaced the latter's principle of conservation of momentum with a creative principle. Leibniz consciously returned to Platonic assumptions but retained the logistic method of Democritus and Descartes. Hume agreed with Democritus, while adopting Berkeley's existential sense of reality. Thus, in whatever direction they went, these thinkers remained within the realm of philosophical intertextuality.

The mutually reinterpreting texts of the Sophists, Democritus, Plato, and Aristotle present the problem of our comparative hermeneutic in miniature. They involve one another even as they displace one another. We seek to map their relationships in a set of transcendental textual principles and to employ the same comparative instrument in a synoptic reading of a wider range of texts, East and West, including contemporary hermeneutical models.

To this end I have identified and characterized four transcendental principles of philosophical texts: authorial perspective, ontological focus, method of articulation, and grounding principle. They are transcendental because they function as semantic factors, or causes of philosophical meaning. But they are drawn synoptically from the history of philosophy.

I will show that while these archic variables may be drawn from any number of major philosophical texts, they can be found all at once, so to speak, in the text of Aristotle. For these presuppositional factors of world-text composition correspond to, and hermeneutically transform, Aristotle's doctrine of the four causes.

First, a philosophical text's material cause is precisely its ultimate ontological reference, as this appears in its definition of its subject matter, however specialized that might be.

Second, its formal cause is its methodological form, which logically orders that subject matter in some definite way. Thus, semantically considered, matter and form are always reciprocal but still distinguishable functions of philosophical worldviews.

Third, a world-text's final cause is its sufficient, grounding principle, which motivates and controls its own interpenetration of material and methodological factors. This kind of telic function is what philosophers usually refer to as the principles of their respective texts. For example, it is what Leibniz identifies as the principle of perfection (which is God's sufficient reason for creating the best of possible worlds); what Hume or Santayana mean when they postulate animal sentiment as the principle of morals; or what Kant refers to when he grounds our cognitive and moral faculties in a principle of pure reason. Or again, without employing the term *principle,* it is what Lao Tzu refers to when he calls the Tao the universal mother; or what Freud postulates as the essentially conservative character of the instincts.

Fourth, a world-text's efficient cause is its authorial perspective. In such a text an author, as theoretical agent, speaks from a certain viewpoint on what is real and its formal constitution. Final and efficient causes are thus also interdependent: the philosopher (theoretical agent) forms a concept of the world according to some principle of interpretation, which simultaneously accounts for his or her text's semantic character.

In the final analysis, however, we do not have two pairs. As Aristotle's various deployments of the four causes already suggest, because of the holistic character of a text each of the semantic factors must coordinate with all the others. Instead of two pairs, we have a set of four reciprocal but distinguishable functions of a philosophical text.

The concept of the text itself, as the subject of this inquiry, corresponds to Aristotle's concept of substance in the primary sense. All along, the text, with its essential modes and properties, has been the substance of these hermeneutical reflections. Thus, while these analytical concepts have generic meanings of their own and can be isolated in specific instances, they function not as meanings in themselves, but rather as the *causes of meanings* in texts. It is the individual world-texts, functioning holistically, that are meaningful in the primary sense and that reveal to us their archic, semantic assumptions.

For the purposes of our comparative hermeneutic, therefore, these archic factors constitute a hermeneutical set drawn from and applicable to the history of philosophy. Conversely, they function only as heuristic factors formally employed in relation to the worldviews. Only in this synoptic sense may they be called archic, or presuppositional, factors, embedded in what I have called the nomothetic utterances of philosophical texts. While they can be learned from Aristotle's text, they transcend it, both in generality and in point of material origin.

I will adduce ample evidence that such hermeneutical principles can be drawn from various texts or groups of texts in the history of ideas. Indeed, the strength of Aristotle's discussion of principles and causes is that it can be cross-referenced in the broader set of philosophical texts.

The Evidence for an Archic Matrix

The body of world-texts provides us with the great books through which we can discover the archic variables of philosophical discourse in general. But we can establish these transcendental points of contact only by a hermeneutical theory general enough to account for the comparability of such texts.

Aristotle's metaphysical causes, I submit, can be reinterpreted as such generic hermeneutical controls. This is not a conclusion that can be deduced from any a priori starting point, however—or even from Aristotle's own text. If our method is synoptic, the painstaking examination of a full range of historical materials and their formal factors will yield this result.

Our comparative hermeneutic, therefore, needs to confirm this interpretation through a series of analyses. In its most local focus, Aristotle's primary heuristic concepts will be seen to pertain to a formal understanding of the principles of his immediate philosophical predecessors and contemporaries. But given the universal character of philosophical discourses, one may then apply Aristotle's primary categories to the broader history of thought.

The ensuing chapters will show how the great texts of philosophy may be illuminated by Aristotle's first principles, reconstituted as hermeneutical causes, and conversely how this broadened field of philosophical discourse substantiates Aristotle's set.

There are no shortcuts to understanding the principles of philosophical thought. The only way to grasp the full range of the formal possibilities of thought—the field of philosophical mind itself—is by studying the entire history of philosophy in a series of synoptic sightings. Contrary to some contemporary hermeneutical models, therefore, I am interested here not in making some narrow stylistic claim, but rather in calling attention to the abundance of world philosophies. The primary fact and point of departure for any truly comparative hermeneutic must be the interrelatedness of the major worldviews. The abundance of world classics outweighs any merely individual claim or omission. Their greatness provides standards for judging contemporary achievements.

In the light of these considerations, let us now assert and exhibit the rich possibilities of comparative analysis opened up by the four archic variables. Allowing for the requisite references to primary sources, I submit that a broadly synoptic reading of the history of philosophy reveals the following divisions among the four archic variables:

PERSPECTIVE

The authorizing voice of a world-text can take one of four possible forms:

Personal. This is the self-referent, idiocentric presence of an author or authors—in the first person singular or plural—that shapes his world-view. The personal perspective is generally preferred by philosophers who promote concepts of irreducible human subjectivity, such as Xenophanes, as well as Protagoras and the other Greek Sophists; Mo Tzu; Erasmus, Descartes, and Hobbes; Voltaire and Rousseau; Kierkegaard, Nietzsche, Scheler, James, Sartre, and Merleau-Ponty.

Objective. This authorial perspective dispassionately observes the world's objects and their practical effects. This is generally the perspective of philosophers who deny that human subjectivity is authoritative in theory-formations—who view such requirements of subjectivity as mere wish-fulfillments or anthropocentric delusions to be replaced by a more realistic cognitive attitude. This perspective is embodied in the texts of such philosophers as Anaximenes, Anaxagoras, and Democritus; Hsün Tzu, the Chinese Legalists, and the skeptic Wang Ch'ung; the Epicureans, Skeptics, and Stoics; Spinoza, Newton, Locke, and Hume; J. S. Mill, Darwin, and Marx; Peirce, Freud, Einstein, and Weber; Wittgenstein, Russell, and Santayana.

Diaphanic. This is the standard voice of religious texts. It bears witness to a higher wisdom or the revelation of an absolute knowledge, of which the text constitutes a transparent, self-transcending medium. This is the authorizing perspective of all sacred scriptures and their theological traditions, and also of various philosophers who speak of and for God or the absolute, such as Heraclitus, Empedocles, and Parmenides; Pythagoras, Plato, and Plotinus; Leibniz, Schelling, Hegel, and Schopenhauer; Bergson, Nishida, and the Kyoto School writers; Heidegger and

Jaspers; as well as most of the classical and modern Taoist, Confucian, Buddhist, and Neo-Confucian writers.

Disciplinary. The disciplinary perspective presupposes an ideal community of like-minded readers; it typically takes the form of the first person plural. In differing versions, the texts of Hippocrates, Aristotle, Aquinas, Machiavelli, Copernicus, Vico, Kant, Fichte, Husserl, Dewey, F. H. Bradley, and Whitehead exemplify this perspective.

In short, a given philosophical text always presupposes its own authorial voice and subordinates the other forms of perspective to itself. Philosophers may agree and disagree about perspectives, but they establish contact with each other on this point of intertextuality.

ONTOLOGICAL FOCUS

Philosophers variously refer to what is real in the subject matters of their texts in the following terms:

Existential. Some philosophers place an ontological priority on historical data—on the acts and affairs of human experience, each of which is "vivid and intense," in Hume's phrase, as it makes its appearance in the stream of an individual or epochal (societal) consciousness. The texts of the Zen Buddhists and Greek Sophists and Skeptics; Erasmus, Berkeley, Voltaire, and Hume; J. S. Mill; William James and F. H. Bradley; Nishida and the Kyoto School; Weber, Sartre, Wittgenstein, Russell, Jaspers, Merleau-Ponty, and Foucault grant precedence to this ontological focus.

Substrative. To other philosophers, the deceptive surface life of existential consciousness has to be traced down to a more fundamental but invisible level of real causality and motivation—of material particles or vitalistic forces; of chemical, biological, and instinctual forces; of forces of production or libidinal economies, and so on. This sense of reality pervades the texts of several of the pre-Socratic *physis* philosophers, as well as those of Hippocrates and Democritus; the Stoics and Epicureans; Mo Tzu, the Legalists, the Taoists, Neo-Taoists, and Wang Ch'ung; Machiavelli, Hobbes, Newton, and Locke; Vico, Rousseau, Adam Smith, Darwin, and Marx; and of Nietzsche, Bergson, Freud, Santayana, and Derrida.

Noumenal. The noumenal sense of reality transcends appearances; it refers to a transphenomenal, supersensible, and eternally perfect realm or activity. One finds this ontological commitment in the New Testament, the Koran, the Hindu scriptures, Parmenides, Plato, Plotinus and the Christian Neoplatonists, Aquinas, Spinoza, Leibniz, Kant, Fichte, Schelling, and Kierkegaard.

Essential. As opposed to the existentialist, the essentialist philosopher sees ideal forms and general, continuous, or enduring traits of nature and experience in the form of gradated patterns, functions, and values. The essentialist describes these as realized or realizable "in" nature and experience (and not "apart," as in the noumenal sense). This ontological focus is found in the Old Testament, in both the Confucian and Neo-Confucian texts, and in Xenophanes, Socrates, Aristotle, Descartes, Hegel, Peirce, Dewey, Husserl, Scheler, Whitehead, and Heidegger, among others.

A worldview always puts forward a dominant sense of what is real, displacing or subordinating other forms of ontological reference to its own.

METHODS

Philosophers assert and exhibit different kinds of concept-formation:

Agonistic or paradoxical. This method obeys the logic of contending forces, or of contrasting concepts, which cannot be reconciled through some higher agreement. It is adversative in formal presupposition. This is the logical method in the texts of the classical Confucians and Legalists; the Taoist Chuang Tzu; the skeptic Wang Ch'ung; Nagarjuna and all other Buddhists; Homer, several pre-Socratics (Anaxagoras, Heraclitus, and Empedocles), the Athenian Sophists, and Hellenistic Skeptics; the Koran; Machiavelli, Erasmus, and Galileo; Berkeley and Voltaire; Kierkegaard, Nietzsche, and Freud; Nishida and the Kyoto School; Scheler and Jaspers; Wittgenstein and the later-phase Wittgensteinians; and Foucault, Derrida, Deleuze, and other postmodern Continental hermeneuticists.

Logistic or computational. The logistic method consists of relating discrete, or simple, units (integers, atoms, ideas, characters, essences, or elementary propositions); it reduces complexes to simples, and then adds or subtracts such homogenous units by the rule of $+1$ or -1 (or of 1, 0), while postulating the logical chain of their exact order of antecedents and consequents. As in computer logic, it is a mechanical model. This is the method in the texts of Mo Tzu, Thales, Anaximenes, Anaxagoras, Democritus, and Epicurus; Descartes, Hobbes, Spinoza, Leibniz, Newton, Locke, Hume, Vico, and Adam Smith; J. S. Mill, Malthus, and Darwin; and Husserl, Frege, Carnap, Russell, and Santayana.

Dialectical or sublational. In the dialectical method one observes a logic of higher agreement, which presupposes and accomplishes a synthetic unity of opposites, contrasts, or multiplicities. Partial, abstract views are subsumed and reconciled—whether aesthetically, actively, or propositionally—in an emerging whole. The Old and New Testaments; Upanishads and Bhagavad Gita; Tao Te Ching, I Ching, Yin Yang theorists, and the Neo-Confucian philosophers; Pythagoras, Plato, the Stoics, Plotinus, and the Christian Neoplatonists; Rousseau; Fichte, Schelling,

Hegel, and Marx; and Royce, Bergson, Bradley, Whitehead, Heidegger, Sartre, and Merleau-Ponty display this method.

Synoptic or problematic. This method converts a problem or subject matter into an analysis of generic and specific, relevant and irrelevant features. The whole and the parts are seen together (hence synoptically) and treated as form and matter of the same holistic function. In differing versions, the texts of Hippocrates, Aristotle, Aquinas, Kant, Schopenhauer, Peirce, James, and Dewey share this approach.

In sum, a philosophical text grants precedence to its method of articulation, subordinating other possible logical forms to its own, and in this way enters into the wider realm of philosophical discourse.

PRINCIPLES

Creative. The creative principle emphasizes making a difference (the opposite of sameness), in which the new replaces the old. It generally functions as an assumption of volitional efficacy or agency in the making of fact—of willpower, work, and effort, whether human or divine; however, it can take the form of some generative cosmic process, as in Thales, Epicurus, or Whitehead. In differing versions, the texts of the Old and New Testaments; Thales, the Greek Sophists, and Epicurus; Hsün Tzu and the Chinese Legalists; Saint Augustine and many other medieval theologians; Luther and Calvin; Hobbes, Newton, Locke, and Berkeley; Adam Smith, Darwin, Marx, and Kierkegaard; William James, Dewey, Bergson, and Whitehead; Weber, Jaspers, Heidegger, Sartre, Merleau-Ponty, Foucault, and Derrida function according to this principle.

Elemental or simple. This is the principle of sameness, identity, indifference, homogeneity, or parity; hence of the conservation of momentum, repetition, and recycling of the same basic element, nature, or essence. The texts of Hinduism, Buddhism, and Taoism; of Mencius, Wang Ch'ung, and Wang Yang-ming; Anaximenes, Parmenides, Empedocles, and Democritus; the Hellenistic Skeptics and Plotinus; Dionysius the Areopagite, Erigena, Meister Eckhart, and Cusanus; Erasmus, Machiavelli, Hume, Voltaire, and Rousseau; Schopenhauer, Nietzsche, Scheler, and Freud; Wittgenstein, Russell, and Santayana exhibit this semantic principle.

Comprehensive. As observed in Plato's idea of the good, Chu Hsi's heavenly principle, Leibniz's preestablished harmony, and Einstein's sense of universal causation, the controlling assumption here involves an ideal set, variety, and multiplicity of forms, with emphasis on the perfect form of the whole, which assigns its members their just and proper places. The texts of the Confucian classics, Mo Tzu, the I Ching, Tung Chung-shu, and the Sung Neo-Confucians culminating in Chu

Hsi; Anaximander, Heraclitus, Aeschylus, Pythagoras, and Plato; Copernicus, Kepler, and Galileo; and Leibniz, Einstein, and F. H. Bradley are examples of this principle.

Reflexive. The reflexive principle may be described as Aristotle's principle of the essential variety of goods and functions, or as the principle of self-sufficiency, autonomy, and self-completion of a specific nature or of a thing's intrinsic form or function. The self-completion of the intellect—of thought thinking itself and generating its own forms—recurs in different versions as the controlling principle of the texts of Descartes, Kant, and Hegel, among others. Xenophanes, Anaxagoras, Aristotle, the Stoics, Aquinas, Spinoza, Vico, Montesquieu, J. S. Mill, Peirce, and Husserl also employ this principle.

In sum, a philosophical text requires a grounding principle to govern the development of its subject matter. In this respect it establishes an affinity with certain philosophical texts and displaces others.

Philosophers are generally well aware of the archic assumptions they bring to their writings. They consciously inquire into the nature of reality, its formal constitution, grounding principles, and valid perspectives. They do not necessarily engage all four semantic factors in one place or at one time, however. They may not envision all four of these variables in their own texts.

Philosophers with alternative hermeneutical projects may even reject, in principle, the possibility of generating such a set of semantic factors. But philosophical disagreement will itself take the form of "text" and will therefore become open to a comparative semantic analysis.

The merit of these variables is that they form a complete set of control concepts, thus allowing for a systematic approach to the various world-view texts. At the same time, the set satisfies the categorial obligation of its own synoptic method. For although it is a formally constituted set, it is drawn from the history of philosophical texts.

As sketched above, the perspectives, ontological references, methods, and principles of philosophical texts can be seen to function as the points of contact, as well as the differential vectors, of all intertextual semantic transferences. The archic matrix drawn from the great world-texts provides a cross-cultural heuristic tool that avoids the disadvantages of the more insular models in use today, and places current deconstructive models in broader perspective as well. It reflects and provides the hermeneutical basis for an architecture of theories, East and West.

Summarily presented here, this synoptic mapping of the specific differences among major philosophical writers generates a complex system of comparative interpretations. It is the result of innumerable hours of teaching and research, and it is subject of course to further insights and correction.[10]

These readings nevertheless offer us the possibility of constructing a comparative hermeneutic of first principles in a cross-cultural approach to the history of philosophy. Together with the transcendental textual modes of human expression, this set of archic variables provides us with a clear guide to any future hermeneutics.

At this point, my readings of the great texts constitute a set of abductory inferences, or predictions, in Peirce's sense. Let us confirm these findings by a closer analysis of the major world-texts.

3

The Principles of Athenian and Hellenistic Philosophy

Democritus, Plato, and Aristotle

There is no ultimate justification for beginning an analysis of the great texts of philosophy with the major Athenian philosophers. One could just as well begin with a period of Indian, Chinese, or Japanese intellectual history—or with another period of Western thought. Any such endeavor simply leads to a larger inquiry, which alone can give shape to the interpretive system.

The story of Athenian philosophy is generally well known and therefore convenient for the present purpose. In addition, our comparative hermeneutic can take advantage of a basic rule of interpretation, that is, to see earlier forms of historical and intellectual experience in the light of later ones. The texts of the Sophists, Democritus, Plato, and Aristotle are the most developed worldviews in Greek philosophy, incorporating the principles of earlier thinkers in many ways.

Aristotle's text represents the culmination of Athenian philosophy, as well as focusing more explicitly on first principles of thought. (One sees this, for example, in Aristotle's survey of the psychological opinions of the many and the wise in *De Anima*, or of the many kinds of constitutions in his *Politics*.)

One should also note that Aristotle tended to see his own text as occupying a middle ground between those of Democritus and Plato. This is an important point for this inquiry. Given the centrality and apriority of the four causes in Aristotle's text, it suggests the possibility of our reconstructing the archic relationships among the texts of Democritus, Plato, and Aristotle himself.

Aristotle must have perceived the differences between the texts of Democritus and Plato. Taking the archic profile of his own text as a guideline, we should be able to construct a schema of at least twelve semantic variables that describe the fundamental assumptions of the texts of Democritus, Plato, and Aristotle.

We can do this in two related steps. First, establishing the archic profile of Aristotle's text, we obtain the preliminary schema:

	PERSPECTIVE	REALITY	METHOD	PRINCIPLE
Plato				
Aristotle	*disciplinary*	*essential*	*synoptic*	*reflexive*
Democritus				

Then carefully studying the career-texts of the other two philosophers, as Aristotle must have done, we will finally be able to intuit the fuller schema:

	PERSPECTIVE	REALITY	METHOD	PRINCIPLE
Plato	*diaphanic*	*noumenal*	*dialectical*	*comprehensive*
Aristotle	*disciplinary*	*essential*	*synoptic*	*reflexive*
Democritus	*objective*	*substrative*	*logistic*	*elemental*

The second schema represents a synoptic reconstruction of one key intertextual profile of Aristotle's text.

Since these archic profiles recur throughout the writings of the three philosophers, we are now in a position to cite their texts at length. Our synoptic method also allows us to cite typical instances where Democritus, Plato, and Aristotle differ.

We begin with the oldest of these world-texts, that of Democritus, reading it through the eyes of Plato and Aristotle. In this regard, Diogenes Laertius reports on the position of Leucippus, Democritus's doctrinal predecessor, as follows:

> The whole is infinite, as aforesaid. Part of it is full and part empty, and these he calls elements. Worlds unlimited in number are formed from these and dissolved into them. The manner of their formation is this. Many bodies of all sorts of shapes are cut off from the infinite and stream into a great void, and these when collected in a mass produce a single vortex, following the motion of which they collide and revolve in all sorts of ways and begin to be sorted out, like to like. But when owing to their numbers they can no longer be carried in equilibrium, the small atoms pass to the void without, as if through a sieve. The rest hold together, become entangled and move in conjunction with one another, so forming a

> first spherical system. From this a kind of membrane becomes detached, containing within itself bodies of every kind. These whirl round in proportion to the resistance of the center, and the membrane becomes thin as the contiguous bodies continually flow together by the contact of the vortex. In this way the earth was formed, by the cohesion of the bodies which had moved to the center. The enclosing membrane in turn is augmented by the influx of atoms from outside; and as it whirls around, it adds to itself those that come into contact with it. Some of these become interlocked and form a system that is wet and muddy at first, but drying out as they are carried round in the universal vortex they finally catch fire and form the substance of the stars. . . . Just as a cosmos is born, so also it grows, declines and perishes by some sort of necessity, the nature of which he does not specify.[1]

In the one other fragment attributed to Leucippus, he is also reported as saying that "nothing comes to be at random, but all things for a reason and by necessity."[2] We shall establish that the concept of necessity in both philosophers, Leucippus and Democritus, can be traced to their elemental principles—principles of an eternal sameness and always antecedent momentum of the world's ultimate constituents, physical atoms in the void.[3]

In this context, Aetius reports: "Leucippus, Democritus, and Epicurus say that sensation and thought take place by the entry of images from without. Neither happens to anyone without the impact of an image."[4] This is confirmed by the testimony of Sextus Empiricus:

> Democritus in some places abolishes the things that appear to the senses and asserts that none of them appears according to truth but only according to opinion: the truth in things that exist is that there are atoms and void. "By convention sweet, by convention bitter, by convention hot, by convention cold, by convention color, but in reality atoms and void." And in his *Confirmations,* although he had promised to assign the power of conviction to the senses, he is none the less found condemning them, for he says, "We apprehend in reality nothing true, but change according to the condition of the body and of the things which impinge on it and resist it."[5]

One can cite an abundance of other texts to fill out Democritus's worldview.

Such excerpts illustrate that Democritus's authorial perspective is paradigmatically an objective one. He holds that just as nothing happens in nature at large except through the action and reaction of material particles, so too neither sensation nor thought occurs without the impact of an image. That cognitive authority is not jeopardized by Democritus's attendant distinction between the "bastard" knowledge furnished by the senses and the "legitimate" knowledge achieved by the intellect.

The latter teaching refers to the methodological operation of the mind, which reduces the phenomenal aggregates of our sensory experiences to their constituent parts. Democritus's logistic method is connected to his substrative sense of the reality of the material particles and the void. The principle governing the resistance, motion, and impact of the material particles is the very sameness of their eternal and indestructible existence and therefore the necessity of their always antecedent motions, which causes the present arrangement of things.

In general, Democritus theorizes, we should note that "animals flock together with animals of the same kind, as doves with doves and cranes with cranes, and similarly with the other irrational creatures. So it is with inanimate things, as one can see with the sieving of seed and with the pebbles on the beaches."[6] These are all metaphors for his basic doctrine of the way in which the substrative atoms attract one another, which underlies his ethical doctrine of human friendship and of the relation between gods and men.[7]

Drawing his archic profile in this way, one discovers a consistent theory of cosmological process and human life in Democritus's worldview. Atoms and the void; being and nonbeing; the origins of knowledge in objective images; truth and opinion; the perfection of human life in cheerfulness, moderation, and friendship; and the materially evolved gods' beneficent relation to the human mind and the cosmos—all are governed by Democritus's elemental principle of necessity and "like attracts like."

This text is a paradigm of pure materialism, perfectly intelligible and self-sufficient on its own presuppositional terms. Although it survives only in fragmentary form, we have enough of these fragments to reconstruct Democritus's powerful theory of the world.

How different this picture of the world is from that of Plato's *Timaeus*, with its comprehensive principle of the perfect pattern to which the demiurge looks in creating the forms of order and life. To Plato, soul is not a whirl of material particles. Soul is self-moving and discovers its eternal participation in a higher, more perfect, intelligible order, of which time is only its moving image, space its receptacle, and material bodies its corruptible facsimiles.

How different again from Aristotle's text, which asserts the autonomy of nature's forms and functions, as they appear in the gradations of natural and human life; in the teleological orders of human knowing, doing, and making; and in the eternal, unmixed self-sufficiency of the divine thinking.

Aristotle comments in many passages on Democritus's principle. In *Generation of Animals*, for example, he writes: "Those are wrong, and fail to state the causal necessity, who say that things have always happened so and think this explains their origin. So Democritus of Abdera says that there is no beginning of the infinite, that a cause is an origin, and what is everlasting is infinite; therefore to ask 'why?' in a case like this is to look for an origin of the infinite."[8] Aristotle clearly states Democritus's elemental principle and seeks to displace it. But like Plato, Aristotle can do so only by putting into play some archic reason of his own.

It would be possible at this point to bypass the texts of Plato or Aristotle and jump to a position (such as Newton's or Freud's) that is at least partially related to that of Democritus. But our heuristic measure is to be the text of Aristotle and, more pointedly, the intertextual relation obtaining among the texts of Democritus, Plato, and Aristotle.

Radically differing from Democritus's doctrine, which authorizes our cognition of phenomena through objective images, Plato's text displays a well-known diaphanic perspective. Socrates is the persona of Plato's Dialogues, who consults the Delphic oracle and through whom the higher wisdom of the gods is revealed. He is represented as turning away from naturalistic speculation. The author, Plato himself, does not voice his own subjective, personal wisdom; nor again does he speak in the disciplinary perspective of Aristotle's text. He speaks in a mythic voice that reveals a higher, spiritual truth. Correspondingly, the ontological focus of Plato's text is the noumenal, supersensible realm (as in the upper division of the "divided line" in the *Republic* 6). This is the realm of the forms, the goal of the self-moving spiritual soul (as in the *Phaedrus* 245C). Memory of this higher kinship of the soul drives the dialogic ascent to the higher universals in Plato's text as a whole. This dialectical method distinguishes the understanding of the senses from that of intellect in an ascending scale of values deriving from Plato's comprehensive principle—the idea of the good, or the beautiful. Plato's principle resurfaces as the principle of justice in the *Republic*, as the principle of psychological and aesthetic integrity in the *Phaedrus*, and of cosmological order in the *Timaeus*.

Contrary to Plato's, the perspective of Democritus's text is objective, even as it repudiates the "bastard knowledge" of existential perception in its affirmation of the massive giveness and causality of material nature. Democritus is the prototypical "scientist," with his impersonal voice of passive sense perception. The ontological focus of his text is correspondingly the substrative one—the whirl of atomic particles in the void underlying the surface world of our sense perceptions. Its discursive form is purely computational; in theory, it adds and subtracts the infinite plurality of the worlds according to a rule of +1 or −1.

Democritus's text logistically orders the theoretical substratum of irreducible material particles according to an elemental principle of sameness, or necessity. The *mutatio rerum* is equivalent to an eternal conservation of momentum, which produces an eternal recycling of the physical atoms in the void. There is no other why or wherefore.

It can be seen at once that Democritus's text has its own powerful coherence. Its elemental principle integrates the other suppositional factors of his text in a way that differs fundamentally from the kinds of telic orders postulated in the texts of Plato and of Aristotle. Its elemental principle thus undercuts Plato's principle of a perfect harmony and system of justice, or Aristotle's principle of the self-fulfillment of natural and human being. But in the wider view, each of these great authors displaces, through the force of his principle, method, sense of reality, and perspective, the presuppositions of the other two.

The classical theories of Plato, Aristotle, and Democritus prove to be mutually exclusive but also mutually defining. The question at this point is whether this distribution of twelve archic elements constitutes a complete set.

Socrates and the Sophists

Relevant to our reading of the Sophists' text is the following citation from Aristotle's *Metaphysics.* Its significance for us is that it analyzes the texts, not of the Sophists themselves, but of Socrates, Plato, and the Pythagoreans.

> Socrates, however, was busying himself about ethical matters and neglecting the world of nature as a whole but seeking the universal in these ethical matters, and fixed thought for the first time on definitions; Plato accepted his teaching, but held that the problem applied not to sensible things but to entities of another kind—for this reason, that the common definition could not be a definition of any sensible thing, as they were always changing. Things of this other sort, then, he called Ideas, and sensible things, he said, were all named after these, and in virtue of a relation to these; for the many existed by participation in the Ideas that have the same name as they. Only the name 'participation' was new; for the Pythagoreans say that things exist by 'imitation' of numbers, and Plato says they exist by participation, changing the name.[9]

This reading by Aristotle, I submit, should put to rest the question of the ontological orientation of the "real Socrates," as distinguished from the fabled character of Plato's Dialogues, on the one hand, and from his contemporaries, the Sophists, on the other.

The first book of the *Metaphysics* remains an excellent example of the concept of philosophical intertextuality. Although necessarily limited in its historical purview, it interprets the texts of other philosophers with an eye to discerning their distinguishing suppositions. Entirely typical is the passage cited above, which performs the hermeneutical function of distinguishing the essentialist ontological focus of the career-text of the historical Socrates of fifth-century Athens from the persona of Plato's Dialogues.

Aristotle clearly distinguishes Socrates' essential sense of reality from Plato's noumenal sense of the supersensible ideas. In the sequel to the same passage, he goes on to distinguish Plato's noumenal from the material, or substrative, sense of reality of the Pythagoreans. As for archic realities, note that only the existential sense is missing in this brief passage. But indebted to Plato's *Theaetetus,* Aristotle does characterize the existential sense of Protagoras and other Sophists in later passages of the *Metaphysics,* as well as in other treatises.

The career-text of Socrates remains one of the clearest cases of a hermeneutical problem in the history of philosophy. The text of Xenophon portrays an existential Socrates; that of Plato, an idealized (noumenal) Socrates; that of Aristophanes, yet another Socrates.[10] The tradition of interpretation of Socrates has continued through the texts of Kierkegaard, Nietzsche, Jaspers, and others to this day. Each philosopher renders the enigmatic Greek philosopher after his own image, or, more accurately, in the service of the archic assumptions of his own text.

Aristotle implies that he has remained true to the essentialist reality of the historical Socrates; and his perception of the kinds of philosophical principles in his *Metaphysics* and other writings illustrates this fidelity. This is an essential point for our comparative hermeneutic. (All the relevant evidence suggests that Socrates' archic profile is diaphanic in perspective, essential in reality, agonistic in method, and comprehensive in principle. Thus he shared an agonistic method with his contemporaries, the Sophists and Aristophanes. He bequeathed his perspective and principle to Plato, and his sense of reality to Aristotle.)

Aristotle's text also demonstrates the correct principle with which to distill the principles of philosophy from the world-texts themselves. This is the principle of active mind, which can reflect on its own principles and rules and thus justify its own essential judgments. This is also the principle (reiterated by Kant, among others) that states that one can always reflect on the rules governing any judgment. Even claims to existential uniqueness or semantic difference fall under a rule of some kind—that is, when we reflect upon the claims themselves.

If we reexamine the materials of Aristotle's predecessors—while pondering again the materials presented in the first book of the *Metaphysics*—we will eventually notice the curious fact that the first book almost completely neglects to mention the Sophists, who in fact inaugurated the development of Athenian philosophy. Aristotle mentions only Socrates' interest in ethical definition, in contrast to the teachings of

Cratylus and the Heraclitean doctrine of the flux of sensible things such that there can be no true knowledge of them.[11]

It is true that Aristotle does not seize the opportunity to put the Sophistic text in its proper place in his discussion of philosophers in the first book of the *Metaphysics.* This may be simply because he thought they had contributed nothing positive to the discussion of metaphysical first principles. But in another place, notably in the fourth book of the same work, he launches a lengthy discussion of the Sophistic position. There he appears to be fully aware of the Sophists' existential and agonistic doctrine as violating the principle of noncontradiction. He pictures the Sophistic position as the corruption of the aims of metaphysics, and its proponents as those who would teach their students to track flying game.[12] In view of this extended and devastatingly critical account of the Sophists here (and elsewhere), it seems that Aristotle's omission of them in the first book of the *Metaphysics* was deliberate—an omission that makes its own philosophical point.

Plato's career-text, for its part, contains a very direct characterization of the Sophistic text. Indeed, it consistently presents its own archic profile in counterpoint to that of the Sophistic text. Plato's text, in fact, by predating Aristotle's, provides an earlier instance of paradigm analysis that is at least implicitly hermeneutical. I will fill out this analysis here, with an eye to establishing the context of the Sophistic paradigm.

First, Plato characterizes the perspective of the Sophists through the humanistic, self-centered proposition, "Man is the measure of all things." Plato constantly contrasts the idiocentric, personal arbitration of opinions, tastes, and values of this Sophistic definition with his own diaphanic perspective, which reveals a higher wisdom. He contrasts just as sharply his noumenal sense of reality with the existential flux of perceptions and opinions championed by the Sophists. He identifies the form of the Sophists' rhetorical art (or "knack") of persuasion as the adversative logic of "is" and "is not"—the method of ambiguation in the service of eristic skills. He sees his own dialectical logic of a higher synthesis of opposites and of reminiscence of true being as the antithesis of the Sophistic form of reasoning. Plato contrasts his principle of the good, or the beautiful—a holistic and hierarchical principle *par excellence*—with the Sophistic principle of sheer human volition, which seeks by dint of its own eristic power to make a difference in the social arena.

Plato's text can be interpreted as characterizing the Sophistic archic profile as personal in perspective, existential in ontological focus, agonistic in method, and creative in principle. Plato's text differs in every respect: it is diaphanic in perspective, noumenal in its sense of reality, dialectical in method, and comprehensive in principle.

Any student of philosophy can remember his or her excitement on reading Plato's *Apology* and other Dialogues for the first time. We can recall feeling that Plato's text was addressing contemporary issues. Those of us fortunate enough to be teachers of Plato's works—of the *Republic,* for example—relive that experience again and again. We have the distinct enjoyment of seeing the younger generation begin to understand Plato's delineation of the real differences between his and the Sophistic position.

Here I am trying to reconstruct how Aristotle, in his own essentialist text, must have regarded the differences between the texts of Plato and the Sophists. He must have seen that from the strength of its own basic presuppositions Plato's text assimilates every variable of the Sophists' text into its own. But from the strength of its own presuppositions, the Sophists' text resists assimilation on every count. It displaces Platonic philosophy in every essential respect.

To be true to his own governing principle—as transformed into the concept of the semantic self-sufficiency of the philosophical text—Aristotle might also have recognized that the texts either of the Sophists or of Plato displace his own semantic priorities. I will show, however, that Aristotle's text contains its own implicit version of the hermeneutical circle—the circle of mind thinking its own possible forms. On the strength of this principle, Aristotle inevitably granted precedence to his own text over Plato's or the Sophists'.

My text seeks to convert the hermeneutical potential of Aristotle's text into a broader architectonic of theories, including contemporary interpretive models. It therefore assigns Aristotle's text a specific place within the realm of possible philosophical paradigms. But it suggests that in establishing the specific intertextual relationships of Aristotle's text, we have the key to disclosing the architecture of theories, East and West, on an unprecedented scale.

Curiously, this hermeneutical potential has lain fallow in the literature of philosophy for over two thousand years. Certain philosophers—Leibniz, Hume, Kant, Nietzsche, and Peirce come to mind—appear to have recognized the possibility for such an architectonic reconstruction of the great texts, only to take the interpretive project in a different direction.

We seek to cultivate this potentially fertile domain of intertextual analysis as Aristotle originally envisioned it. We do so by transforming Aristotle's own textual principles into a "first philosophy" and prolegomena to any comparative hermeneutics. Thus, one of the first tasks must be to reconstitute and to rechart, perhaps more thoroughly than Aristotle did, the primary sources of Greek philosophy for their first principles.

By taking the text of the Sophists into account, I can now construct a matrix of sixteen archic variables, as follows:

	PRINCIPLE	METHOD	REALITY	PERSPECTIVE
Sophists	*creative*	*agonistic*	*existential*	*personal*
Democritus	*elemental*	*logistic*	*substrative*	*objective*
Plato	*comprehensive*	*dialectical*	*noumenal*	*diaphanic*
Aristotle	*reflexive*	*synoptic*	*essentialist*	*disciplinary*

Each of these sixteen variables represents an archic factor that is irreducible to any other.[13]

The question is now whether this chart fully represents the variety of hermeneutical variables. If it does, it will by implication describe the essential features of all texts. If it does not, it will be necessary to expand or redefine the chart until it is a self-completing set.

But I suggest that we do in fact have a complete set. The "control" (or archic) concepts of this set are Aristotle's four causes, forming a matrix of reciprocal yet distinguishable semantic factors. The four Aristotelian causes are synoptically related, although they represent essentially different subfunctions of mind. Each is its own kind of final cause of textual formation, yet functions interdependently with the others.

For our comparative hermeneutic, this conclusion is of prime importance for understanding the possibility of philosophy itself. It embodies a claim that is very likely to be met with disbelief and resistance: that Aristotle did in fact think metaphysics, or "first philosophy," through to its first principles. He did achieve the "end" of metaphysics.

Aristotle himself conceived of the four causes as a complete set of ontological and cognitive principles. He encountered stiff resistance in his own day. Any philosopher remains of course at liberty to challenge Aristotle's hermeneutical judgment by adding or subtracting such causes and principles. Each philosopher must, at least implicitly, either assimilate or displace Aristotle's first principles—and every other philosopher's as well—thus contributing to (and presupposing) some matrix of first principles. But such a philosophical strategy and our perception of its success (or failure) will take the form of other philosophical texts, thus regenerating the essential intertextual problem that Aristotle addressed in his own terms in the first place.

For our comparative hermeneutic, Aristotle's four causes, transformed into a set of archic variables of philosophical texts, suffice to generate a multivariate typology of the formal possibilities of philosophical interpretation. In this light, the archic profiles of Plato, Aristotle, the Sophists, and Democritus—differing as they do in all respects—represent pure archic types comprising the essential variety of suppositional factors of world-texts.[14] While mixed types of archic profiles have their own semantic integrity, they do not have the full theoretic generality of the pure modes.

As expected, in the Greek context the pre-Socratic texts display a variety of mixed modes that were eventually resolved in the texts of the four pure Athenian types. Reserving this complex topic for the next chapter, let us turn to the major Hellenistic and Roman worldviews.

Archic Transformations in the Hellenistic Worldviews

The Platonic and Aristotelian schools lived on through the Hellenistic period, and their presence is discernible even in later Roman times. With the conquests of Alexander and the rise of imperial Rome, however, we witness major transformations in the social and existential bases of ancient civilization. In due course newer, more cosmopolitan schools of philosophy emerged, most notably those of the Skeptics, Epicureans, and Stoics.

The Skeptics begin with Pyrrho of Elis (365–272 B.C.), a younger contemporary of Aristotle (384–322 B.C.). Major names in this school range from Arcesilaus (315–241 B.C.) and Carneades (215–130 B.C.) to Sextus Empiricus (180–210 A.D.).

The Epicureans claim an even more venerable ancestry in the philosopher Aristippus (ca. 435–355 B.C.), who was a disciple of Socrates. Their actual founder, Epicurus (341–270 B.C.), was also a younger contemporary of Aristotle and flourished in Athens. Epicurus's philosophy can be traced through Hellenistic and Roman schools, culminating in the *De Rerum Natura* of Lucretius (96?–55 B.C.), one of the most influential texts of all times.

The Stoics also claimed a disciple of Socrates, Antisthenes (445–365 B.C.), as their philosophical ancestor. Diogenes the Cynic was another forerunner of this school, but their true founder was Zeno of Citium (ca. 340–265 B.C.), of the generation after Aristotle's, a full contemporary of Pyrrho and Epicurus. The careers of Cleanthes (b. 250? B.C.), Chrysippus 280–207 B.C.), Polybius (ca. 204–122 B.C.), Cicero (106–43 B.C.), Seneca (ca. 4 B.C.–65 A.D.), Epictetus (dates unknown), and Marcus Aurelius Antoninus (121–80 A.D.) bear witness to an essential continuity in the ancient Stoic worldview. Indeed, an analysis of the extant texts of Skepticism, Epicureanism, and Stoicism reveals that the doctrinal transmission and amplification in these several schools remained essentially homoarchic for centuries.

The historical record shows that the archic shifts embodied in these schools were already effected in the texts of Pyrrho, Epicurus, and Zeno. While these three philosophers' careers coincided with the decline of the Athenian city-state, they predated the full-scale shift to Hellenistic and Roman civilizations. When their texts first appeared in the fourth century B.C., each represented a complete worldview.

By a series of comparative analyses we can establish that the Epicurean text introduces only one change in the pure Democritean paradigm; and the later texts of Plotinus and Saint Augustine, one change each in the pure Platonic paradigm. The Skeptic text has two Sophistic and two Democritean elements. The Stoic text has two Democritean, one Platonic, and one Aristotelian element.

The Skeptic text is objective in perspective, existential in its sense of reality, agonistic in method, and elemental in principle. Thus it achieves a certain suspension of judgment, and consequent ethic of tranquillity (or insensibility) of mind. "Pyrrho denied that anything was honourable or dishonourable, just or unjust. And so, universally, he held that there is nothing really existent, but custom and convention govern human action; for no single thing is in itself any more this than that."[15] This principle of "custom or convention" is elemental in that it presupposes a governing force of repetition, a mechanical tendency at work in the existential reality at large. The same principle was to recur in the text of that "moderate sceptic," David Hume, among others.

The Skeptics, in other words, traded the creative principle and personal perspective of the Sophists for the elemental principle and impersonal perspective of Democritus. Consequently, while the ancient Sophists practiced their art at the borderline of philosophy and politics, the Skeptics refrained from taking any position: "The Skeptics . . . were constantly engaged in overthrowing the dogmas of all schools, but enunciated none themselves; . . . they themselves laid down nothing definitely, not even the laying down of nothing. So much so that they even refuted their laying down of nothing, saying, for instance, 'We determine nothing,' since otherwise they would have been betrayed into determining. . . ."[16] This is a far cry from the voluntarism of the Sophists and others who sought not to understand the world but to change it.

The Skeptic text nevertheless represents a worldview and has its place within a range of theories of the Sophistic and Democritean types. It recurs in the writings of Wittgenstein and has specifiable relations with other philosophical texts as well.[17]

Turning to the text of Epicurus, one sees another mixed, or contracted, form of one of the pure Athenian paradigms. Like that of Democritus, Epicurus's text is objective in perspective, substrative in ontological focus, and logistic in method. But it rejects Democritus's elemental principle for the creative principle of the Sophists.

The *locus classicus* for this Epicurean doctrine occurs in the second book of Lucretius's *De Rerum Natura:*

> If every motion of atoms is always continuous with another, if new motion always originates from old in determinate sequence, and if it is the case that the primal bodies do not swerve and at least begin to break the bonds of determinism, thus preventing cause from following cause in perpetuity, then why do living creatures throughout the world have freedom of the will, this freedom torn from necessity that allows each of us to go where his pleasure bids? . . . Thus it is this slight deviation of the primal bodies, at indeterminate times and places, that keeps the mind as such from experiencing an inner compulsion in doing everything it does and from being forced to endure and suffer like a captive in chains.[18]

Epicurus's central injunction to study nature was designed to "make men defiant and self-sufficient and proud of their inalienable goods instead of the goods of circumstance."[19] The same principle of liberty informed Epicurus's sense of the freedom of the gods, which in any case exercised no constraints upon human freedom.

Individual freedom determines the attitude of Epicurus toward law and government, and well as his negative attitude toward public careers. In lieu of the latter, Epicurus advocated freedom of friendly association in the pursuit of a simple rustic life, as celebrated by the Roman Epicureans Lucretius and Horace. Archically considered, Epicurus's position has all the elements of what was to become the social contract theory of Locke.[20]

Lucretius develops Epicurus's principle not only in the doctrine of swerving atoms, but also in his concept of their generative character. We meet this principle in the opening lines of *De Rerum Natura,* which celebrates the fecundity of nature and is dedicated, most appropriately, to the goddess Venus.[21] Lucretius even formulates a doctrine of human progress.[22] Not only Lucretius and Horace, but Vergil and Ovid were to invest significantly in this creative principle in their various works. The four Roman poets exercised a considerable influence on Western literature and thought.

If the archic text of Hellenistic and Roman Stoicism is now introduced into our comparative picture, the following schema of sense-constituting elements is obtained:

	PERSPECTIVE	REALITY	METHOD	PRINCIPLE
Skeptics	*objective*	*existential*	*agonistic*	*elemental*
Epicureans	*objective*	*substrative*	*logistic*	*creative*
Stoics	*objective*	*substrative*	*dialectical*	*reflexive*

The text of Stoicism is a rather rare combination of two Democritean values, a Platonic method, and an Aristotelian principle. The force of its dialectical method holds together archic values that are heterogenous to one another according to the pure texts of the former Athenian thinkers.

Famous for their objective perspective, the Stoic thinkers appropriated the substrative fire of Heraclitus to form their material sense of reality. Their dialectical method is conspicuous in their sense of an all-pervasive, harmonious cosmos; and they produced doctrines of man's cosmopolitan, rational nature. This is the sense in which both the slave Epictetus and the emperor Marcus Aurelius could declare that, while their local habitat was Rome, their truer city was the universe.

The Stoics' dialectical writings are governed by a reflexive principle of reason, which takes the form of the eternal decrees of Zeus, or of providence, and of the autonomy of our rational faculties. Their concept of the sage proceeded from the principle of the autonomous activity of reason. The Roman Stoics bequeathed to Western civilization doctrines of natural law (*jus naturale*) as governing the law of nations (*jus gentium*) on the same basis.[23]

The two major philosophies produced at the end of the Roman empire were those of Plotinus and Saint Augustine. Both incorporated variations on the basic Platonic paradigm, but in different respects.

Plotinus assimilated the Stoic logic of a harmonious cosmos into his own doctrine of world-soul, while also reinterpreting Plato's doctrine of the *Timaeus*. He took over the Aristotelian doctrine of reason, but subordinated it as the level of the divine intelligence in his system of emanations of "the One, or Good." Diaphanic in perspective, his text requires that one "strike forward yet a step," beyond the intellectual level, to mystical union with the One: "This, therefore, is the life of the Gods, and of divine and happy men, a liberation from all terrene concerns, a life unaccompanied with human pleasures, and a flight of the alone to the alone."[24] Plotinus's text functions through an elemental principle of absolute metaphysical identity, the One, which is a variation on the Democritean paradigm of eternal sameness.

Saint Augustine reinterpreted the New Testament and Pauline concepts of the first creation, while developing a trinitarian theology and preserving a distinction between creator and creatures in his own dialectical articulations. In his doctrine of the freedom of the will he also produced another version of the voluntary principle of the Epicureans, while transforming their materialistic ontology into his own noumenal one.

Thus the intertextual relation between Plotinus and Saint Augustine shows the following distribution of archic elements:

	PERSPECTIVE	REALITY	METHOD	PRINCIPLE
Plotinus	*diaphanic*	*noumenal*	*dialectical*	*elemental*
Augustine	*diaphanic*	*noumenal*	*dialectical*	*creative*

Radically differing in principle, each author produced a form of spirituality that was to have a profound effect on Western history. Each displaced Plato's comprehensive principle, thereby contracting the full generality of the pure mode of Plato's text.

One sees this relationship between pure and mixed archic paradigms in the texts of the pre-Socratics as well. The pre-Socratic worldviews are built on distinctive archic configurations. Despite the claims of Nietzsche, Heidegger, and other postmoderns, however, the later worldviews of the Sophists, Democritus, Plato, and Aristotle are clearly the more developed ones, having had the advantage of drawing upon the legacies of their predecessors. We pursue this multifaceted topic in the following chapter.

4

Archic Configurations in Pre-Socratic Philosophy

Aristotle's Pre-Socratic Predecessors

In Western philosophy, the Sophists were the first humanists. They broke away from the cosmological theories of their predecessors and formulated questions about human perception and language. This new orientation, which claimed to achieve revolutionary perceptual and linguistic turns, resurfaces in any number of philosophical epochs. In the Greek setting, it emerged in the great age of Athenian philosophy, which eventually included Socrates, Plato, and Aristotle.

Plato portrays Socrates as a participant in the humanistic trend inaugurated by the Sophists. But while the Sophists propounded existential ontologies from personal perspectives, Socrates focused on essential ethical definitions in the service of his divine muse.

Plato's own diaphanic text rejected even more sharply the narrow humanism of the Sophists. He, rather, broadened the entire domain of philosophical discourse to encompass the texts of the Sophists and Socrates, on the one hand, while at least partially reappropriating the traditions of the pre-Socratic philosophers—notably, Heraclitus, Parmenides, and the Pythagoreans—and of Homer and the other poets, on the other.

Aristotle's text proved to be more broadly architectonic, exhibiting a pluralistic interest in the general principles of philosophy and the other sciences and arts. Aristotle's theoretical attitude was a function of his disciplinary perspective, which presupposes a community of individuals sharing a given purpose and proficiency. He conceived of metaphysics as the first philosophy and therefore as the foundational science of sciences. Here too he endorsed the viewpoint that the various forms of knowledge energize their own communities of knowers, doers, and makers.

From this authorizing perspective, Aristotle's definition of methodological inquiry was deeply humanistic. True methods, he insists, are problematic, proceeding from things known to things unknown—and thus from what is first in the order of human acquaintance to what is first in the order of being and knowing. Scientific inquiries and technical achievements are historical and social products. The substance of such inquiries and practices always derives from real processes and products, which progressively reveal their true shapes and functions through developing institutions of learning and intercommunication.

As modeled in the third book of *De Anima,* Aristotle's description of mind is obliquely self-referent. The passive mind is *mens capax omnium*—a capacity that refers precisely to its world-orientation, or worldhood. Active mind then transforms the worldly matters of cognition into its own intellectual principles. Aristotle's philosophical activity epitomizes the reflexive principle.[1]

If all men by nature desire to know and are capable of sharing mental life at various levels, then the philosophical texts of his predecessors contributed to Aristotle's hermeneutic of first philosophical principles. Aristotle studied and appreciated the essential principles of other philosophical minds. At the same time, he reworked these concepts in his own text.

It is important to note that this did not force Aristotle to take, as it did the Sophists, a different linguistic or perceptual direction from his predecessors, or to launch a project of semantic deconstruction of their texts. Nor does he endorse Socrates' abandonment of the models of naturalistic philosophy of his predecessors. Nor, again, does he reject the poets and other witnesses to the truths of man, as did Plato. Rather, Aristotle sought in the main to account for the variety of philosophical interests in their diverse domains. His own text thus became a prism in which the primary-source materials of ancient Greece remain refracted in their abundant variety.

By contrast, Plato (and later Plotinus) tended to adapt the thoughts of his predecessors for his own purpose, acting from a belief in the unitary perspective of a higher, or diaphanic, science. Most of the medieval Neoplatonists followed suit in this regard. Aquinas, who restored Aristotle's definition of science, is an exception to this rule.

In contrast to Aristotle's liberal attitude toward the plurality of sciences, many of the world's philosophical texts have been "illiberal" in character. Examining contemporary experience, we can say that many philosophers remain insulated in their own special, technocratic styles. Many of them denounce the natural sciences and arts, as well as other philosophies. Aristotle's hermeneutical attitude was different because he sought reflexively to tap the principles of mind itself, which generously displays its own forms.

It is also important to note that the archic elements of Aristotle's text are found in his philosophical predecessors as well. Aristotle explicitly acknowledges, for example, his affinity with the essentialist reality of Socrates and the reflexive principle of Anaxagoras, although he does not acknowledge a similar affinity with the essentialist reality and reflexive principle of Xenophanes' text.

In point of archic precedent, if not also of direct, local influence, Aristotle's philosophy especially represents a transformation of some of the semantic assumptions of Hippocrates (460–390 B.C.) and of the school that originated on Hippocrates' native island of Cos. (Aristotle was born in approximately 384 B.C.; his father, a court physician of Hippocrates' generation, died when he was a child.) The Hippocratic Corpus represents perhaps the first school of medicine dedicated to the investigation and application of scientific first principles and methods.

The extant literature of this school shares the substrative sense of nature as *physis*, an underlying reality of material nature, to be found in different versions in the texts of the Milesian philosophers, the Pythagoreans, Heraclitus, Empedocles, Anaxagoras, and Democritus. For the followers of Hippocrates this took the form of the doctrine of the body's vital fluids, as manifested in the four humors of blood, yellow and black bile, and phlegm. When the body dies, each component must return to its own elemental nature; "moist to moist, dry to dry, hot to hot, cold to cold."[2] Aristotle departed from this materialist assumption, as one can observe in his *Physics, De Anima, De Partibus Animalium*, and other treatises. He transformed the Hippocratic substrative reality into his own sense of an essential reality.

In other respects Aristotle draws on Hippocratic assumptions. Hippocratic teaching repudiates both the diaphanic perspective of "magicians, ritualists, charlatans, and exorcists, all of whom lay claim to great piety and special wisdom" (from *The Sacred Malady*) and the "inferior practice" of private quackery (from *On Ancient Medicine*).[3] These are subordinated to the disciplinary perspective, exemplified in the Hippocratic oath, the basis for which we find in an exemplary text such as the following:

> Medicine, on the other hand, in dealing with its problems, possesses a long-established start-point (*arché*) and method of procedure. Thereby it has been making many excellent discoveries for quite a while; and what remains will be discovered provided the investigator is competent and sets out from a knowledge of discoveries already known. But when anyone neglects or casts aside these requirements and seeks to make discoveries in an arbitrary way of his own, then he will only deceive himself if he claims to have discovered anything.[4]

Hippocrates distinguished medicine from other human arts, some superior and others inferior, in an architectonic attitude that underwent further generalization with Aristotle.

As for method, in the Hippocratic tradition one finds the following exemplary text:

> He who would be a healer should be guided not primarily by plausible-looking theories, but by practice combined with reason. Properly, a theory is a sort of composite memory of data that have been received by sense-perception. After the phantasms of sense have been received by us their details are sent up to the intellect, which, receiving them again and again and noting what kind they are, stores them up in itself—which is to say, remembers them. Accordingly I approve of theorizing as far as it finds its initial principle in, and draws its conclusions from, a variety of actual phenomena. For if a theory has its starting-point in discoverable facts, it then partakes of the power of intellect to receive into itself particulars from various sources.[5]

This passage could be transferred verbatim into the closing paragraphs of Aristotle's *Posterior Analytics,* which describes the process whereby the universal is formed.[6]

Aristotle assimilated another maxim of the Hippocratic teaching: "But leisure and a focused activity of mind produce a tensive condition which makes for the beauty of life. . . . A more graceful kind of thinking is that which, whatever it may be about, has been fashioned into an art, provided it be such an art as will lead to wise behavior and good repute."[7] Another precept of the Hippocratic school holds that

> A physician who is a lover of wisdom (*philosophos*) is equal to the gods. There is no sharp distinction between wisdom and the healing art; for in the latter are to be found all the qualities that constitute wisdom—disinterestedness, conscience, modesty, reserve, sound opinion, judgment, calm, straightforwardness, purity, a dispensing of what cleanses, freedom from superstition, and godlike superiority.[8]

Spinoza could also have written these last two passages, which now reveal the reflexive principle of reason.

In archic analysis, we see that the reflexive principle is broadly inscribed in the Hippocratic text, just as it is prominently displayed in Aristotle's. It underlies both philosophers' sense of teleological nature, such that the forms of life realize certain discoverable biological goals. "For each of them has a nature (*physis*) and a power (*dynamis*) of its own, and there is none which is utterly incapable of being investigated and subjected to medical treatment."[9] Every organism tends by nature to play its part in the cycle of its species in a healthy manner.[10]

The same telic principle is considered to function pluralistically: "In actuality, however, cures are of many kinds. . . . That is why the characteristics of illness are many and accordingly the ways of curing are many."[11] And just as the characteristic properties of the humors are essentially different—"phlegm being quite unlike the blood, blood unlike bile, and bile unlike phlegm; how could they be like one another when their colors appear different to the eye and their textures to the hand?"—so there can be different arts, and inferior and superior kinds of wisdom.[12]

In archic terms, Aristotle was an essentialist Hippocratic; the Hippocratics were physicalist Aristotelians. By shifting the ontological focus, Aristotle transformed the theoretical potential of the Hippocratean text. He thereby achieved a pure paradigm of theory-formation. It is a theory of qualitative functions of natural and human processes at the limit of philosophical generality.

In a broader but still local picture, one finds the following continuities in the archic modes of pre-Aristotelian texts:

	PERSPECTIVE	REALITY	METHOD	PRINCIPLE
Xenophanes		*essential*		*reflexive*
Anaxagoras				*reflexive*
Hippocrates	*disciplinary*		*synoptic*	*reflexive*
Socrates		*essential*		
Aristotle	*disciplinary*	*essential*	*synoptic*	*reflexive*

This intertextual synopsis also allows one to see that Aristotle's text is composed of archic elements that are comparatively rare even in Greek philosophy.

Plato's Pre-Socratic Predecessors

Just as one can reconstitute the archic profile of Aristotle's text from the reflexive principle of Anaxagoras, the essentialist reality of Socrates, and the reflexive principle, problematic method, and disciplinary perspective of Hippocrates, so too can one discover that every element of the archic profile of Plato's text is presaged in his pre-Socratic predecessors.

Plato was closest to the Pythagorean text, rejecting only its substrative, or material, sense of the reality of numbers and of the soul. The material ontology of the Pythagoreans is attested to by Plato's *Phaedo* and by Aristotle's *Metaphysics* and *Physics*.[13]

I have already spoken of the Pythagorean dialectical method of circularity, proportionality, and harmonic attunement of the soul with the cosmos, which may even attain to a mystical participation in the celestial music of the spheres. The same mystagogical element figures in their diaphanic perspective, stemming from the cultist interests and personality of Pythagoras himself.

The governing principle of the Pythagorean text is that of the perfect number, the decad, as witnessed in the report of Hippolytus:

> What Pythagoras principally taught about number was this. Number is the first-principle: it is unlimited and indefinable, and it contains within itself the infinite series of numbers. The decad, the perfect form of the sacred number ten, is present in the essence of each of the first four numbers, since they (when added) become ten. He declared that this sacred tetractys is the fountain which has its source in ever-flowing nature. In the tetractys all the numbers have their first-principle.[14]

The perfect number ten also appears in Chinese and Japanese numerologies and signifies the same semantic intention. A comprehensive principle of an all-embracing totality recurs in various Eastern philosophies as well.

Notice that Plato's comprehensive principle has its immediate precedent in the text of the Pythagorean school. Indeed, Plato's encompassing principle of a perfect and just order has a longer history in pre-Socratic thought. A comprehensive principle already functions in the text of the Milesian philosopher, Anaximander: "The Unlimited is the first-principle of things that are. It is that from which the coming-to-be of things and qualities takes place, and it is that into which they return when they perish, by moral necessity, giving satisfaction to one another and making reparation for their injustice, according to the order of time."[15]

Aristotle does not mention Anaximander in the first book of his *Metaphysics*. In his *Physics*, however, he supports this reading of Anaximander's principle when he writes: "The Unlimited encompasses and governs all things. On this basis the Unlimited is equivalent to the Divine, since it is deathless and indestructible, as Anaximander says."[16] Further corroboration is given by Diogenes Laertius, who says that the Milesian philosopher was "the first to draw a map containing all the outlines of land and sea, and he constructed a global chart of the sky also."[17]

Anaximander also held that the earth is spherical or cylindrical in shape. He conceived of a primordial cosmic evolution taking the form of a flame surrounding the air that surrounds the earth, like the bark of a tree. "This sphere became broken into parts, each of which was a different circle; which is how the sun, the moon and stars were generated."[18] These images of circularity predominate in the doxographical commentaries on his doctrine; they are also images of orders of encompassment, presaging the semantic principle that recurs in the more sophisticated cosmological doctrines of the Pythagoreans and Plato's *Timaeus.*

Anaximander's comprehensive justice that redresses the excesses of things also sets the precedent for Plato's idea of justice, which assigns each social function its proper place in the *Republic*'s well-ordered community. But such a principle is also inscribed in Heraclitus's doctrine of the hidden harmony of the *logos,* which unites agonistic opposites in a paradoxical unity. Heraclitus says that all things come to pass in accordance with this *logos,* which is common to all, although most men live as if each one had a private intelligence of his own.[19]

To Heraclitus, whose sense of primary reality is substrative, the universe is "an ever-living fire, kindling itself by regular measures and going out by regular measures."[20] Thus wisdom is one—"to know the intelligence by which all things are steered through all things."[21] All things come in their due season. Even the sun will not overstep his measures; were he to do so, the Erinyes, handmaids of justice, would seek him out for punishment.[22]

In this archic analysis, the texts of Anaximander and Heraclitus are similar not only in their comprehensive principles, but in their agonistic methods and substrative realities. They differ only in perspective. The objective perspective, which breaks with the mythic (or diaphanic) perspective of Homer and Hesiod, can be considered to be the common perspective of the three Milesian philosophers, Thales, Anaximander, and Anaximenes, who in turn set the precedent for the texts of Anaxagoras and Democritus. Heraclitus's diaphanic perspective already breaks with this proto-objectivist trend and, in that respect, presages the perspectives of the texts of Parmenides, Empedocles, Pythagoras, Socrates, and Plato.

The comprehensive principle of Pythagoras and Plato appears to have lain fallow in the Christian medieval world, subordinated to the orthodox (that is, biblical) creationist principle of Augustine, Anselm, and Bonaventure; to the various strains of Neoplatonic thought that reiterated Plotinus's elemental principle of the One, and to Aquinas's reflexive principle.

The mainstream of transmission of the comprehensive principle in the West travels from the Pythagoreans, through Plato, to Copernicus, Kepler, and Leibniz. In retrospect, the epochal work of Renaissance philosophy can be attributed to Copernicus's *De Revolutionibus Orbium Coelestium* (1543), which contains the following passage:

> For who could give the sun another and better place in this splendid temple of the universe than the center, whence it can illuminate the whole in its totality. Nor without reason have some called it the candle of the world, others the mind, and others the director, Trimegistus the visible god, and the Electra of Sophocles the viewer of all. From its royal throne it rules the swarms of stars, as they circle about it, so that there is manifest to us in this order a wonderful symmetry of the world and a strong and harmonious connexion between the movement and size of the single heavenly spheres, such as in found nowhere else.[23]

As is well known, Kepler proved to be even more neo-Pythagorean in his own text.

A century later, Leibniz combined the concept of a perfect number—namely, God the supreme monad—with an archic assumption concerning a perfect creation distributed as an "infinite series of numbers." Thus, in our archic analysis, Plato was a noumenal Pythagorean, and Leibniz a logistic Platonist.

The sense of a perfectly structured universe runs from the fragments of the Pythagorean Philolaus, a contemporary of Socrates, to Einstein. (Plato is said to have visited this Philolaus on a journey to Italy in about 388 B.C.) Such passages as the following are to be found in the latter's text:

> In the universe everything is fitted together and harmonized out of the limited and the limiting—both the universe as a whole and all the things that it contains.
>
> . . . .
>
> We must obviously conclude that the universe and its contents are fitted together and harmonized by a combination of the limiting and the unlimited.
>
> . . . .
>
> In studying the operations and the essence we must take account of the power and role of the Decad: it is great, completely self-realizing, and all-accomplishing; it is the first principle of human life, in which it participates, and of which it is the leader. Its power is such that without it all things are unlimited, obscure, and indiscernible.[24]

In more recent times, Einstein speaks from this comprehensive principle when he writes of his "cosmic religious feeling," which he says is the strongest and noblest incitement to scientific research.[25] Einstein rejected an indeterministic interpretation of quantum physics, saying that God doesn't throw dice. Commentators have linked his sense of universal causation to that of Spinoza. But in an archic analysis Einstein's text reveals a principle that aligns him with the tradition of Pythagoras and of Plato's *Timaeus*.[26]

Not only Pythagoras and Philolaus, but in other inscriptions Anaximander, Heraclitus, Aeschylus, and Herodotus bequeathed this comprehensive principle to Plato. Plato transformed it into the principle of the beautiful in the *Symposium*, the idea of the good and the principle of justice in the *Republic*, and the principles of rhetorical composition and of the procession of Zeus and the other gods in the *Phaedrus*; it becomes the cosmic principle of the *Timaeus*.

In one archic variable Plato departed from Pythagoras and turned to his "venerable father," Parmenides. Parmenides taught that perfect being suffers no admixture with nonbeing and therefore entirely transcends the appearances of our perceptions. One sees how consciously selective Plato was in aligning his thinking with that of his predecessors. He established an archic relationship with the Pythagoreans, the only exponents of the dialectical method, and with Parmenides, the only other major exponent of a perfect noumenal reality.

The archic precedents of Plato's text can be traced schematically to the following pre-Socratics:

	PERSPECTIVE	REALITY	METHOD	PRINCIPLE
Anaximander				*comprehensive*
Parmenides	*diaphanic*	*noumenal*		
Heraclitus	*diaphanic*			*comprehensive*
Empedocles	*diaphanic*			
Pythagoras	*diaphanic*		*dialectical*	*comprehensive*
Plato	*diaphanic*	*noumenal*	*dialectical*	*comprehensive*

We see again that the pure Platonic paradigm represents a rare combination of archic elements. Indeed, Plato's text remains unique in the history of philosophy.

Democritus's Pre-Socratic Predecessors

Returning now to the text of Democritus, one observes that it too illustrates the theme of continuity in the first principles (*archai*) of the pre-Socratic philosophers. Democritus's text selects from that tradition and grants priority to semantic assumptions that were explicitly subordinated by Plato and Aristotle.

The Democritean text, we noted, is a paradigm of pure materialism:

objective in perspective, substrative in ontological focus, logistic in method, and elemental in principle. It is pure because of the natural affinity among its archic elements. But this text is itself prefigured in that of the Milesian philosopher, Anaximenes. Both Anaximenes and Democritus, and later Santayana, were pure materialists in the sense I am about to reestablish.

For Democritus, the concept of air or ether functions as both material reality (as noted by Aristotle, Anaximenes treated air "as prior to water and the most fundamental of all simple bodies") and as elemental principle.[27] "As our souls, being air, hold us together, so breath and air embrace the entire universe," writes Anaximenes.[28]

The ancient commentaries help fill out the meaning of Anaximenes' text. "He says that all things, even gods and daemons, come-to-be as products of air," reports Hippolytus.[29] Anaximenes agreed with Anaximander that the essence of things is one and unlimited, reports Simplicius, but he disagreed with Anaximander by holding that the ultimate element has "the specific nature of air, which differs in rarity and density according to the kinds of things into which it forms itself."[30] In the words of Plutarch: "Or should we, as Anaximenes of old maintained, accept neither hot nor cold as real things but regard them rather as epiphenomena and temporary states which occur in any material thing when it undergoes certain inner alterations?"[31] "Motion, according to Anaximenes, has existed forever. He adds that the earth came-to-be from a compression of air. . . ." (Pseudo-Plutarch).[32] "Anaximenes said that air is a god, that it is infinite and always in motion" (Cicero).[33] ". . . but instead of believing that the air had been created by the gods, he held on the contrary that they themselves were products of air" (Saint Augustine).[34]

I suggest that Democritus refined the methodological factor in Anaximenes' text (the logistic concept of "condensation and rarefaction" of the material substance) into the idealization of "atoms and the void." But, like Anaximenes, he believed that the ultimate material element(s) existed forever, or, as one should say, the material substance (*physis*) preexisted forever—it is primordial and always antecedent. Even the gods and daemons, who play agential roles in the world, are products of this eternally preexisting material flux. Our own souls are composed of this eternal element.

From Homer through Anaximenes, Empedocles, and Anaxagoras, to Democritus, Epicurus, and Lucretius, the philosophers agree in this materialist interpretation. Saint Augustine, while a spokesman for the noumenal reality and creative principle of the orthodox Christian text, accurately portrays the presuppositions of the same tradition.

Empedocles' version of the elemental principle is as follows:

> They are fools, with no ability to reach out with their thoughts, who suppose that what formerly Was Not could come into being, or that What Is could perish and be utterly annihilated.
>
> And I shall tell you something more. There is no birth in mortal things, and no end in ruinous death. There is only mingling and interchange of parts, and it is this that we call "nature."
>
> . . . .
>
> In the All there is nothing empty; whence, then, could there be any increase?[35]

Both Empedocles and Democritus agree on the doctrine of eternal material nature (*physis*), although the latter understood the former's agonistic conception of the "mingling and interchange" of the parts in a logistic manner.

Empedocles' full archic profile is identical to that of Homer—diaphanic in perspective, substrative in reality, agonistic in method, and elemental in principle. Democritus subordinated their texts' perspectives and methods, while retaining their realities and principles.

As these last citations also indicate, Empedocles' text is further indebted in its elemental principle to the "All" of Parmenides. The "All" dictates that whatever is, is, such that whatever apparently comes-to-be or ruinously ceases-to-be is a merely supervenient epiphenomenon of our consciousness. Like Empedocles, Democritus adopted the same Parmenidean assumption as to an eternal self-sameness, identity, and self-conservation of the "All," while disagreeing with Parmenides' noumenal sense of its perfect reality.

There is a global tradition—composed of the Hindu and Neoplatonic texts, and a modern variant in Schelling—that perpetuates Parmenides' elemental sense of a noumenal reality; so too is there another tradition that reproduces Democritus's elemental sense of a material reality. Like Homer and Empedocles, Parmenides had a diaphanic perspective, which was subordinated by the objective perspective of Democritus's text, but shared with it a logistic method of articulation, conjoined with elemental principles.

Democritus's text is irreducible to either Plato's or Aristotle's because it deploys first principles that are different in kind. Democritus's text, in our comparative analysis, is built on two Parmenidean variables (principle and method), while it is heteroarchic with respect to reality and perspective. But so conspicuous and strong are the former semantic variables in Parmenides that they shed valuable hermeneutical light upon Democritus's otherwise pure text.

In method, Parmenides attacks such agonistic-minded predecessors and contemporaries as Homer, Anaximander, and Heraclitus when he writes: "There are crowds of them without discernment, maintaining that to be and not to be are the same and not the same, and that everything is in a state of movement and countermovement."[36] In broader perspective, this passage and others like it attack the agonistic logics not only of such pre-Socratics as Empedocles and Heraclitus, but of the Taoist Chuang Tzu and of the Mahayana Buddhists, of the Greek Sophists and Skeptics, and their postmodern counterparts in contemporary circles of the East (Nishida and the Kyoto School) and West (Wittgenstein, Derrida, Deleuze, and so on).

The elemental principle of the texts of Leucippus and Democritus, with antecedents in Homer, Anaximenes, and Empedocles, is that of the sheer necessity of things, grounded in the eternal pregiveness of the ontological elements, the atoms in the void, and their eternal motions. Epicurus retained Democritus's basic materialism, but introduced a new basis of cosmic evolution in the creative principle of the built-in declension (or swerving) of the atoms. Newton wanted to retain Democritus's inertial physical system, but he also grounded it on the principle of God's creative power and will.

The immediate antecedent for Democritus's elemental principle is again that of Parmenides, who said that "Never shall it be proven that not-being-is" and ". . . you cannot cut off being from being: it does not scatter itself into a universe and then reunify."[37] There remains, then, but one word by which to express the true road: "And on this road there are many signs that What Is has no beginning and never will be destroyed: it is whole, still, and without end. It neither was nor will be, it simply is—now, altogether, one, continuous. How could you go about investigating its birth? How and whence could it have grown? . . . Necessarily therefore, either it simply Is or it simply Is Not."[38] The Parmenidean text goes on to say that both creation and destruction are driven away by this true belief. For "strong Necessity holds it in bonds of limit, which constrain it on all sides; Natural law forbids that Being should be other than perfectly complete."[39]

Democritus's text improves on this doctrine by changing the Parmenidean sense of the perfect simplicity of the noumenal whole into the simplicity of the material particles (each a perfect whole, as Newton was to emphasize later in his own fashion), while retaining the sense of their eternal, pregiven fate and necessity. Democritus's cognitive attitude was that of the morally neutral, naturalistic observer, who perceives the flux of material bodies that cause the epiphenomenal states of our sense perceptions.

Recapitulating our findings on Democritus's archic antecedents in Greek thought, we have the following schematic representation:

	PERSPECTIVE	REALITY	METHOD	PRINCIPLE
Homer		*substrative*		*elemental*
Thales	*objective*	*substrative*	*logistic*	
Anaximander	*objective*	*substrative*		
Anaximenes	*objective*	*substrative*	*logistic*	*elemental*
Parmenides			*logistic*	*elemental*
Anaxagoras	*objective*	*substrative*	*logistic*	
Empedocles		*substrative*		*elemental*
Democritus	*objective*	*substrative*	*logistic*	*elemental*

In retrospect, the Democritean strain of Greek philosophy proves to have been the prevalent one, just as its modern version, derived from Newton, Locke, Adam Smith, and Darwin, is in our times.

Antecedents to the Sophistic Text

I now turn more briefly to the text of the Sophists in order to trace its antecedents in the pre-Socratic philosophers.

The Sophists, as I have noted, took perceptual and linguistic turns, thereby shifting the focus of philosophy to human activities. In the sentence of Prodicus of Ceos: "Sophists reside in the borderland between philosophy and statesmanship."[40] They are depicted in Plato as grammarians and rhetoricians who understood very well the logical possibilities of that "borderland between." Masters of the art of paradox and ambiguity, they taught the techniques of the eristic art through sheer force of personality. They were the first to put their personalities on the line, so to speak, by charging fees for their philosophical services.[41]

Despite their emphasis on personal flair and style, however, the textual fragments of Protagoras, Gorgias, Prodicus, Thrasymachus, Antiphon, Critias, and other Sophists have a common archic identity. Their text is personal in perspective, existential in reality, agonistic in method, and creative in principle.

If the Sophist movement effected a radical turn, it was in their ontological focus. There is no instance of the existential reality in any of the known pre-Socratic philosophers. Some philosophers are thought to have made an existentialist out of Heraclitus, but his ontological reality centers on a substrative fire (as interpreted by Aristotle and appropriated by the Stoics). The other semantic characteristics of the Sophists are also comparatively rare, which lends credence to their insistence on the novelty of their philosophical principles.

Closest to the Sophists and their true forerunner in certain respects is

Xenophanes, whose text is personal in perspective and agonistic in method. The text of Thales has a creative principle, while the agonistic method appears in the texts of Homer, Anaximander, Heraclitus, and Empedocles.

Aristotle did not acknowledge the text of the Sophists in the first book of his *Metaphysics,* but he did discuss the Sophistic position in later passages of the same work and throughout his philosophical writings in general. The Sophists, according to Aristotle, violated the principle of noncontradiction. He says, for example, that if on Protagoras's principle a man's existential awareness were the measure of all things, and if it were equally possible to affirm and deny anything whatever on any subject, then a given thing could be a trireme, a wall, and a man.[42] Aristotle, the essentialist *par excellence,* clearly rejected the theoretic assumptions of the Sophistic paradigm; he appears to have held that Xenophanes' text does not exhibit first principles. For he wrote: "Xenophanes, who first upheld the doctrine of the one, and whose pupil Parmenides is said to have been, produced no definite doctrine. . . ."[43]

But for this comparative hermeneutic, Xenophanes' fragments outline an important archic profile, whose influence can be traced to the Sophists and other figures in the history of philosophy. Two of the semantic principles of Aristotle's text draw on Xenophanes' text, which is essentialist in its sense of reality and reflexive in principle.

Evidence of Xenophanes' reflexive principle is furnished by Diogenes Laertius: "Xenophanes holds that God is spherical in substance, and that he is unlike man; for the whole of him sees, the whole of him hears, he does not breathe, he is totally mind and thought, and is eternal."[44] In Galenus there is the report: "Xenophanes was an eclectic philosopher who had skeptical doubts about everything except his own dogma that all things are one, and that this One is God, who is limited, rational, and immovable."[45] There are several reports to the effect that Xenophanes believed that the concept of God and gods implied supremacy and self-rule.

Personal in perspective, essentialist in reality, agonistic in method, and reflexive in principle, Xenophanes' text is that of an agonistic Cartesian. While Descartes's text is logistic in method, following Parmenides and Democritus in that respect, he shared the sense of real essences to be found in the archic profile of Xenophanes. Xenophanes' personal perspective and methodological element appear in his constant denunciations of the opinions of other philosophers. As we read in Galenus's testimony, "Xenophanes was an eclectic philosopher who had skeptical doubts about everything except his own dogma . . ."; or in Pseudo-Plutarch's, "Xenophanes of Colopon, going his way and differing from all who preceded him. . ."[46]

Nonetheless, we have set out to discover the archic antecedents of the Sophistic text in pre-Socratic thought. The principle of the Sophistic text is its doctrine of the power of human beings to effect changes in existential life. The Sophists' creative principles of discourse run counter to the naturalistic strains of pre-Socratic thought that are governed by elemental principles, with their various doctrines of necessity. They oppose the comprehensive principles of Anaximander, Heraclitus, Pythagoras, and Plato, with their sense of antecedent cosmic rationality, as well. Aristotle, who has a reflexive principle, also criticizes the creative principle of the Sophists' rhetoric.

The precedent for this creative principle, albeit in the setting of naturalistic speculation, can be traced to the text of Thales. At the very beginning of the Greek philosophical tradition Thales held that "All things are full of gods" and "The magnetic stone has soul because it sets the iron in motion."[47] The magnetic stone has the godly power of active force.

Aristotle seems also to have read Thales' text as having a generative principle: "Thales, the founder of this type of philosophy, says the principle is water (for which reason he declared that the earth rests on water), getting the notion perhaps from seeing that the nutriment of all things is moist, and that heat itself is generated from the moist and kept alive by it (and that from which they come to be is a principle of all things)."[48] Thales is even depicted in the ancient accounts as a practical man who, with a keen objective perspective, predicted an eclipse, dug a deep channel to divert the course of a river for King Croesus's army, and profited financially by predicting a large olive crop on the basis of his astronomical observations.

The Sophists reinterpreted Thales' principle of effective force in their own careers. In a broader intertextual analysis, we can trace the same principle to the originary texts of the Jewish biblical tradition where God and man together are depicted as creative agents in natural and moral processes. Variations on this central religious theme can be observed in the New Testament, the Koran, and the traditions of Augustinian theology, from Anselm, Bonaventure, and Luther to Calvin.

Heidegger, as a modern example, would have us believe that his philosophy appears in a fullness of time. He calls into question the tradition of representational thinking, which he alleges runs from Plato to Nietzsche. His own form of originary *Andenken* turns out to be a meditative thinking that takes place in the horizon of *Ereignis,* the event of appropriation. As such, it turns out to be a form of mythopoetic, revelatory discourse whose antecedents can be traced not to Athens, but to Jerusalem. His philosophy centers on a version of the creative word. But in another respect, Heidegger's self-serving declaration of the end of metaphysics recalls the creative eloquence of the

Greek Sophists. In its rhetorical originality Heidegger's text tends to gloss over its own antecedents in both Athens and Jerusalem.

Another modern philosopher, Whitehead, by contrast, openly acknowledges his debt to the biblical tradition in his concept of cosmological process and of Christ, the poet of the world, the fellow sufferer who understands. In that respect, Whitehead reminds us of Newton, Locke, and Berkeley, who grounded their respective texts' creative principles in biblical citations. They availed themselves equally of the semantic principle of Thales and of the Greek Sophists.

We can summarize the archic antecedents to the Sophistic text in the following schema:

	PERSPECTIVE	REALITY	METHOD	PRINCIPLE
Homer			*agonistic*	
Xenophanes	*personal*		*agonistic*	
Thales				*creative*
Anaximander			*agonistic*	
Heraclitus			*agonistic*	
Empedocles			*agonistic*	
Sophists	*personal*	*existential*	*agonistic*	*creative*

Such an archic synopsis gives further insight into the uniqueness of the pure Sophistic paradigm.

Archic Profiles of Pre-Socratic Philosophy

In the end, as every professional philosopher knows, it is not productive to write the history of philosophy in a merely consecutive fashion. Such a story degenerates into the historian's account of names and dates and into the philosopher's appropriation of cannibalized concepts. In the historical model (which often has a creative principle), since the texts of each of the major authors represent archic shifts, it is impossible to develop a consistent account of the philosophical endeavor. Such histories make sense only according to the grounding principle of their authors. But for others, they serve only to present raw materials for further philosophical analysis, which must take place in some other hermeneutical act.

I have suggested above that Aristotle's reading of his predecessors and contemporaries provides a more viable hermeneutical model. It converts the material variety of the "opinions of the many and the wise" into their formal distribution of first principles.

Adapting Aristotle's own methodology for the purpose, I have endeavored in this chapter to show that the texts of Aristotle, Plato, Democritus, and the Sophists can serve as guides for recovering the rich legacy of archic variables in the texts of the pre-Socratic traditions. Conversely, the pre-Socratic philosophers provide a wealth of archic precedents for the forms of Athenian philosophy. In either respect, we can observe the evolution of the major texts of Greek philosophy toward the pure modes of the four Athenian philosophies.

As every beginning student in philosophy knows, there is a certain pleasure in first reading the archaic texts of the pre-Socratic philosophers. This must be because these fragmentary texts are indeed replete with *archai,* the principles of philosophy, which find their counterparts in our own minds.

With the exception of the text of Anaximenes, the worldviews of the pre-Socratic philosophers represent configurations of mixed modes, that is, archic profiles having at least one heterogenous archic element. The eventual appearance of the pure modes illustrates the point that archic elements can be combined in naturally related combinations. The mixed modes therefore contract the theoretical possibilities that are available in the pure ones.

Reviewing our findings thus far on the theoretical presuppositions of pre-Socratic philosophers, we obtain the following distributions of archic profiles:

	PERSPECTIVE	REALITY	METHOD	PRINCIPLE
Thales	*objective*	*substrative*	*logistic*	*creative*
Anaximander	*objective*	*substrative*	*agonistic*	*comprehensive*
Anaximenes	*objective*	*substrative*	*logistic*	*elemental*
Pythagoras	*diaphanic*	*substrative*	*dialectical*	*comprehensive*
Parmenides	*diaphanic*	*noumenal*	*logistic*	*elemental*
Xenophanes	*personal*	*essential*	*agonistic*	*reflexive*
Heraclitus	*diaphanic*	*substrative*	*agonistic*	*comprehensive*
Empedocles	*diaphanic*	*substrative*	*agonistic*	*elemental*
Anaxagoras	*objective*	*substrative*	*logistic*	*reflexive*

The archaic texts of the Indian, Chinese, Japanese, and other great traditions will yield the same sorts of analyses as their Western counterparts. The rich legacy of such texts will shed further light on philosophical first principles. We need a hermeneutical approach, then, that approaches the texts of world philosophy precisely as expressions of a universal quality of mind.

5

The Principles of Confucian Philosophy

Peirce wrote of the transmission of thought as a self-forming and self-continuing process. Amplification, ramification, and thus generalization are tendencies immanent in the universe at large and vividly illustrated in the history of the human sciences, arts, and crafts. The growth of mind from the randomness of "certain one-idea'd philosophies," which fill in the available niches in an ephemeral landscape, to those that become enduring habits of higher civilization exemplifies what he called the synechistic process.

This recombinant process of intellectual history can be observed in the synoptic analyses of the preceding two chapters. Although necessarily abbreviated, these readings of pre-Socratic, Athenian, and Hellenistic worldviews confirm Peirce's formulation of historic continuities in the great ideas of philosophy. Our ability to establish such a theory of the essential semantic structures of Greek philosophies presupposes the same synechistic process of intellectual history.

Peirce based his formulation of the generalities of mind on his exhaustive researches into the histories of the logical, mathematical, and natural sciences, and tended to highlight the methods and aims of these disciplines. The comparative hermeneutic of this work seeks to expand the potential generality of Peirce's sense of the transmission of thought by encompassing a wider variety of philosophical texts, East and West, while maintaining Kant's definition of the philosophers as the very lawgivers of human reason. By contrast, Kant argued, logicians, mathematicians, and students of nature produce only technical concepts. In the light of this distinction one can see that the history of the sciences, however instructive they were for Peirce's phenomenological reflections, could not provide the final generalizations he sought. Their merely technical concepts still presuppose nomothetical sciences, which finally hold them in their own foundational theories.

These considerations have a special relevance as we turn to a cross-cultural analysis of the principles of Asian thought. Here again we can only endeavor to establish the fuller program in condensed form, while proposing the scope of a broader research enterprise. In contrast to this program, the tendency of many styles of humanistic scholarship to ape the technocratic methods of the various sciences has already been noted. Nowhere is the deleterious effect of this kind of specialization more conspicuous than with respect to the traditions of Asian religions, philosophies, and literatures. The average Western philosophical stylist today remains professionally out of touch with the great works of Eastern civilizations. Meanwhile, the richness of the Asian civilizations provides the potential for unprecedented insights into, if not also for a reconstruction of, the very practice and pedagogy of philosophy today.

What the many forms of Asian philosophy offer us is a world stage on which to complete a reflection on the essential variety of philosophical principles. They command our attention and challenge, indeed oblige, us to integrate their insights and pedagogies with those of the Western traditions. Everywhere we go, we encounter the coexistence and recurrence (reenactment and transmission) of enduring Asian worldviews, which also inevitably intertwine with, clarify, and confirm our readings of the Western worldviews. The net result can only be illumination of the systematic relationship among the great philosophies, East and West. By contrast, the entrenched forms of stylistic chauvinism methodically cut off from these abundant resources have succeeded only in constricting the potential generality and significance of their own localized achievements.

To return for a moment to Peirce's sense of the transmission of general ideas, clear precedents for this formulation can be found in such universal theorists as Aristotle and Hegel. To such thinkers, the world's enduring philosophies and religions are the very substance of our higher mental life. Authentic intellectual activity clarifies but does not break with the achievements of the past. Rather, we reinterpret the concepts and judgments of earlier traditions in our own apprehension of these resources, which enrich rather than limit the possibilities of contemporary life.

From this perspective, it is easy to note that this kind of essentialist reading of the transmission of intellectual history has always been a hallmark of the Confucian traditions of China, as well. In East Asia, the Confucian scholars played the historical role of keepers of the books of higher human culture. Revering antiquity, they preserved its paradigmatic lessons as a mirror for the present. They succeeded admirably, producing along the way some of the most learned traditions of all time.

(We remain appallingly unaware of their philosophical concerns and scholarly accomplishments.)

Like other philosophers, of course, the Confucian scholars gave precedence to their own perceptions of the world, systematized into a full program of cognitive, practical, and aesthetic disciplines. In some instances they too have drawn narrower conclusions than their premises required. But from the vantage point of contemporary intellectual life we can more fully appreciate the potential universality of the Confucian disciplines. Because the Confucians are essentialists, they contribute directly to a hermeneutic of the first principles of philosophy. In connection with the ontologies of such central figures as Aristotle, Hegel, and Peirce, the Confucians force us to reflect again on the theme of intellectual transmission that is at the heart of philosophy.

This point will receive further treatment in the following discussion of the forms of Chinese philosophy. For now we need only indicate a connection to the central Confucian themes of "manifesting the clear character," "illuminating illustrious virtue," and the like. In modernized form, these ideas can be adapted to align the essentialist orientation of this hermeneutic of texts, East and West. Note that the Confucians' transmission of the great books of classical antiquity stands in marked contrast to the book-debunking and book-burning strategies of the Taoists, Ch'an Buddhists, and Legalists. (Whether they are aware of it or not, postmodern deconstructionists are taking a page or two from the Taoists and Buddhists.)

We are now in a position to draw conclusions about Confucianism, Taoism, Hinduism, Buddhism, and the many other forms of Asian thought, having provided a structure for bridging the gap between these traditions and those of the classical and modern West. Such generalizations will involve a reappreciation of religious and secular concepts of sagehood and genius as contemporary models of the integrative functions of human wisdom. To achieve such wisdom surely remains the first business of philosophy, just as it still provides the raison d'être of its many subcultures.

Let us now attempt a series of archic readings of the Chinese philosophical traditions. The abundance of the materials requires us to do so in stages. In this chapter, we examine the archic relationships among the classical Moist and Confucian worldviews, and some of the Yin Yang theories of the Han dynasty. In chapter 6, we go on to compare the more evolved forms of Chinese Taoism, Legalism, the miscellaneous schools, and Neo-Confucian orthodoxies. In discussing the world religions, we will refer to certain Indian (Hindu, Jain, Buddhist) and Japanese (Shinto, Buddhist, Confucian, Neo-Confucian) worldviews.

Comprehensive Principles in Confucius and Mo Tzu

The two great rivals of the early Chinese philosophical tradition were Confucius and Mo Tzu. Their texts differed in perspective, ontological focus, and method, and these disagreements provide glimpses into various aspects of ancient Chinese culture. Nevertheless, both thinkers grounded their texts in comprehensive principles, which link them to world-texts of similar cast within and without the Chinese traditions.

After Confucius and Mo Tzu, comprehensive principles can be seen in the *Great Learning* and *Doctrine of the Mean;* in the Confucian interpretations of the Book of Changes and the classics of ancient poetry, history, and ritual; in the works of the influential Han dynasty systematizer Tung Chung-shu; as well as in the Sung dynasty's reinterpretation of these classical texts in the School of Principle, culminating in Chu Hsi.

Since the Confucian scholars have tended, as an institution, to dominate the intellectual classes, we need to circumvent the scholastic debates between the Confucian, Moist, and other camps to establish independent readings of the major texts.

In its archic analysis the text of Mo Tzu is unique in the Chinese intellectual traditions in that it combines a personal perspective and substrative reality (both typically seen in its concept of "the needs of the people") with a logistic method (of "enriching" the commonwealth and "economizing" in the case of extravagant expenditures), under a comprehensive principle of the common good.[1]

Mo Tzu's doctrine is governed by all of these semantic factors and is typified in the following: "Therefore, if one clearly understands how to obey the will of Heaven and put it into practice in the world at large, then the government will be well ordered, the population harmonious, the state rich, and wealth and goods plentiful. The people will all have warm clothes and plenty to eat, and will live in comfort and peace, free from care."[2] Mo Tzu speaks elsewhere of a heavenly plan for ordering the social world from the top down, resulting in the redistribution of the roles, functions, and commonwealth of the people.

Mo Tzu's program has been described as paternalistic in the sense that its comprehensive principle governs all the political variables in the production of its own intrinsic meaning. The resultant text envisions the career of a sage-king as the paradigm of "universal love," who treats all the people as his own family and establishes the criteria of righteousness and unrighteousness. The "Son of Heaven" receives the mandate of heaven; but even the tip of a hair is the work and concern of heaven.[3]

In another respect, the fundamental concepts of Mo Tzu's text reinforce a populist perspective. If Wing-tsit Chan is correct, this is a text of the working people, which attacks social privilege in the name of a universal rule of righteousness.[4] It is hierarchical in principle and egalitarian in reference.

The Moists attacked the Confucians, depicting them as proponents of conspicuous consumption in the matters of funerals, music, and other ceremonial functions.[5] Confucius himself is painted as an "all too human," rather than a diaphanic, individual—like the Socrates of Aristophanes', as opposed to Plato's, text.[6]

The somewhat monotonous reiteration of Moist themes and tropes stands in contrast to the rhetorical (Sophistic, or paradoxical) brilliance of the chief Confucian texts. This again is a function of the logistic method of the Moist school, which developed treatises on logic and military science in the same methodological form.

Like the Confucians, the Moists predicate their political and social philosophy on the analogy of the family ruled by the father (or both parents). The biological and emotional needs of the children are met through the generous love of the parents. One can envision the organization of families and villages today and, by extension, the organization of the small-scale political communities of Mo Tzu's and Confucius's day along these lines.

Confucian philosophers vigorously attacked Mo Tzu's position. But like any other dissenting philosophical position, their rejection of the altruism of the *Mo Tzu* text was reflexively self-serving. The Confucians' reaction to Mo Tzu's political views was a function of their own essentialist sense of human reality, agonistic method, and comprehensive principle, through which they expressed a foundational sense of the gradations of love and obligation in contrast to the universal love of Mo Tzu's text.

But it should be noted that the Moist text displays a hierarchical principle of its own. It does not say that heaven and its surrogate, the son of heaven, should employ every member of the society alike. It asserts that every person should be treated as a member of the family; but the members of a family are distinguished by age, gender, talent, and other factors. Mo Tzu plainly teaches us to honor the worthy and competent and to assign the titles of office accordingly.[7] He teaches inferiors to identify with their superiors and ranks every member in a society according to a scale that measures the rightness and wrongness of their activities and functions.[8]

These intertextual lessons reconfirm the point that philosophers do not refute one another except by granting priority to their own semantic assumptions. Sophistic in method, the major Confucian texts—notably, of Mencius and Hsün Tzu—contentiously "take the action to" the Moist text, and Confucian-minded historians claim the victory in the eventual demise of the Moist school. But such refutations and claims, reenacted even today, take place in texts that define the relation between the two schools on their own terms.

The *Analects*, like the *Mo Tzu*, reveals a comprehensive principle of government. This principle typically appears in Confucius's teaching that both society and individual are to be governed and judged by the rules of propriety, grounded in overarching concepts of the Way, heaven, the mandate of heaven, and the like. Confucius's words produce an even more authoritative effect than Mo Tzu's because of the diaphanic perspective of his text.

The Chinese character employed for both "ritual" and "propriety" already carries this diaphanic connotation, as scholars have pointed out.[9] At the same time, Confucius uses it to order essential realities—not the noumenal reality of Plato's text or the material realities of Mo Tzu's text, but categories of human relevance and significance. In the *Analects*, this semantic combination underlies every concept of rule and governance, whether social or personal, and every corresponding description of political and moral regulation, measurement, order, and pattern—in brief, every discussion of the civilizing forms of "rites and music."

Thus, a recurrent theme of the *Analects* is that the sages Yao and Shun demonstrated the proper regulation of the empire through the moral and aesthetic ritualization of human life.[10] Book 10 of the *Analects*, which depicts Confucius in his village, describes an idealized lifestyle that is comprehensive in its ritualistic performances and essentialist in ontological orientation.[11] It exemplifies his teaching that "the superior man, extensively studying all learning, and keeping himself under the restraint of the rules of propriety, may thus likewise not overstep what is right."[12]

In Confucius's teaching, moreover, the superior man must be a complete person.[13] There is an intrinsic relationship between the exemplary leadership of a morally developed individual and the completion of civilized society.

Ideally, it will be the "Son of Heaven" who embodies the Way of heaven and sets in motion its pervasive moral energy through the orders of his ministers. Before his divinely bestowed virtue the people will bend like grasses in the wind. A corresponding dynamic of moral interaction is envisioned within the structure of the five constant relationships. Confucius's fondness for learning, as well as the connection between benevolence and knowledge, is also predicated on this orientation to a transformation of the entire social fabric.[14]

These fundamental Confucian concepts are perpetuated in the *Great*

Learning and *Doctrine of the Mean* and are reinterpreted in the Neo-Confucian texts of Chu Hsi and others. They are all variations on the theme of an "all-pervasive unity" in Confucius's teaching.[15] In the final analysis, it is the Tao itself that penetrates and comprehensively circulates through the orders of nature and human life.

Thus in the *Great Learning,* it is said that things have their roots and their branches, and affairs have their end and their beginning.[16] The ancients who wished to show their illustrious virtue throughout the kingdom established order in their own states first. In order to do this they regulated their families; but to accomplish this they first cultivated their persons. In order to cultivate their persons they first purified their hearts and made their thoughts sincere. They could achieve such sincerity only by extending their knowledge to the utmost, and this in turn required an exhaustive investigation of things.[17]

This passage of the *Great Learning* then lists a number of such illustrious performances in a symmetrical fashion. Chu Hsi elucidates the principle of this passage when he writes of the Confucian sage: "After exerting himself in this way for a long time, he will suddenly find himself possessed of a wide and far-reaching penetration. Then, the qualities of all things, whether external or internal, the subtle or the coarse, will all be apprehended, and the mind, in its entire substance and its relations to things will be perfectly intelligent. This is called the investigation of things. This is called the perfection of knowledge."[18]

The Doctrine of the Mean reasserts this all-pervasive principle. In the opening lines of the work, it is heaven that confers the moral nature.[19] As in the *Analects,* the concept of heaven's mandate functions here as both the comprehensive principle and diaphanic perspective of Confucius's teaching.[20]

The same principle informs the *Doctrine of the Mean*'s teaching of the coordinate relation of equilibrium and harmony: "This equilibrium is the great root from which grow all the human actings in the world, and this harmony is the universal path which they all should pursue."[21] "Equilibrium" refers to the mind before the stirring of the human feelings, and "harmony" to the state when the feelings have acted to the appropriate degree. Accordingly, the text goes on to say, the superior man does what is proper to the station in which he finds himself.[22] For all the gradations of human love and worth are measured by this principle of propriety.

In the *Doctrine of the Mean,* the five constant relations form another comprehensive set of ethical relationships, embedded within the all-completing Way of the sages. Passages depicting King Wen and the Duke of Chou also exemplify the diaphanic, essentialist, and comprehensive teaching of the text.

The Principles of Mencius and Hsün Tzu

Let us now describe the archic profiles of the classical Confucian texts in greater detail. By classical I mean the pre-Han texts, as opposed to the Neo-Confucian documents of the Sung and the Ming dynasties. For the present purposes I will concentrate on the five philosophical books—the *Analects, Mencius, Great Learning, Doctrine of the Mean,* and *Hsün Tzu* of the classical Confucian tradition. A wider-ranging study would include the *Book of Odes, Book of History, Spring and Autumn Annals,* and the *Book of Rites.*

We observe first that the texts of Mencius and Hsün Tzu are formally heteroarchic not only with one another, but also with the *Analects, Great Learning,* and *Doctrine of the Mean,* in their grounding principles. I have shown that the elemental principle takes the form of some primordial element, substance, or nature, which acts through its intrinsic oneness and enduring self-sameness. It produces differences out of its own undifferentiated substance and returns them to itself in their fundamental identity, rather than establishing, as does a comprehensive principle, their hierarchical distribution in a complete set. Such was the elemental principle of the Taoist classic, the Tao Te Ching, in contrast with the contemporary texts of Mo Tzu and Confucius. The text of the second great Taoist classic, the *Chuang Tzu,* follows Lao Tzu in this archic respect, but then so does the text of the second great Confucian classic, the *Mencius.*

The creative principle, on the other hand, is the principle not of some identical nature or element, but of voluntarily "making a difference." The emphasis here is on the generative process and product through which the new replaces the old. In Chinese philosophy, the creative principle appears first in the text of the Confucian Hsün Tzu and then in that of the Legalist Han Fei Tzu. In terms of historical influence, the latter took over the former's principle, while diverging in all other archic respects, thereby producing a text hostile to all the streams of Confucian learning.

Confining ourselves here to the unfolding of the Confucian Way, Mencius's discourse illustrates a shift from the comprehensive axiom of Confucius to an elemental concept of the intrinsic moral heart-and-mind (*pen hsin*). Thus in Mencius the first step in royal government is for the king to respect the seasons of husbandry, which have their own cycles and determine the livelihood of his people in natural ways.[23] The king's respect for the rhythms of nature and his compassion for his people are traced to their moral basis in the king's own mind.[24] Various passages of the text bring out the connection between fathoming the moral resources of the king's mind and the possibility of achieving kingly dignity.[25] These are interwoven with another set of passages, which articulate the theme of the pleasure enjoyed by the virtuous ruler and his people in sharing the wealth of his kingdom.[26] The sage and the people are said to have the same benevolent sensibility of mind, which flowers spontaneously in life's moral attitudes—a theme that was to become central to the Wang Yang-ming school in later centuries.[27]

At the core of Mencius's teaching is a reversion, through self-examination, to the depths of one's innately moral element.[28] Reminiscent in this respect of Lao Tzu, Mencius says that the great man does not lose his child's heart.[29] Echoing Meister Eckhart's little castle, he calls it the quiet home in which all men should dwell.[30] For all three authors, Lao Tzu, Eckhart, and Mencius, it is not a matter of breaking out of, but of breaking through to our innermost heart of hearts.

Thus in Mencius the superior man discovers and preserves benevolence and righteousness in his own heart.[31] The people will turn to such a person as water flows downward or as wild beasts fly to the wilderness.[32] In various passages Mencius contrasts his position with that of Kao Tzu's text, which appears to be creative in principle (as well as existential in its sense of reality and personal in perspective).

"Exhausting his mind, knowing the nature, knowing Heaven, . . . and thus establishing his Heaven-ordained being," the sage of Mencius realizes a different model of moral development within the Confucian tradition.[33] The principle of sagehood is man's own "passion nature,"[34] a Mencian concept that was to be elaborated in the Wang Yang-ming schools of China and Japan. We see it again in Mencius's assertion of our intrinsically commiserating mind and the other equally innate "four beginnings" of virtue; or even, in the old funeral arrangements through which the ancients satisfied the natural feelings of their hearts.[35]

The comprehensive principles of the *Analects, Great Learning,* and *Doctrine of the Mean* are noticeably absent in such passages. Instead, the integrative principle of Mencius's text shows affinity with that of the Taoists, in the form of the spontaneous flow of natural feeling. In broader perspective, Mencius's elemental principle of innate moral sentiment is archically convergent with that of Hume's *Enquiry Concerning the Principles of Morals.*

This is radically different from the case of Hsün Tzu. His text also advocates a program of moral reform, but it does so through a creative principle. In this respect Hsün Tzu brings to mind the Sophists' emphasis on the power of conscious activity, ultimately a form of action, to "make a difference" among men. The *Hsün Tzu* stresses the dogged effort required to acquire learning and virtue, and the corresponding efficacies of the Confucian rituals and Confucian teachers.[36] Creative in principle and essentialist in sense of reality, the *Hsün Tzu* ranks with the philosophical program of John Dewey in envisioning the transformation of human life through melioristic institutions and agencies.

Hsün Tzu envisions the Confucian gentleman as literally instituting the ritual principles in the historical process and thereby forming a triad with heaven and earth to bring the natural processes to their fulfillment.[37] He actively works to produce consummatorily moral organizations of human living, thus perfecting all that is necessary between heaven and earth.[38]

In section 23 of the work Hsün Tzu makes a radical departure from Confucius and Mencius with his paradoxical doctrine that human nature is evil—an assertion that stands out in rhetorical effect against the main Confucian definitions of human nature and openly contradicts Mencius in particular. It is at the same time an expression of Hsün Tzu's moral agonism, since the creative principle operates to establish goodness as the result of conscious human activity. He attacks Mencius for precisely this reason—namely, for not distinguishing between the basic nature and the products of conscious activity.[39]

Such archic differences will become clearer as we investigate the perspectives, ontological commitments, and methods of the classical Confucian texts.

The Five Confucian Classics

In the *Mo Tzu* there is a chapter entitled "Against Confucians." In one passage Duke Ching of Ch'i asks Master Yen, "What sort of a man is Confucius?" His reply has outraged Confucians for centuries. Confucius is depicted as an arrogant, self-righteous schemer, a corrupter of innocent people. He and his followers are further branded as fatalists who teach that long life or early death, wealth or poverty, safety or danger, order or disorder are all decreed by the will of heaven and cannot be modified.[40]

An archic analysis of this remarkable chapter of the *Mo Tzu* reveals that it is governed by a personal perspective. Mo Tzu advances the view that the Confucian type of person does nothing to meet the vital needs of ordinary people. This is a good example of the heteroarchic appropriation of one philosophical text by another. Outrageous as it must be to Confucian-minded scholars, it is of a piece with such reductions of sage and hieratic wisdom found in a variety of personalists from Protagoras to Erasmus, Voltaire, Kierkegaard, Nietzsche, James, and Sartre.

Thus Nietzsche, for one, brands the hieratic types of philosophers and religionists as "God's ventriloquists," whose ascetic ideals conceal covert wills to power. In like manner the Chinese Legalist philosopher

Han Fei Tzu castigated the Confucian counselors at court as "the shaman priests of the rhetoricians." This is an apt but heteroarchic designation within the parameters of the Legalist text.

Nonetheless, it is outrageous to the followers of Confucius to see the life and teaching of their sage reduced to a merely private will to power. They are right within the parameters of their own text, which is diaphanic in perspective. The *Analects* depicts Confucius as "a man among men," warm and genial with his intimate friends. He is a paradigm of humanism in passages exhibiting the essentialist sense of reality (the actualized moral personality) of the text. But the issue here is that of the epistemic authority of the *Analects* and the other classics of the Confucian tradition. Confucius, like Plato's Socrates and the Buddha, is a vehicle for the transmission of a higher, more-than-human wisdom. The temples later erected to Confucius in China, Korea, and Japan bear witness to the same diaphanic character of Confucius's teaching.

Thus in the *Analects* Confucius's fondness for learning is a function of his diaphanic perspective. His learning is ordained to transmit the Way, as epitomized in the sage-kings of antiquity. This also applies to Confucius's "fondness for antiquity" and his reverence for old knowledge even as he pursues the new.[41] He insists that the wise regulations of the Hsia, Yin, and Chou dynasties can be known, and he considers heaven to be using him as its wooden tongue.[42] He thus describes his mission in life as "a transmitter and not a maker, believing in and loving the ancients."[43] He stands in awe of the ordinances of heaven and the words of the sages.[44]

It is heaven that knows Confucius and has produced the virtue in him.[45] Therefore Confucius had no fear of K'wang, because heaven had entrusted the truth to him. The last passage of the present edition of the *Analects* depicts a Confucius who recognizes the ordinance of heaven, establishes his character through the rules of propriety, and knows men by knowing the force of words.[46] Confucius's own words are forceful, like those of Socrates, because they presuppose and transmit a higher authority.

In this archic analysis, the same perspective carries over into the texts of the *Mencius*, the *Great Learning*, and the *Doctrine of the Mean*. It is conspicuously absent in the *Hsün Tzu*, which demythologizes the Confucian concept of heaven and reorients the civilizing work of the Confucian gentleman in an objective perspective.

Many passages in these four texts confirm this interpretation. In the *Mencius*, such themes as delighting in heaven, knowing heaven, receiving employment from heaven, accomplishing a great result through heaven, following the ordinances of God, and accepting benevolence and dignity from heaven[47] are linked with Confucius's perspective, which draws its inspiration from the sage-kings of antiquity. Mencius therefore says: "The compass and square produce perfect circles and squares. By the sages, the human relations are perfectly exhibited."[48] That is to say, they are diaphanically and essentially revealed. Key passages on establishing one's destiny, and on heaven's mandate or heaven's correct appointment, with their revolutionary political connotation, presuppose this diaphanic form of legitimation.[49] Paralleling the *Doctrine of the Mean,* the *Mencius* also highlights the concept of sincerity as the way of heaven.[50]

In the *Great Learning* we see the same perspective functioning as an epistemic attitude that knows and transmits the teaching of heaven. The sage is depicted as contemplating and studying the illustrious decrees of heaven.[51] Through his translucent sincerity of character the superior man overcomes the disguises and self-deceptions of the evil man.[52]

In the *Doctrine of the Mean* the correlation between illuminative intelligence and sincerity is also pronounced. Some of its key passages depict the transparency and brilliancy of the sincere man—and his powers of foresight by signs and portents—in memorable terms.[53] It echoes the Mencian theme that sincerity is the way of heaven and sagehood.[54] Thus the superior man awaits the appointments of heaven: he also receives from heaven the emoluments of dignity.[55] All of these passages establish the authority of the text as a diaphanic transmission of the Way. This theme is already sounded in the text's opening sentence: "What Heaven has conferred is called the nature; an accordance with this nature is called the Way; the regulation of this Way is called instruction."[56]

The *Hsün Tzu* departs from the texts of Confucius and Mencius in its creative principle as well as in its objective perspective. It is significant that no commentary was written on this text until the ninth century A.D.; thereafter, it was virtually excluded from the canon by Chu Hsi and other Neo-Confucian hermeneuts of the classical Confucian tradition. These developments constitute other instances of heteroarchic intertextuality in the Chinese philosophical traditions.

For his part, Hsün Tzu transformed the diaphanic perspective of his Confucian predecessors into a hard-headed orientation to the causalities of the real world. His attitude toward human nature is reminiscent of Freud's well-known "reality principle," which rejects the validity of subjective wishes and idealistic illusions. Hsün Tzu's chapter, "On Dispelling Obsessions," clearly illustrates this attitude.[57] He inevitably clashed with the diaphanic perspective and elemental principle of Mencius, especially with his doctrine of the innate goodness of the human heart. Hsün Tzu also clashed with the diaphanic mysticism of Chuang Tzu; he did so while stressing the general narrowness of other philosophical views in the objective perspective of his own text.[58]

In effect, Hsün Tzu's text takes its point of departure from empirical observations of natural phenomena and realistic assessments of the possibilities of human action. Empirical observation forms the basis of his doctrine of "Rectifying Names": Names are not fixed, but only the means by which one attempts to understand different realities.[59] This perspective carries over into Hsün Tzu's radical demythologization of the Confucian concept of heaven, which functions for him neither as a (comprehensively) grounding principle nor as a (diaphanically) illuminating epistemic authority.

In the chapter entitled "A Discussion of Heaven," Hsün Tzu asserts that what men attribute to heaven is only the natural result of their own actions.[60] Accordingly, the sage does not seek to understand heaven; he seeks only to understand the regularity of natural phenomena. Hsün Tzu rejects both the Confucian prognostication of portents and the practice of praying to heaven: "You pray for rain and it rains. Why? For no particular reason, I say. It is just as though you had not prayed for rain and it rained anyway. The sun and moon undergo an eclipse and you try to save them. . . ."[61]

Hsün Tzu treats the former kings more as creative pioneers of higher civilization than as diaphanic individuals. He does not restrict their appearance to high antiquity or a mythical golden age, the standard legitimating tropes of the diaphanic perspective (from Plato to Confucius and Lao Tzu).

In archic analysis, however, Hsün Tzu rejoins Confucius and Mencius in exhibiting an essentialist ontological focus in an agonistic form. All authentically Confucian and Neo-Confucian texts give precedence to essentialist realities. Thus, all the passages of the Confucian schools that celebrate learning, friendship, filial piety, benevolence, rites, and music, as well as all the vignettes illustrating Confucius's ways of thinking and behaving in concrete situations, are essentialist in focus.

The hallmark of the essentialist philosopher is generally to be found in his appreciation of universal qualities of mind, their possibilities of full development, and their self-sustaining powers. Confucius was interested in the *Book of Odes*, the Histories, and the *Book of Rites* for the exemplary lessons they provided. Not an existentialist, Confucius advocated the continuity of these essential forms of civilized behavior in the historical transmission of the true Way. In like manner, the Confucian historiographers of the Chinese and Japanese traditions have always held up the lessons of the past as a mirror for the present.

For the same reason, Confucian culture is energetically this-worldly in moral and political implication. Confucius taught that the civilized character is molded by education and strengthened by obeying the rules of propriety, with the emphasis on actual performance of one's duties in office and, in general, on observing "rites and music" as the habitual forms of civilized life.

The discourse of Mencius is essentialist when he is represented as saying, in the opening passage of the text, that "benevolence and righteousness are his only topics."[62] Like Confucius, he emphasizes the potential for benevolence and righteousness that distinguishes men from the lower animals.[63] Against the Moists he upholds Confucius's teaching of gradations in love and kindness to relatives, the people at large, and the lower creatures.[64] Mencius's essentialism is typically exhibited in all passages in which he speaks of the king's attaining royal dignity, that is, realizing a specifically moral character.[65] There are numerous passages illustrating the merits of upholding the supremacy of the noblest part (the moral nature) and of bringing the "four beginnings" of virtue to maturity.[66]

The generically Confucian teaching of the "accumulation of virtue" is continued in Hsün Tzu, who stresses the moral lessons of the classics and the completion of one's character through rituals.[67] Honoring the rites, understanding the moral relations and categories, persevering in virtue, and in general observing the "ritualization of life" are dominant themes of this text. "Rites are the markers: he who does away with the rites blinds the world."[68]

Central to Hsün Tzu's text is the chapter entitled "A Discussion of Rites," which takes as its theme the origins of ritual in our emotional nature and defines rituals as developed forms satisfying that nature and producing the institutions of civilized life.[69] Mankind forms a triad with heaven and earth, completing the natural and vitalistic processes through the formation of higher human civilization.[70]

The essentialist ontological focus prevails in the texts of the *Great Learning* and *Doctrine of the Mean* as well. It is conspicuous, for example, in the latter's teaching on the full development of one's nature and that of other men, and the nurture of the myriad creatures, which combine to form a triad with heaven and earth.[71] The sage is a diaphanic individual as he contemplates the illustrious decrees of heaven; he is essentialist in embodying the teaching of the *Great Learning*—which is to personify illustrious virtue, restore the people's spirit, and rest in the highest excellence.

As for method, a careful grammatical analysis of the *Analects* reveals that the memorable sayings of Confucius are expressed in an agonistic form. For example, the mildly adversative particle *ehr*—meaning "but" or "and yet"—and equivalent constructions and tropes occur throughout the text, conditioning the reader to think in that way. This kind of paradoxical effect can be produced with or without particles in the Chinese language. It functions when Confucius's uncommon ways are portrayed. Thus, Confucius is a transmitter, not a maker. He does not herd with beasts, he is a man among men. The gentleman does not depart from the Way for the interval of a single meal. When the stables burnt down, Confucius did not ask about the horses. He honors the ghosts and spirits, but keeps them at a distance. If he does not know about life, how can he know about death?[72]

A grammatical analysis of the *Analects* inevitably becomes a grammatological one, revealing the remarkable consistency among the text's three modes of expression. The gentleman, or superior man, exhibited in the citations above, is contrasted in various ways to the mean, or inferior, man.[73] In the active mode of judgment, the same moral agonism impels the career of the Confucian gentleman in the moral and political spheres. East Asian Confucianism certainly represents one of the oldest enduring schools of thought in recorded history.

A purportedly "unitary thread" of transmission of the Confucian heritage is preserved in certain commentaries, which exemplify the hermeneutical process in their own ways. The first step in this interpretive process usually consists of jettisoning the text of Hsün Tzu, leaving it in a state of limbo outside the orthodox line of transmission. But the *Mencius* remains heteroarchic in its principle, with the predictable result that formulations of Neo-Confucian orthodoxy split along two main lines, in the schools of Chu Hsi and Wang Yang-ming, respectively.

To summarize the analyses of the ancient Chinese schools thus far, one finds that the Moist and Confucian classics already represent a rather diverse set of semantic assumptions. Charted schematically, they are as follows:

	PERSPECTIVE	REALITY	METHOD	PRINCIPLE
Mo Tzu	*personal*	*substrative*	*logistic*	*comprehensive*
Confucius	*diaphanic*	*essential*	*agonistic*	*comprehensive*
Mencius	*diaphanic*	*essential*	*agonistic*	*elemental*
Hsün Tzu	*objective*	*essential*	*agonistic*	*creative*

Significant analogues to these archic elements will be found in the history of world philosophy. The ancient Chinese classics illuminate and are illuminated by the wider interrelationships of philosophical texts.

Yin Yang Theories and the Book of Changes

Another branch of classical Chinese philosophical thought deals with Yin Yang theories, whose affiliations with the traditional schools of Confucianism (and Taoism) can be further elaborated.

The principal text in this category is the I Ching, or Book of Changes, an ancient classic that has inspired a complex body of interpretations by rival schools.[74] Here again we must attend to the changes of the books—

the hermeneutical changes—by analyzing the archic profiles of the texts involved. The problem is compounded by the fact that the keepers of the books have traditionally claimed the I Ching as a Confucian classic, even attributing its appendices, or "Ten Wings," to the hands of the master himself.

It is clear that the Yin Yang theory (or theories) represents the efforts of generations of Chinese philosophers to identify fundamental forces, elements, and principles. Since these comprise binary pairs of *yin* (that is, passive, female, weak, negative) and *yang* (that is, active, male, strong, positive) forces, their relationship in philosophical texts inevitably took the form of two-voiced logical operations.

Confucians and Taoists were prepared to divide the interpretation of the Yin Yang theory in several ways. Chuang Tzu, an agonistic Taoist, preferred to stress paradoxical dislocations of *yin* and *yang* in the substrative reality; in contrast, Lao Tzu, a dialectically minded Taoist, envisioned their harmonious interaction. Both are possible readings, but Chuang Tzu's takes a more rhetorically brilliant *tour de force* to read the relationship between *yin* and *yang* forces as a logical series of disjunctions.

Lao Tzu's reading appears to be the more natural one, and it agrees with the prevailing body of literature, which describes the dialectical resolution of *yin* and *yang* tendencies. Perhaps this explains why the Yin Yang and Five Agents theories are not to be found in the chief Confucian classics—the *Analects, Mencius, Great Learning*, or *Doctrine of the Mean*—whose methodology is agonistic.

Wing-tsit Chan summarized the relevant historical facts in this regard. Originally the Ying Yang and Five Agents, or Elements, theories formed separate texts, and joined to form a single doctrine only later.[75] The five elements are ostensibly material elements (metal, wood, air, fire, and water), which lend themselves to a substrative interpretation. The theory contributed another archic feature, namely, that of the "mutual succession" of the five elements in natural and cosmical rotation or progression, which suggests an assumption as to a complete, comprehensive set.

The same material elements or forces, however, can be conceived of as operations with the five elements symbolizing the five agents of cultural transformation. The Confucian philosophers took this tack. The thrust of their essentialist ontologies was to interpret the forms of human civilization, manifested in such generic concepts as rites and music, as culminating forms of the cosmical processes.[76]

The branch of Confucian thought that developed especially from the *Analects* could therefore reasonably adapt the combined Yin Yang theory to its own purposes by granting precedence to its own semantic factors of essentialist reality and comprehensive principle. But, to repeat, the later Confucian tradition of the Han dynasty did so despite the complete silence about the Yin Yang theory in the texts of Confucius and Mencius, as well as in the *Great Learning* and the *Doctrine of the Mean.*

This essentialist reconstruction may account for the co-opting of the I Ching as a Confucian classic, supposedly edited by Confucius himself. The later Confucian tradition could then read the I Ching as a guide to the starry heavens above and the moral law within, while giving ontological priority to the latter over the former. It is perhaps easiest to do this in a text that dialectically unites the natural and human agents by means of a language describing their harmonious interaction, as in the interpretation of Lao Tzu.

In historical fact, the Yin Yang theory is a sedimented one. As Wing-tsit Chan documents it, Yin Yang configurations occur in the *Tso Chuan,* Tao Te Ching, *Chuang Tzu,* and *Hsün Tzu;* the Five Agents, or Elements, theory appears in the *Book of History, Mo Tzu, Hsün Tzu, Tso Chuan,* and *Kuo-yü.*[77] But despite the importance of these concepts, there is not a single ancient treatise on them or even a good passage displaying them in an essential form. As for the composition of the I Ching itself, it is most probably the product of many hands over a long period of time, extending from the fifth or sixth century to the third or fourth centuries B.C. The combined Yin Yang and Wu Hsing theories take definite shape only in such latter-day interpreters as Tsou Yen and Tung Chung-shu.

This hermeneutical fact even governs our access to the ideas of Tsou Yen (305–240? B.C.), who is reported by Ssu-ma Ch'ien (145–86? B.C.) to have produced essays totaling more than one hundred thousand words. As portrayed by the Grand Historian, Tsou Yen's text appears to have been objective in perspective: "He invariably examined small objects and extended this to larger and larger ones until infinity. He first described the present and then traced back to the Yellow Emperor, all of which has been recorded by scholars."[78] But is this objective perspective Tsou Yen's or Ssu-ma Ch'ien's?

Tsou Yen at any rate appears to have been a world-mapper in the mode of Anaximander and others. A comprehensive principle and objective perspective combine in this charming account, also mediated by the text of Ssu-ma Ch'ien:

> He first made a list of China's famous mountains, great rivers, deep valleys, birds and animals, things produced on land and sea, and select objects. On the basis of these he extended his survey to what is beyond the seas, to what men are unable to see. He mentioned and cited the fact that ever since the separation of heaven and earth the Five Powers (Five Agents) have been in rotation. The reign of each power was quite appropriate and how has it corresponded to fact![79]

In working out the ontological status of his Five Agents theory, Tsou Yen appears to follow the Confucian interpretation of the I Ching. He taught that heaven gave Great Yu its nine categories, through which the various virtues and their relations were regulated. The essential properties of the five agents, five activities, five arrangements of time, and so on are thus treated categorically and correlated with the properties of the five directions, the five musical instruments, the five colors, the five grains, the five sense organs, the five atmospheric conditions, the five metals, the five ancient emperors, the five virtues, the five feelings, and the five social relationships.[80]

This fascinating symbolism of correspondences is rendered by Tsou Yen as a dynamic process of natural and human exchanges. The methodological model for these operations is the interaction of *yin* and *yang*, dialectical opposites that harmonize in the unity of man and nature.[81] In this respect Tsou Yen can be considered to have set the stage for Tung Chung-shu and for the Neo-Confucian masters of the Sung.

Tung Chung-shu (ca. 179–104 B.C.) created his intellectual synthesis by retaining Tsou Yen's dialectical method, in contrast to the classical Confucian authors, but returning to the diaphanic perspective of Confucius and Mencius. His text is an unorthodox one from the standpoint of any of the five Confucian classics, but orthodox from the standpoint of Neo-Confucianism.

As in the case of Tsou Yen, the decisive factor for Tung Chung-shu's theory seems to be the influence of the I Ching's formulation of the relation of *yin* and *yang*. Tung also produces another version of Tsou's correspondence theory based on a doctrine of interacting similarities in kind. The Confucian emphasis on humanity and righteousness is another sign of his essentialist ontological focus.[82]

All of these teachings are governed by Tung Chung-shu's principle of preestablished harmony, from the authorizing perspective of a pristine wisdom. Thus the same principle and perspective control in turn his theory of the mutual succession of the five agents and their various categorial correspondences, his rotational theory of historical cycles, as well as his theory of the correspondences of man and the numerical categories of heaven.[83]

Having come this far in reconstructing the archic assumptions of a number of Chinese philosophical paradigms, let us conclude on a general hermeneutical note. Some scholars may be inclined to dismiss ancient views in favor of the fresh ideologies in vogue today. This is a mistake, if only for the reason that the forms of thought are recurrent and branch out along established lines. Accordingly, we will suffer a loss in philosophical awareness if we confine ourselves to present existential forms alone. We may also possibly fail to recognize relevant analogues among the intellectual forms of our common heritage.

Related to this problem is the penchant of some scholars to draw a line of demarcation between religious and philosophical texts. The East will have its mysticism and the West its morals. But in our comparative hermeneutic there is no viable reason for making a distinction between religious and philosophical texts, any more than there is for making one between ancient and modern ones.

In the foregoing account I have traced various lines of evolution in the principles of Confucius and Mo Tzu, Mencius and Hsün Tzu, the *Great Learning, Doctrine of the Mean,* and the I Ching. In the next chapter we will examine in greater detail the Legalist and Taoist traditions, two prominent branches among the Hundred Schools that underwent hermeneutical transformations in the Han dynasty. For now, we have begun to discern a shift in the Confucian texts of the Han dynasty toward the dialectical method:

	PERSPECTIVE	REALITY	METHOD	PRINCIPLE
I Ching	*diaphanic*	*essential*	*dialectical*	*comprehensive*
Tsou Yen	*objective*	*essential*	*dialectical*	*comprehensive*
Tung Chung-shu	*diaphanic*	*essential*	*dialectical*	*comprehensive*

In the first and the last of these we also have the archic profiles of the texts of the masters of the Sung dynasty (from Chou Tun-i to Chu Hsi) and of their Korean and Japanese counterparts.

6

Chinese Philosophies in World Perspective

Studying the ancient schools of Chinese philosophy confirms the perception that any developed mental culture or civilization is comprised of a rich variety of texts and subtexts. The more we search for subtexts, the more often we will find them. Pursued along such a trajectory, a properly philosophical perspective eventually becomes attenuated or transmuted into the interpretive work of special sciences. Conversely, the more we seek the higher forms of a prevailing culture of texts, the more they stand out as well.

In China, these governing worldviews came to coexist in a definite set of interrelationships. Contemporary interpretive projects can now organize them in logistic, agonistic, or dialectical sets; but it is equally possible to reconstitute them in a synoptic set of their sheer generality of worldviews. The latter approach, I argue, can alone exhibit the full power of ideas in their routes of historical transmission. Capitalizing on their exemplary status as historical essences, the synoptic approach can also better appreciate the Chinese worldviews as vital resources of thought in general.

To borrow a phrase of Galileo's, there is no way to charm these new—that is, old—planets out of the sky. Scholars are elucidating the tenets of Confucianism, Taoism, Buddhism, and the other forms of Chinese tradition as enduring insights into the world and human life; a larger student population is finding these Chinese worldviews perfectly relevant to their intellectual needs. The work of my comparative hermeneutic arises from these kinds of experiential exigencies. Chinese and other Asian philosophies confirm the point that the principles of thought harbor their own potentialities for ramification, amplification, and translation across any present boundaries of thought.

What has been lacking to this point have been the bridge concepts to go with a world perspective. I will further suggest the possibility of this transcultural work by sketching the archic iconography of some of the other forms of Chinese intellectual history. Illuminating even some of these will enable me to focus many larger research projects with regard to both indigenous intertextual linkages and the wider networking of world philosophies. I will do this by a series of brief archic readings of the texts of Lao Tzu, Chuang Tzu, Han Fei Tzu, certain miscellaneously classified philosophers, and finally the Neo-Confucian masters of the Sung and Ming dynasties.

The Tao Te Ching

The Tao Te Ching articulates a philosophy thought to originate in the fifth century B.C.; thus its reputed author, Lao Tzu, would have been a contemporary of Confucius and Mo Tzu. Whatever its precise date, the Tao Te Ching is a seminal text whose influence can be discerned in Chuang Tzu, Mencius, Han Fei Tzu, the I Ching, Wang Ch'ung, the Neo-Taoists, and Neo-Confucians.

The archic profile of the Tao Te Ching gives it a definite place within the wider array of texts. The Tao Te Ching is a diaphanic text and figures prominently among the great texts of world religion. It is also a paradigm of substrative ontology, dialectical method, and elemental principle. That it yields to analysis within the network of world-texts corroborates the philosophical intertextuality in which it, and our readings of it, coexist.

An older generation of Western translators and scholars tended to misread the naturalistic ontology of the Tao Te Ching. Max Weber has contributed to another kind of misinterpretation by classifying Taoism in his "world-fleeing" typology, suggesting that certain transcendent and transcendental Taoist concepts were invested with the noumenal senses of Platonism and Christianity. Other interpreters have sought to find similarities with the texts of Mahayana Buddhism, particularly those of a supposedly unique Chinese variety (for example, Ch'an). Thus art historians have tended to link certain Taoist and Zen aesthetic forms. It is always possible to combine divergent worldviews, of course, and many scholars seem to settle for that. But we can gain more from reading the Tao Te Ching first on its own terms and then in terms of its relationships to other works of philosophy.

Contrary to earlier interpretations, the Taoist classic is an exemplarily substrative text. This naturalistic sense of reality is already met in its opening verses:

In the beginning of heaven and earth there were no words,
Words came out of the womb of matter;
And whether a man dispassionately
Sees to the core of life
Or passionately
Sees the surface,
The core and the surface
Are essentially the same,
Words making them seem different
Only to express appearance.
If name be needed, wonder names them both;
From wonder into wonder
Existence opens.[1]

The same passage is also wonderfully elemental in principle. The "womb of matter" underlying all superficial "appearances" of the false surface of individual consciousness serves to establish the priority of the substrative mode, while the essential sameness of the core and the surface is elemental in presupposition.[2] The entire text can be considered a series of variations on this theme.

To Lao Tzu, the return of all things into their natural element is a process of the going forth and returning of the Tao itself. The Taoist sage reveals the dialectical movement of the Tao:

As the soft yield of water cleaves obstinate stone,
So to yield with life solves the insoluble:
To yield, I have learned, is to come back again.
But this unworded lesson,
This easy example,
is lost upon men.[3]

. . . .

Be so charged with the nature of life that you give your people birth,
That you mother your land, are the fit
And ever-living root of it:
The seeing root, whose eye is infinite.[4]

Elemental and dialectical factors also account for the text's ubiquitous themes of rustic simplicity and friendship with one's fellow wayfarers in life:

If the sign of life is in your face
He who responds to it
Will feel secure and fit

As when, in a friendly place,
Sure of hearty care,
A traveler gladly waits.[5]

In abandoning certain artificially ritualized forms of human life, Lao Tzu could only intensify the emphasis on spontaneous feelings and genuine friendships. In connection with this, the Tao Te Ching offers a version of the "ethics of cheerfulness" found in the works such naturalistic philosophers as Democritus and Santayana. But in addition to its diaphanic perspective, it differs from those texts in the dialectical logic through which it constantly affirms the unity of natural and human life.

The Tao Te Ching is a good example of a world-theory that simultaneously reveals exhibitive, assertive, and active modalities. We enjoy its poetic beauty, but appreciate its other two dimensions. The Chinese have always viewed it as a political and moral tract. It has become a favorite text of certain countercultures of our times, perhaps because its archic profile is identical to Rousseau's except in its perspective.

As a political and religious philosophy the Tao Te Ching instructs the world's princes to "take no action," but rather to let their peoples live in rustic simplicity, as described in the last rhetorical trope of the text.[6] The point being made here is not that Lao Tzu is a passive, rustic recluse. He is a prince among philosophers, who would govern the political discourse of ancient China. Substrative in sense of reality, the Tao Te Ching subordinates the essentialist focus of the Confucian texts to its own ontological ground. Dialectical in methodological form, it reorders the presuppositional models of the agonistic Confucian and Legalist writers, and of the logistic models of the Moists. Elemental in principle, it displaces the comprehensive principles of Mo Tzu and Confucius, or the creative principle of Hsün Tzu and Han Fei Tzu. Diaphanic in perspective, it departs from the epistemic horizons of Mo Tzu, Hsün Tzu, or Han Fei Tzu.

In its archic profile, the Tao Te Ching consists of two Platonic (dialectical and diaphanic) and two Democritean (elemental and substrative) elements. Despite the efforts of Western translators and other hermeneuts to coopt it, therefore, the Tao Te Ching remains a rather rare mix of archic assumptions in the world history of philosophy. In its religious naturalism, which requires a sympathetic communion with the forces of life, it may compare most directly with the indigenous Shinto religions of Japan. But Lao Tzu must also be recognized as one of world philosophy's oldest dialectical materialists, although the Tao Te Ching may reflect some early influences in the composition of the I Ching in this regard.

Lao Tzu holds his own even among those philosophers who can be properly called dialectical materialists. Such a set includes the Pythagoreans, Shao Yung, the Hellenistic and Roman Stoics, Rousseau, Marx, Bergson, and Mao. The Pythagoreans and Bergson display significant similarities with Lao Tzu, but differ in comprehensive and creative principles, respectively. Shao Yung, influenced by Neo-Confucian interpretations of the I Ching, also has a comprehensive principle. The texts of the Stoics proceed from reflexive principles and objective perspectives, while those of Marx and Mao use creative principles and objective perspectives. This leaves Rousseau, whose career-text parallels Lao Tzu's masterpiece in its elemental principle, dialectical method, and substrative reality although it differs in perspective.

The Chuang Tzu

The other Taoist classic is the *Chuang Tzu,* one of the more aesthetically brilliant texts in world philosophy. Its rhetorical force is a function of its agonistic, or paradoxical, form of expression; in this methodological respect it even partially displaces the dialectical philosophy of the Tao Te Ching.

The *Chuang Tzu*'s pages abound in images of an astounding, superhuman wisdom embodied in the "perfect and true persons of the Taoist way." These diaphanic characters also possess magical powers, undergo trancelike states, and experience intimations of immortality.[7] Some of these attributes became standard in the repertoire of the Taoist tradition inspired by both Lao Tzu and Chuang Tzu.

Typical is Chuang Tzu's holy man on faraway Ku-she Mountain, whose skin is like ice or snow and who is gentle and shy like a young girl. "He doesn't eat the five grains, but sucks the wind, drinks the dew, climbs up on the clouds and mist, rides a flying dragon, and wanders beyond the four seas. By concentrating his spirit, he can protect creatures from sickness and plague and make the harvest plentiful."[8] Superhuman qualities are attributed elsewhere to another such person, who "rides the clouds and mist, straddles the sun and moon, and wanders beyond the four seas." He is one who "leans on the sun and moon, tucks the universe under his arm, merges himself with things . . . takes part in ten thousand ages and achieves simplicity in oneness."[9] Such a person "of ancient times" is said to be like a child, companion of heaven, and equal of the son of heaven.[10]

In a perfect diaphanic expression, Chuang Tzu says that these Taoist sages "illuminate all in the light of Heaven."[11] Heaven here refers to nature, the Tao itself, which the sage embodies in his mystical illumination. But Chuang Tzu often depicts the Taoist sage, not in Lao Tzu's harmonious, rustic simplicity but in such "transcendent wanderings."[12]

These wanderings of Chuang Tzu's perfect men are in turn semantic functions of the text's agonistic form, which establishes a discontinuity between the affairs of ordinary men and the activities of the sages "who climb up to heaven and wander in the mists, roam in the infinite, and forget life forever and forever."[13] The "nameless man" thus rejects ruling the empire and "rides off on a Light-and-Lissome Bird out beyond the six directions." "Vague and aimless, he wanders beyond the dirt and dust"; free of responsibilities, he "wanders beyond the realm."[14]

The Taoist sage does not subscribe to the comprehensive moral essentialism of Confucius, but rather repudiates it through his wanderings into the substrative realms of the Tao: "Chuang Tzu at this very moment is treading the Yellow Springs or leaping up the vast blue; to him there is no north and south."[15]

Another function of these anecdotes is to present overt "dislocations of the yin and the yang." The opposite of the beautiful people, or even of the cultivated literati of the Confucian traditions, Chuang Tzu's sages are typically hunchbacks, cripples, mutilated criminals, ugly men and women, old persons with the complexions of children, lunatics, or children.[16] Like comic-strip characters, these people at once delight us and set our minds free from conventional wisdom.

Thus in a variety of ways Chuang Tzu develops the concept of disorder, a companion to his concept of the humanly useless. In a famous passage of the chapter entitled "Fit For Emperors and Kings" he depicts an emperor of the central region named Hun-tun (meaning chaos) who did not have the customary seven human orifices. His well-meaning emperor friends of the south and the North Sea proceed to bore seven holes in him over seven days. On the seventh day Hun-tun died.[17] Such passages poke fun at the various concepts of political and moral order to be found in the writings of Confucians, Moists, and Legalists. Chuang Tzu's frequent references to the Taoist sage who refuses to take the reins of government serve the same purpose.

Chuang Tzu uses a metaphor that the old Ch'an masters and later-phase Wittgensteinians have wittingly or unwittingly adopted. The fish trap and the rabbit snare, he says, exist because of the fish and the rabbit; once you've caught them, forget the snares. Similarly, "words exist because of meaning; once you've gotten the meaning, you can forget the words. Where can I find a man who has forgotten words so I can have a word with him?"[18] One could logically do this if language functioned as a series of semantic displacements. Under such a methodological assumption, one could learn to stop talking, having returned language to its irrational and senseless source, if one's textual principle were also an elemental one. (And, as Aristotle says in the fourth book of his *Metaphysics*, one doesn't always practice what one preaches.)

A combination of substrative reality and elemental principle shape the meaning of Chuang Tzu's text. In the first sentence of the text a tiny K'un fish unaccountably turns into a giant P'eng bird.[19] Names, it turns out, are only guests of reality, which goes through endless transformations.[20] Anticipating the bantering tropes of Santayana, Chuang Tzu says that the "great clod" belches out breath, whose name is wind.[21] Human emotions are like musical sounds escaping through empty holes or like mushrooms springing up in the dampness.[22] The human body is a temporary form of a formless force; any injuries to it are only apparent ones. Human words are not transactions in the existential forms of life; rather, they are like the peeps of small birds. The rights and wrongs of Confucians and Moists are equally vain.[23]

Chuang Tzu accordingly joins the world's substrative philosophers in depicting the surface life of human consciousness as an illusory play of appearances. From Democritus and Lao Tzu, or Epicurus and the Stoics, to Schopenhauer, Nietzsche, Freud, and Santayana, these thinkers insist on an underlying flux of material or vital energy, with human consciousness merely an epiphenomenal form of its own physiological basis. They typically express an *amor fati* while asserting that loving life and resenting death are both delusions of either an egocentric or a theocentric consciousness. They compare apperceptive consciousness (or spirit) to a dream state and emphasize our inability to distinguish between waking and dreaming. Democritus, Epicurus, the Stoics, Freud, and Santayana, however, transmute the mystical tendencies of this doctrine through the use of an objective perspective.

Chuang Tzu's own religious liberation takes the form of embracing the substrative reality of nature and celebrating its marvelous permutations and confusions. Passages depicting the death of Taoist sages are generally comic in effect. Chuang Tzu treats the death of his wife in this fashion: she was born and she died in the mysterious and wonderful jumble of nature. Skulls and skeletons appear in Hamlet-like graveyard scenes to expound the same message.[25]

In the opening passage of the text we see the little quail laughing at the great P'eng bird—a metaphor for the necessity of natural forms and of the indifference of the Tao that generates them. The "great clod" makes all things equal, yet gives each thing a different purpose. The sage understands that the true master of all difference has identity but not form.[26] He learns that the essence of the Way is the state in which all differences and opposites dissolve into their underlying identity. The Way makes them all one—the little stalk and the great pillar, the leper and the beautiful Hsi-shih. Nature is the great equalizer, and Chuang Tzu calls for the equalization of all philosophical theories on the same basis.

Chuang Tzu shares a similar attitude with Nagarjuna, the Ch'an and Zen masters, and other Buddhist apologists in seeming to abandon the battle over theories for a diaphanic indifference. Passages recommending such yogic practices as "sitting down and forgetting everything," the "fasting of the mind" for the cultivation of emptiness or indifference,[27] or regulating one's breathing, and the like are common to both Taoist and Buddhist traditions. The sage, in both traditions, lets things be in his mirrorlike mind and takes no purposeful action.

It appears that the Chinese Ch'an masters adopted Chuang Tzu's language in this area. Both Taoist and Ch'an masters can speak, for example, of wandering in the single breath of heaven and earth, of encompassing the six directions in the twinkling of an eye, of absolute indifference to life and death, and so on. In the final analysis, however, Chuang Tzu and the other Taoists affirm the Tao's substrative reality, which the Buddhists replace with an existential reality.

If we define Chuang Tzu's text as diaphanic in perspective, substrative in reality, agonistic in method, and elemental in principle, then his Western counterparts are Homer and Empedocles. The texts of the Han dynasty skeptic Wang Ch'ung and of his modern Western counterpart, Sigmund Freud, alter this profile by employing objective perspectives. Nietzsche's profile differs only in its personal perspective. The *Chuang Tzu* yields many other comparisons of interest.

The Han Fei Tzu

Together with the *Book of Lord Shang,* the *Han Fei Tzu* is the representative text of ancient Chinese Legalist philosophy. The name is a misnomer, unless one recognizes that the Chinese characters connote the sense that might makes right through political strategies and subterfuges.

The *Han Fei Tzu* reflects the influence of Hsün Tzu, the Taoists, and Mo Tzu. Although it drew steady criticism from the Confucianist camp, it played an influential role in Chinese historiography, especially in the works of such historians as Ssu-ma Ch'ien and Pan Ku.

The *Han Fei Tzu,* whose subject is political power, is worth analyzing in relation to several key texts of the Western traditions. In archic profile, the *Han Fei Tzu* is half Sophistic and half Democritean: it displays a creative principle and agonistic method, with a substrative reality and objective perspective. (It differs only in method from the Marxist text.)

Han Fei Tzu partially appropriated the philosophy of his reputed teacher, Hsün Tzu, retaining his creative principle, agonistic method, and objective perspective, but replacing his moral essentialism with a substrative sense of human nature. In this respect Han Fei Tzu agrees with Mo Tzu. Mo Tzu's text, however, proceeds from a principle of the ruler's universal love for his people. The Legalist text shifts emphasis to a ruthless will to power of the "enlightened prince," who keeps his potential rivals (including his own wife and children) at bay by a shrewd but impersonal regimen of rewards and punishments.[28]

The Taoist element in the Legalist text also manifests itself in a substrative sense of causation that operates silently and invisibly. Han Fei Tzu, like Lao Tzu and Machiavelli, sees politicians as driven by ambition and greed and concealing murderous thoughts behind their obsequious behavior.[29] His prince draws on hidden reserves of schemes and tricks, like Derrida's Theuth in "Plato's Pharmacy." Like the Taoist sage, therefore, Han Fei Tzu's Legalist sage does not reveal his inner thoughts and desires but sits in stillness and reserve.[30] Unlike the Taoist sage, however, the Legalist prince works to manipulate human needs and passions to his own advantage. His inscrutability is a function of his insight into human frailty and folly.[31]

This Legalist position stands in sharp contrast to the moral essentialism of both Aristotle and the Confucian philosophers, who argue for virtuous citizens and a virtuous ruler. Han Fei Tzu's political discourse reinforces the substrative reality of Machiavelli, Hobbes, Locke, Vico, and Rousseau and anticipates the agonistic method of Machiavelli and Nietzsche and the creative (or volitional) principle of Hobbes and Locke. It shares an objective perspective, substrative reality, and voluntary principle with the texts of Marx and Mao.

These analyses must be carried out in detail. For example, a scholar can examine the implications of the *Han Fei Tzu*'s divergence from the "political" text of Foucault in ontological focus (Foucault's being existential), or its correspondences with such ostensibly distant texts as those of the Roman poet Ovid and the French deconstructionist, Derrida.

A Miscellany of Unorthodoxies

So far we have examined the classic Moist, Confucian, Legalist, and Taoist texts in the light of our comparative hermeneutic. In such an endeavor we are particularly indebted to the Confucian scholars, ancient and modern, who have preserved the records of the ancient Chinese traditions. Confucians are essentialists: they believe in the consummatory forms and continuities of mind. We can contrast their preservation of the great texts of the past with the book-burning and book-debunking strategies of the Legalists and Taoists, while drawing the appropriate analogies with their counterparts in Western history.

In preserving these works, however, both Confucian and Neo-Confucian scholars have insisted on granting precedence to an essentialist reality and a diaphanic perspective. These variables surface in their text's constant references to the "orthodox transmission" of the Confucian Way. Exceptions to their interpretive rules are branded as "unorthodox."

Let us briefly analyze the unorthodox texts of the logician Kung-sun Lung (b. 380? B.C.), the Han skeptic Wang Ch'ung (27–100?), and the so-called Yang Chu Chapter of a later Taoist work called the *Lieh Tzu*.

Kung-sun Lung appears in Chinese anthologies in an eclectic category called the School of Names, or Scholars of Names and Debates. Like many pre-Socratics texts of ancient Greece, Kung-sun Lung's must be reconstructed from other ancient documents. In particular, it must be disentangled from those of a fellow logician, Hui Shih (380–305? B.C.), and other figures mentioned by Chuang Tzu, Hsün Tzu, and the Grand Historian, Ssu-ma Ch'ien. Wang Ch'ung's text is an established, extensive, and unproblematic document. The Yang Chu Chapter is a fragment attributed to Yang Chu (440–360? B.C.), whose position is already under attack in the *Mencius;* but it is probably a later text. Its archic analysis, at any rate, gives it a semantic status independent of the *Lieh Tzu*.

These texts allow us a glimpse of the philosophical principles employed by the ancient Chinese thinkers. It is crucial for our comparative hermeneutic that we not dismiss these fragments by calling them "unorthodox" or "miscellaneous," but rather try to reconstruct their archic profiles as completely as possible.

In the case of Kung-sun Lung, Wing-tsit Chan indicates that he subscribed to the Moist doctrine of universal love.[32] In that case Kung-sun Lung must have elaborated his own version of the comprehensive principle of Mo Tzu and Confucius. His doctrine of "the correspondence of names and realities" appears to resemble in method that of the logicist Moists, while also sharing the objective perspective of Hsün Tzu and the Legalists. Kung-sun Lung's discussion of the attributes of whiteness in horses, of hardness and whiteness, of the marks of things, and so on is a model of logicist thinking.[33] He also appears to express an essentialist ontological focus, as found in the classic Confucian works. Objective, essentialist, logistic, and comprehensive factors are illustrated in the following passage:

> Heaven, earth, and their products are all things. When things possess the characteristics of things without exceeding them, there is actuality. When actuality fulfills its function as actuality, without

> wanting, there is order. To be out of order is to fall into disorder. To remain in order is to be correct. What is correct is used to rectify what is incorrect. To rectify is to rectify actuality, and to rectify actuality is to rectify the name corresponding to it.[34]

The text goes on to say that the wise kings of old were perfect because they examined names and actualities and were careful in their designations. This is a sound teaching even today.

In this reading, except for its method, Kung-sun Lung's text gives priority to archic elements also found in the logical propositions, but reads as a political and moral discourse as well.

Hsün Tzu, a political and moral agonist, went out of his way to attack Kung-sun Lung's text; for some of the same reasons, so did Chuang Tzu. Note that Chuang Tzu, who transmogrifies Kung-sun Lung into his "frog in the well," was a friend of the above-mentioned Hui Shih, whose name is associated with Kung-sun Lung's as a debater of the School of Names.[35]

Hui Shih's own books are said by Chuang Tzu to contain enough tricks to fill five carts.[36] Indeed, the extant fragments of these works accord with Chuang Tzu's methodology. Hui Shih says, for example, "The eye does not see," and "The pointing of the finger does not reach a thing; the reaching never ends." Or: "When the sun is at noon, it is setting; when there is life, there is death."[37] Many of his other paradoxes remind us of the obscure sayings of Heraclitus. Like Heraclitus and Chuang Tzu, Hui Shih appears to express a substrative sense of reality in a diaphanic perspective; from this vantage point the sage experiences the oneness of all things. But what we know of Hui Shih's debates with his friends comes from Chuang Tzu's text, whose own perspective places a barrier between Hui Shih and us.

Let us turn now to the text of the Han dynasty skeptic Wang Ch'ung (27–100?). Compared to the fragments of Hui Shih's paradoxes, Wang Ch'ung's *On Balanced Inquiries,* a sustained treatise of eighty-four chapters in thirty books, provides a substantial material for our comparative hermeneutic.[38] Wang Ch'ung, like Chuang Tzu, is a master of the counterargument. But although he shares this Sophistic trait with the Taoist sage, his text clearly replaces Chuang Tzu's diaphanic perspective with an objective one, thereby acquiring a critical tone.

Further evidence of Wang Ch'ung's skepticism is his relentless debunking of cherished popular beliefs in life after death or the existence of ghosts and spirits. He has a formidable sense of human folly and fabrication. He devotes special chapters to criticizing Confucius, Mencius, and the Legalist Han Fei Tzu. He refutes nearly all previous theories of human nature and produces a counterargument to the syncretic

Confucian cosmology of his Han dynasty predecessor, Tung Chung-shu (ca. 179–104 B.C.).[39]

It goes without saying that Wang Ch'ung is not popular with Confucian historians. Wang Ch'ung's ontological focus echoes the Taoist doctrine of "material force," inspiring his attitude toward the vanity and emptiness of human ideals. His archic profile resembles Chuang Tzu's, but with an objective perspective.

Like Hume and Santayana, those latter-day critics of idealistic theories, Wang Ch'ung also asserts an elemental principle. Custom or habit, the necessity of our instinctive nature with its "animal faith," and thus the sameness of men's motives are different expressions of this principle for Hume and for Santayana alike. If you want to know the motives of the ancient Greeks or the Romans, Hume suggests, study the French or the Germans of today. In like manner Wang Ch'ung writes:

> The virtue of sages earlier or later was not different, and therefore good government in earlier ages and today is not different. The Heaven of earlier ages was the same as the Heaven of later ages. Heaven does not change, and its material forces do not alter. The people of earlier ages were the same as those of later ages. All were endowed with the original material forces, which are pure and harmonious and are not different in earlier or late ages. . . . In ancient times there were unrighteous people, and today there are gentlemen of established integrity. Good and evil intermingle. What age is devoid of them?[40]

This passage demonstrates several aspects of Wang Ch'ung's philosophy. Conspicuous is his elemental principle, which equalizes past and present manifestations of a substrative reality. The same semantic factors underlie his theory of innate nature—namely, "that in nature, some people are born good and some born evil." He therefore condemns the creative principles of such theorists as Kao Tzu, Hsün Tzu, and Han Fei Tzu, as well as the comprehensive principles of Mo Tzu, Confucius, and Tung Chung-shu.[41]

The Yang Chu Chapter of the *Lieh Tzu* offers us another glimpse of the diversity of philosophical principles behind the official interpretations of the Chinese traditions. The *Lieh Tzu,* the original of which has been lost since the second century B.C., promotes a species of skepticism and fatalism that appears to fall, like Hui Shih's text, within the archic profile of the *Chuang Tzu.* In significant contrast, the three major texts of philosophical Neo-Taoism—the Pure, or Light, Conversational School of Wang Pi (226–249), Ho Yen (d. 249), and Kuo Hsiang (d. 312)—all appear to follow Lao Tzu. It is true that Wang Pi wrote commentaries on the Tao Te Ching and the I Ching, while Kuo Hsiang wrote on the *Chuang Tzu;* but all three texts appear to follow a dialectical method in the manner of Lao Tzu. The same can be said of earlier thinkers such as Yang Hsiung (53 B.C.–18 A.D.) and Hai-nan Tzu (d. 122 B.C.). Neither of these thinkers displays the rhetorical wizardry of Chuang Tzu, Hui Shih, and the *Lieh Tzu*.

Because of the brevity of the Yang Chu Chapter, only a tentative reading can be made of its semantic elements. But it would appear that its perspective is personal, its reality substrative, its method logistic, and its principle elemental. "Men of great antiquity knew that life meant to be temporarily present and death meant to be temporarily away. Therefore they acted as they pleased and did not turn away from what they naturally desired. They would not give up what could amuse their own persons at the time. Therefore they were not exhorted by fame. They roamed as their nature directed and would not be at odds with anything."[42] The text idealizes feudal lord, Po-ch'eng Tzu-kao, a contemporary of the Confucians' beloved Emperor Yao, for saying that he would refuse to pluck even one of his own hairs to benefit the world around him. The wise Emperor Yu, by contrast, is ridiculed for having devoted himself to humanity and justice, only to die half paralyzed.[43]

According to the *Huai-nan Tzu,* a Han dynasty Taoist compilation, Yang Chu would not injure nature with material desires. As reported in the *Chuang Tzu,* the hedonistic Po-ch'eng Tzu-kao gives up his kingdom and becomes a hermit farmer. The Yang Chu Chapter itself reports:

> Yang Chu said, The myriad things are different in life but the same in death. In life they may be worthy or stupid, honorable or humble. This is where they differ. In death they all stink, rot, disintegrate, and disappear. This is where they are all the same. However, being worthy, stupid, honorable, or humble is beyond their power, and to stink, rot, disintegrate, and disappear is also beyond their power. Thus life, death, worthiness, stupidity, honor, and humble station are not of their own making. . . . Thus they all become rotten bones just the same. Who knows their difference? Let us hasten to enjoy our present life. Why bother about what comes after death?[44]

This is reminiscent of Santayana, particularly of his views on life's natural moments and the solipsism of the present moment. The difference between the two philosophers lies in their perspective, Santayana's being objective and Yang Chu's personal.

One often hears the West's materialism contrasted with the East's spiritual idealism. Such statements overlook the texts of the Moists, Taoists, Legalists, Hui Shih, Wang Ch'ung, Yang Chu, and the Yang Chu Chapter. Such a sweeping generalization of mainstream Chinese philosophy cannot account for twentieth-century Chinese Marxism, which extends the substrative ontology and objective perspective not to mention the creative principle and dialectical method, of several indigenous Chinese philosophical traditions.

The Neo-Confucian Orthodoxies

The Confucians, we have noted, acted as the preservers of Chinese philosophy. Their traditions of scholarship produced a conservative moral culture, in the best sense. In their works of historical interpretation, however, we encounter a problem for our comparative hermeneutic, namely, the problem of the "orthodox transmission" of the Confucian way inscribed in their texts.

The Neo-Confucian school that appropriated the Chinese philosophical legacy was the Ch'eng-Chu school, which gained official patronage and determined the rules of pedagogy for the Chinese civil servant examination system between 1313 and 1905. It achieved other kinds of official institutional status in Korea and Japan, exercising thereby a degree of control over the mainstreams of philosophy and scholarship. We may say that this status has continued into our own times through English translations of leading works of Chinese philosophy belonging to the Chu Hsi school.

Sung Neo-Confucianism can be traced from Chou Tun-i, Shao Yung, Chang Tsai, Ch'eng I, and Ch'eng Ho to its culmination in Chu Hsi. Chu Hsi synthesized Confucius's concept of humanity, Mencius's doctrines of humanity and righteousness, the idea of the investigation of things in the *Great Learning*, the teaching of sincerity in the *Doctrine of the Mean*, the Yin Yang and "five agents" doctrines of the Han dynasties, and virtually all the important ideas of the other masters of the Sung.[45]

However, Chu Hsi's text excluded certain thinkers—Hsün Tzu and Shao Yung, for example—from the line of orthodox transmission of the Confucian way. Although he retained its diaphanic perspective, Chu Hsi also tended to downplay the I Ching, regarding it primarily as a book of divination, whereas the other Sung masters venerated it as a philosophical text. Chu Hsi selected the *Analects*, the *Mencius*, the *Great Learning*, and the *Doctrine of the Mean* as a special canon of four books and promoted this controversial reading through his own comprehensive scholarship.[46]

Chu Hsi disparaged the Chinese Taoist and Buddhist schools of thought, which had flourished for centuries in a variety of indigenous forms. This tendency derives from the archic profile of Chu Hsi and other Neo-Confucian masters of the Sung. The Taoists, Buddhists, and Neo-Confucians all use the diaphanic perspective, which infuses their texts with a sense of ultimate spiritual legitimation, although the Taoists have substrative realities and the Buddhists are existentialists (or, in the case of Pure Land Buddhists, noumenalists).

One side effect of the spiritual forms of legitimation is to diminish the forms of philosophy that do not have diaphanic perspectives—the *Hsün Tzu* and the texts of Wang Ch'ung and the miscellaneous schools. Diaphanic orthodoxies subordinate the other schools of thought to their own. In exploring the intellectual history of a civilization, one's viewpoint must not be limited to any one orthodoxy, but must describe various developments as they appear from the records.

With the exception of Shao Yung, the Neo-Confucian masters of the Sung share an archic profile composed of one Aristotelian (essential) and three Platonic (diaphanic, dialectical, and comprehensive) elements, which had already crystallized in the texts of the I Ching and Tung Chung-shu. The Sung masters developed its theoretical implications into a number of new disciplines. In general, however, this archic profile signals a kind of diaphanic cultural essentialism and therefore tends to redefine the very historical process that it seeks to explain. This effort to gather and conserve the branches of the Confucian tradition continues even today.

Chu Hsi's concern for an orthodox transmission of the Way becomes clearer in an archic analysis. We see that the Aristotelian component in the Neo-Confucian worldview produces a mixed model from an otherwise pure Platonic profile. (By contrast, the noumenal reality of Plato's text produces a symbolic remythologization of all historically generated texts, such that they can never finally solidify into a this-worldly transmission of a particular pedagogical culture.) In many respects, the Western counterparts of the Neo-Confucians are the prophets of the Old Testament and such philosophers as Hegel and Heidegger.

As the Neo-Confucian doctrines were transmitted through the centuries, a number of regionally based schools developed. By the time of the Ming dynasty these had divided into two main branches, often referred to as the Ch'eng-Chu and the Lu-Wang schools. The Lu-Wang school originates in the philosophical career of Wang Yang-ming, who replaced the comprehensive principles of the Sung masters with the elemental principle of Mencius—the principle of the innately moral mind-and-heart.

Within the Ch'eng-Chu school of the Ming, such figures as Lo Ch'in-shun adopted some of the vocabulary of the Wang Yang-ming school while continuing to adhere to the Chu Hsi form of orthodoxy. In broader perspective, Lo Ch'in-shun revived the theory of the primacy of a unitary cosmic energy, the precedent for which can be found in Chu Hsi's Sung predecessor, Chang Tsai. The two main branches, the Ch'eng-Chu and Lu-Wang, as well as the Chang-Lo variant of the former, inspired generations of Neo-Confucian scholars through the nineteenth century in Japan as well.[47]

As the work of Wm. Theodore de Bary and others has shown, these schools of thought provided the categories in which the modernization of East Asian civilizations was conceived.[48] They instilled in generations of scholars habits of judgment and learning that would play an important part in the eventual confrontation with Western civilization. When that confrontation first took place in nineteenth-century China and Japan, the slogan "Eastern morals and Western science" was popularized by the first modernizers, who were in fact comprehensively minded Neo-Confucians.

If we examine the historical record, we see that the Han traditions of Confucian interpretation of the I Ching influenced the formation of the Neo-Confucian worldviews. The Han interpretations were conspicuously dialectical in method, in contrast to the agonistic form of the *Analects,* the *Mencius,* and the *Hsün Tzu.* The Neo-Confucians needed a dialectical method to achieve the revitalization of the Confucian traditions in new forms.

For their diaphanic perspective the Neo-Confucians also drew upon the Confucian classics, perhaps most notably on the concept of sincerity in *The Doctrine of the Mean.* The Sung version of this perspective first appears in Chou Tun-i's *Explanation of the Diagram of the Great Ultimate* and *Penetrating the Book of Changes.* "Sincerity is the foundation of the sage," Chou writes, and "Sagehood is nothing but sincerity."[50] All the other Neo-Confucian writers followed suit in this regard. This ideal informs Shao Yung's concept of the tranquillity of the penetrating mind in his *Supreme Principles Governing the World,* and it is the validating perspective of Chang Tsai's *Western Inscription* and *Correcting Youthful Ignorance.*[51] We find the same perspective to be the legitimating voice of the texts of the Ch'eng brothers and Chu Hsi, as well as of Lu Hsiang-shan and Wang Yang-ming. The Neo-Confucian writers share this perspective with the authors of all religious traditions.

With the exception of Shao Yung, all the Neo-Confucians adopted the essentialist sense of reality found in the Confucian classics, the Han interpretations of the I Ching, and the text of Tung Chung-shu. Thus, while they are cosmological in general orientation, the Neo-Confucian texts always underscore the superiority of man in bringing to moral and aesthetic completion the teleological processes of the natural universe. Shao Yung was considered to have failed to discuss such central Confucian problems as humanity and righteousness. For this reason, reported by Wing-tsit Chan, Shao Yung's Taoist-sounding doctrines were not propagated by later Neo-Confucians.[52]

We can establish that, with the possible exception of Lu Hsiang-shan, who appears to use Mencius's agonistic method in his critique of Chu

Hsi, all the Neo-Confucians formulated doctrines of a dialectical universe unfolding from primordial unity into greater complexity, culminating in the human order. Chu Hsi's assertion of the priority of principle over material force, or concrete realization, addresses the question of the governing principle of this entire process. But his doctrine of cosmic, historical, and personal realization is a function of the archic elements of this worldview.[53] Essential reality, for these Neo-Confucian philosophers, is something that becomes concrete in dialectical form.

Chou Tun-i's *Explanation of the Diagram of the Great Ultimate* sets the tone for the entire tradition. Chang Tsai's monistic material energy culminating in a universal moral ecology is another version of this basic doctrine. Ch'eng Hao expresses the same view when he says: "The investigation of principle to the utmost, the full development of one's nature, and the fulfillment of destiny are one thing."[54] Chu Hsi's synthetic doctrine of the cooperative functionings of principle and material force and Wang Yang-ming's doctrine of "the unity of knowledge and action" are other variations on the basic theme of the Neo-Confucian worldview.

For similar reasons Chu Hsi's adherents in the Ming and Ching dynasties would strive to reconcile the differences between the Ch'eng-Chu and Lu-Wang schools. Again, the same discursive practice recurs in some of the leading anthologies of the Chinese philosophical traditions, as well as in the conference volumes and other scholarly compilations devoted to the Neo-Confucian philosophers.

In the matter of textual principles, we have noted that Wang Yang-ming, influenced by Lu Hsiang-shan, diverged from the official text of the Ch'eng-Chu school.[55] His text returns Neo-Confucian theory to elemental principles, reinterpreting the Mencian doctrine of a moral mind-and-heart that manifests itself in the four beginnings of virtue. Wang Yang-ming distinguished this principle of the "original good mind" with its "innate good knowledge" from the comprehensive principles of Chu Hsi and others. He rejects Chu Hsi's emphasis on exhausting the principles of things, and related concepts.[56]

Some of Wang Yang-ming's followers sought to portray the Ch'eng-Chu scholars as bookworms and rigid legalists, which was unfair to Chu Hsi and his followers, who held their own doctrine of "the unity of knowledge and action" and were seeking to reconcile the teachings of Confucius and the Book of Changes to those of Mencius. In general, we can say that Neo-Confucianism branched into two major directions, the Ch'eng-Chu schools with their comprehensive principle and the Wang Yang-ming schools with their elemental principles.[57]

In Japan Neo-Confucianism vied with Buddhism as the prevailing pedagogical culture of Japan at the beginning of the Tokugawa period

(1600–1867). Japanese Neo-Confucianism developed several strains, some officially sponsored by the Tokugawa and related daimyo families, and others paralleling Neo-Confucian developments in China and Korea. (These strains tend to recur in the archic assumptions of contemporary schools of interpretation as well.)

Scholars have also cited the influence of Korean Neo-Confucianism on the two principal Tokugawa trends known as *rigaku* (school of principle) and *kigaku* (school of material force). The former emerged from the ideas of Fujiwara Seika (1516–1619), who was influenced by the Korean Yi Toe'gye (1501–1570), among others. The *rigaku* strain corresponds to the line of the Sung masters from Chou Tun-i to Chu Hsi. The *kigaku* strain propagated the teaching of the Korean Yi Yulgok (1536–84) and of such Ming Neo-Confucians as Lo Ch'in-shun (1465–1547) and Wang T'ing-hsiang (1474–1544). Although it adopted the Ming Neo-Confucian language of the primacy of material force (*ch'i;* Jap., *ki*), the *kigaku* school continued to function on comprehensive principles.

However, Japanese culture of the earlier Heian, Kamakura, and Muromachi periods encompassed a variety of philosophical traditions—noumenal Pure Land Buddhism; existential Tendai, Shingon, and Zen schools; essentialist Confucian teachings; and various substrative cultures of aesthetic naturalism. These philosophies inspired the complex tapestry of Tokugawa culture.

The differences among these theories led to polemics in the transmission of official and unofficial orthodoxies in this period of centralized feudalism.[58] Most of the Japanese Neo-Confucian schools absorbed Shinto religious concepts. But in short, the *rigaku* school of Tokugawa Neo-Confucianism originated with Fujiwara Seika and was further developed by Yamazaki Ansai (1618–82), Arai Hakuseki (1657–1725), and Muro Kyūsō (1658–1734), among others. The *kigaku* school was represented by such thinkers as Hayashi Razan (1583–1657), Kaibara Ekken (1630–1714), and Andō Shoeki (1622–1701). Its influence can even be perceived in such Ancient Learning (*kogaku*) scholars as Yamaga Sokō (1622–85), Itō Jinsai (1627–1705), Itō Tōgai (1670–1736), and Ogyū Sorai (1666–1728). (These *kogaku* scholars, however, favored the agonistic method, which they used to oppose Neo-Confucian speculation while advocating the pristine doctrines of the Confucian classics.)[59]

We can discern another form of the *kigaku* philosophy in the Japanese Wang Yang-ming school (*Yōmeigaku*). This tradition remained a quieter undercurrent during the Tokugawa period, until it emerged dramatically in the political maneuverings accompanying the fall of the shogunate in the early nineteenth century. Prominent *Yōmeigaku* scholars were Nakae Tōju (1608–48), Fuchi Kozan (1617–86), Kumazawa Banzan (1619–86), Miyake Sekian (1665–1730), and Ōshiō Heihachirō (1793–1837), among others. A new Wang Yang-ming (*shin Yōmeigaku*) line traceable to Satō Issai (1772–1859) played an important role in synthesizing the Ch'eng-Chu and Lu-Wang schools at the end of the Tokugawa period.

Most of the influential figures of the late Tokugawa and early Meiji period had samurai backgrounds, with intellectual pedigrees in the several Neo-Confucian schools I have mentioned. Judging from the case of Fukuzawa Yukichi (1835–1901) and other "civilization and enlightenment" figures of the Meiji period, the Neo-Confucian heritage survived in altered form. Modernizers tended to abandon the diaphanic perspective of the ancient orthodoxies, while retaining all or most of the other semantic elements of the older Neo-Confucian texts. Comparative analyses will reveal the similarities and differences between older and newer Neo-Confucian texts in modern Japanese culture. At the same time, such studies may uncover resemblances among philosophical texts of many different cultures.

The archic profiles of Chu Hsi and the other Sung masters will be illuminated by comparisons with Western texts such as those of the Old Testament prophets, Hegel, and Heidegger. All these texts employ diaphanic perspectives, essential realities, and dialectical methods. Therefore each contains its own version of the historical transmission and fulfillment of cultural ideals, expressed in a language of authentic revelation. Where they diverge is in their principles—Chu Hsi's is comprehensive, the Old Testament prophets' and Heidegger's are creative, and Hegel's is reflexive. Wang Yang-ming's text differs from all these in granting precedence to an elemental principle. Still, each of these five world-texts achieves its own form of diaphanic cultural essentialism.

7

Early Modern Western Philosophy

Every philosopher hopes to make a lasting contribution to civilization. Not every philosopher achieves this goal, although even a minor figure may still affect the course of major careers. In the Renaissance, Francis Bacon (1561–1626) and René Descartes (1596–1650) laid the foundations of modern Western philosophy.

It is significant for our comparative hermeneutic to note that Bacon and Descartes shared Aristotelian principles and Democritean methods. The complete analysis of their intertextual relationship is as follows:

	PERSPECTIVE	REALITY	METHOD	PRINCIPLE
Bacon	*objective*	*substrative*	*logistic*	*reflexive*
Descartes	*personal*	*essential*	*logistic*	*reflexive*

Bacon's text mirrors the archic profile of the pre-Socratic philosopher Anaxagoras.

Bacon's Great Instauration

Anaxagorean elements underlie Bacon's project of laying a new foundation for scientific progress. At the end of the second book of his *Novum Organum* Bacon wrote: "Man by the fall fell from his dominion over creatures. Both of these losses however can even in this life be in some part repaired; the former by religion and faith, the latter by arts and sciences."[1] In this passage Bacon echoes his own preface to the *Great Instauration,* in which he envisioned that "the commerce between the mind of man and the nature of things might be restored, if not to its perfect and original condition, yet reduced to a better state than it is now."[2]

In the preface to the same work Bacon laments that contemporary knowledge is neither prosperous nor greatly advanced. Accordingly he states that a way must be opened for a new form of human understanding, "in order that the mind may exercise over the nature of things the authority which properly belongs to it."[3] This is the human mind's prerogative. Thus Bacon writes that he intends to establish a "true and lawful marriage between the empirical and rational faculty, the unkind and ill-starred divorce and separation of which has thrown into confusion all the affairs of the human family."[4] To achieve this goal, he advances his new method of induction, which is "to proceed regularly and gradually from one axiom to another" and "by due process of exclusion and rejection lead to an inevitable conclusion."[5] Bacon thus anticipated Descartes's revolution in logistic method, and precisely on that line of classical British thought, to which Hume, among others, would later refer as "natural philosophy."[6]

In an archic analysis, Bacon gives precedence to an objective perspective. "And all depends on keeping the eye steadily fixed on the facts of nature and so receiving their images as they are. For God forbid that we should give out a dream of our own imagination for a pattern of the world."[7] In regard to his own project he therefore writes: "I open and lay out a new and certain path for the mind to proceed in, starting directly from the simple sensuous perception."[8] To the mind, the universe is a labyrinth, and the senses are frequently seduced by its appearances. But the senses, Bacon is quick to add, can be reeducated with the help of the intellect. "For certain it is that the senses deceive; but then at the same time they supply the means of discovering their own errors."[9]

Along with this objective perspective, Bacon grants priority to a substrative reality. This ontological presupposition underlies Bacon's doctrine of the "idols, or phantoms," which beset the human mind.[10] There are four classes of such idols—idols of the tribe, the cave, the marketplace, and the theater. The idols of the theater include "the playbooks of philosophical systems and the perverted rules of demonstration."[11]

In his attack on the received philosophical systems Bacon also reveals a physicalist aspect of his substrative ontology. He denounces equally "the sophistical, the empirical, and the superstitious systems." He condemns Aristotle as one of the sophistical philosophers for having contaminated physics with logic. By contrast with all of these, Bacon asserts: "The *homoeomera* of Anaxagoras; the atoms of Leucippus and Democritus; the Heaven and Earth of Parmenides; the Strife and Friendship of Empedocles; Heraclitus' doctrine how bodies are resolved into the indifferent nature of fire, and remoulded into solids; have all of them some taste of the natural philosopher,—some savor of the nature of things, and experience, and bodies. . . ."[12] Bacon's references to the ancient philosophers always demonstrate a solid learning and perspicacious judgment and prove that he understood their various ontological commitments. He consciously related his own thought to the pre-Socratic *physis* philosophers on many occasions.[13]

To overcome the difficulties presented by the substrative nature of things, Bacon combined a reflexive principle of human understanding with a logistic method of true induction. In several passages he calls attention to the fact that God on the first day created light only, giving to that work an entire day; in like manner we must strive "to discover true causes and axioms"—that is, "to seek for experiments of Light, not merely of Fruit."[14] In the investigation and discovery of what he calls the latent process and latent configurations of bodies, "a separation and solution of bodies must be effected, not by fire indeed, but by reasoning and induction, with experiments to aid; and by a comparison with other bodies, and a reduction to simple natures and their forms, which meet and mix in the compound. In a word we must pass from Vulcan to Minerva, if we intend to bring to light the true textures and configurations of bodies."[15]

Bacon insists that the mind can establish positive scientific conclusions. After rejecting and excluding inessential properties by the power of negative assertions, it can finally achieve "a Form affirmative, solid and true and well defined."[16] "When I speak of Forms, I mean nothing more than those laws and determinations of absolute actuality, which govern and constitute any simple nature, as heat, light, weight, in every kind of matter and subject that is susceptible of them."[17]

The *Novum Organum* is devoted to the doctrine of positive induction. In a flurry of logistic formulations Bacon speaks of "Instances Agreeing" within a "Table of Essence and Presence." He also develops a "Table of Deviation, or of Absence in Proximity," as well as a "Table of Degrees, or Table of Comparison." He then sums up these tables under the heading of the "Presentations of Instances to the Understanding."[18] Hume, for one, considered Bacon the forerunner of his doctrine of the association of ideas in this methodological form.[19]

Bacon's logistic method, empowered by the human mind, works to interpret the substrative *physis* of things and thus to control the virtues and actions of bodies. His text is Democritean, except for an Aristotelian principle.[20] Bacon endeavored to lay a true foundation for the natural sciences, in which knowledge and power are one and the same thing. His pioneering work had a major influence on early modern Western philosophy.

For this study, however, perhaps the most important point is that Bacon's text agrees in all archic elements with that of Anaxagoras. Aristotle criticized Anaxagoras, saying that he did not explain how mind can direct nature. He nevertheless stated that Anaxagoras's principle of mind, eternal and unmixed with the material substrate of things, made him the one sober philosopher among the pre-Socratic thinkers.[21] In Anaxagoras's now fragmentary text, the requirements of an effective logistic method are not spelled out. Bacon in effect described in Anaxagoras's terms how the scientific mind functions in interpreting the physical substratum.[22] He thus inaugurated the modern traditions of philosophy, preparing the way for such British naturalists as Hobbes, Newton, and Locke.

In his *Great Instauration* and *Novum Organum* Bacon envisioned a renewal and legitimation of the mind's power to know and direct the nature of things. He did so by reinterpreting an ancient paradigm. His writings reinforce the observation that a reflexive principle tends to provide a theoretical foundation for the sciences and arts. This point will become clearer as we turn to the works of Descartes, which in turn inspired such philosophers as Spinoza and Leibniz.

Descartes, Spinoza, and Leibniz

Like Bacon, Descartes set out to lay a new foundation for the sciences on a series of axiomatic intuitions—the mind's intuitions of its own true ideas. He returned these intuitions to three kinds of metaphysical ideas: thinking substance, infinite substance, and extended substance. Descartes thus concerned himself with the various kinds of being and their gradations.[23] He brought to this endeavor a sense of the reflexivity of mind that thinks these foundational concepts, its own possibilities of true reference, and determines their necessary truth according to the order of their appearance in his meditating consciousness.

Descartes's archic profile differs from Bacon's in reality and in perspective. Radically un-Baconian were Descartes's rejection of the evidence of his senses and his program of transcendental analysis conducted in the solitude of his own *cogito*. The net result for our comparative hermeneutic is that the works of Bacon and Descartes become mutually exclusive, yet also mutually defining. Later philosophical developments will give us a better sense of the interrelationships of these two philosophers' views.

In his *Rules for the Understanding, Discourse on Method,* and other writings Descartes elaborated another version of the methodological revolution that Bacon started. "By commencing with the objects easiest and simplest to know, I might ascend by little and little, and, as it were, step by step, to the knowledge of the more complex," Descartes wrote of his logistic method, now translated into an epistemological organon of scientific and philosophical progression.[24] He exhibited the same method in the sequential order of true ideas elaborated in his chief metaphysical work, the *Meditations.*

But if the methodological variable of Descartes's text was logistic (that is, Democritean), its perspective was personal (that is, Sophistic). Descartes wrote, for example: "I have never contemplated anything higher than my own opinions, and basing them on a foundation wholly my own . . . I do not by any means, therefore, recommend to anyone else to make a similar attempt."[25] This is very different from Bacon, the Anaxagorean naturalist. In Descartes's various writings, the wealth of autobiographical detail, doubts and dreams as a means of testing the implications of a universal skepticism, his references to his own fallibility, and his sense of dependence on divine truth should be read as manifestations of his personal perspective.[26]

Descartes's personal reconciliation of traditional concepts of God and the spiritual soul with the Renaissance's new physical sciences inspired his philosophical project, as announced in the title page of the *Meditations*. However, for our comparative hermeneutic, Descartes's text, like Bacon's, is a case study in archic elements drawn from and continuous with ancient Greek sources. The Democritean element in Descartes's text influenced the worldviews of such thinkers as Spinoza, Leibniz, Hobbes, Newton, Locke, Vico, and Hume. Together with Bacon's, Descartes's text also transmitted the reflexive principle (of Anaxagoras, Hippocrates, Aristotle, the Stoics, and Aquinas) to modern Western philosophy. Furthermore, Descartes's career-text appears to be the only prominent instance of an essentialist sense of reality in the West after Aristotle and before Montesquieu, Hegel, Peirce, Husserl, Dewey, Whitehead, and Heidegger.

The brilliance and ingenuity of Descartes's writings soon stimulated other works of major import. Foremost among these was the philosophy of Spinoza, who professed himself to be a Cartesian in some respects. What are those respects, given the unique system that Spinoza formed? In archic terms, we see that Spinoza retained both the logistic method and reflexive principle of Descartes, while radically diverging from him in perspective and in primary sense of reality.[27] Spinoza's textual perspective is objective, and his ontological focus is noumenal.

	PERSPECTIVE	REALITY	METHOD	PRINCIPLE
Descartes	*personal*	*essential*	*logistic*	*reflexive*
Spinoza	*objective*	*noumenal*	*logistic*	*reflexive*

If Descartes's text is a paradigm of the personal perspective, Spinoza's is a model of the objective perspective. Spinoza's perspective emerges in the appendix to the first book of his *Ethics,* where he repudiates as subjective superstition every anthropomorphic version of *Deus sive Natura*. He argues that "nature has no particular goal in view, and that final causes are mere human figments."[28] He says that people, not understanding the mechanical order of nature, foolishly take refuge in "the will of God, that is, the sanctuary of ignorance," looking for miracles and other manifestations of divine and supernatural skills. People also impute to nature such human attributes as goodness, badness, order, confusion, warmth, cold, beauty, deformity—as though any of these qualities were inherent in nature.[29]

Spinoza's perspective also contributes to his elusive sense of the indwelling of the divine substance in all forms of life. For Spinoza, there is only one true idea—namely, that of the reality of God's eternal and infinite perfection—of which the infinite and finite attributes and modes known to the human understanding must all be its subaltern parts and coefficients. Wisdom consists of understanding that everything happens by the perfect necessity of the divine nature. On the basis of this objective sense of God's perfect reality, Spinoza committed himself to the monumental task of developing a human ethics. The principle governing this enterprise was a reflexive one—a version of thought thinking itself—in which man's intellectual love of God reflects the infinite love with which God loves himself. Spinoza established the identity of God and man on the basis of this Aristotelian principle.

Spinoza therefore begins his *Ethics* with a variant of the ontological argument that derives from Anselm and Bonaventure in the Middle Ages, and from Descartes in Spinoza's own times. He writes, "By that which is *self-caused,* I mean that of which the essence involves existence, or that of which the nature is only conceivable as existent."[30] The whole work flows from this premise, which gives precedence to a noumenal sense of infinite reality as that which is self-caused, or pure actuality.[31] With this one stroke, Spinoza reclaimed the principle, formulated earlier by Aristotle and Aquinas, that "a being does not move from potency to act except under the influence of a being already in act." At the same time Spinoza grounded his ethics of man's return to God on an active intellectual love of God.[32]

For our comparative hermeneutic, Spinoza's sense of God's self-causing, noumenal reality profoundly affects his text. The various naturalistic interpretations of Spinoza are unable to account for the movement of ideas in his *Ethics* through the stages of passivity, or the bondage of the emotions, to human blessedness, characterized by a godlike, intellectual love. Nor are they capable of comprehending Spinoza's noumenal sense of the human mind *sub specie aeternitatis.* Thus in *Ethics* 5, Spinoza writes, "In God there is necessarily an idea, which expresses the essence of this or that human body under the form of eternity."[33] He continues, "The human mind cannot be absolutely destroyed with the body, but there remains of it something which is eternal."[34]

Spinoza also states that "the intellectual love of God, which arises from the third kind of knowledge, is eternal."[35] In the decisive expression of his noumenal ontology, he concludes: "The intellectual love of the mind towards God is that very love of God whereby God loves himself, not in so far as he is infinite, but in so far as he can be explained through the essence of the human mind regarded under the form of eternity; in other words, the intellectual love of the mind towards God is part of the infinite love wherewith God loves himself."[36] This passage reaffirms his reflexive principle as well. When Spinoza writes that "God loves himself with an infinite intellectual love," he adds that God is absolutely infinite and therefore "the nature of God rejoices in infinite perfection"; such rejoicing is "accompanied by the idea of himself," that is, "the idea of his own cause."[37]

The same reflexive principle underlies Spinoza's sense of the human mind's completion in the intellectual love of God. "Since the essence of the mind consists only in knowledge, whereof the beginning and the foundation is God, it becomes clear to us, in what manner and way our mind, as to its essence and existence, follows from the divine nature and constantly depends on God."[38] (Here he echoes Descartes's reflexive principle.) In book 5 of the *Ethics* Spinoza applies this view specifically to the human mind. Spinoza's deepest insight into the possibility of human blessedness asserts that "there is nothing in nature, which is contrary to this intellectual love, or which can take it away."[39]

The reflexive principle controls Spinoza's definition of the self-causality of God, its logistic development of God's attributes and modes, and his vision of the human mind's relationship to the divine nature.

In Leibniz, we find another internally complete and unique world-view. Like Spinoza's, his works are metaphysical but, unlike Spinoza's, they "suffer anthropologies." Leibniz shares Spinoza's noumenal sense of reality and his logistic method. Leibniz's *ars characteristica,* or calculus of integers, and his definition of each monad as a "complete substance" containing all its predicates reveal the influence of this method on his thinking. But Leibniz differs from his contemporaries in his diaphanic perspective and comprehensive principle.

To Leibniz, God is a moral being who creates a perfect order, an infinite plenum of expressive monads. Each monad is an "eternal reason" in the divinely creative calculus—a sufficient reflection of God's wisdom, love, and power. God is the supreme simple monad, who encompasses all other possible monads. These monads are not in time and space, which are properties of appearance and not things in themselves. The confused evidence of the senses must yield to the moral calculus of God's perfect creation. This already occurs at the level of scientific and mathematical theories, which provide the best kinds of propositional languages of identity we are likely to have.

Leibniz therefore departed from Spinoza in insisting on the moral necessity of God's perfect creation and on the resultant (that is, eternally preestablished) perfect distribution of creation into an infinite number of harmoniously synchronized monads or essences. Spinoza had expressed contempt for philosophers who believed that "God himself takes pleasure in harmony."[47] Leibniz, however, emphasized this very point in his concept of God as the supreme monad, the harmony of harmonies, and the moral architect of the perfect metaphysical order. He claimed on the basis of this concept to have achieved the principle of all principles in metaphysics.

As we read at the end of his *Monadology*, Leibniz portrays God as an architect and a lawgiver, recapitulating ancient and medieval conceptions of justice with their gradations of metaphysical and moral values. The philosophy of Leibniz, a logistically minded Platonist, is a prism through which are refracted many tendencies of world philosophy. It functioned as a conduit not only for ancient Greek and medieval Christian ideas, but also for Confucian and Neo-Confucian ideas in the modern West.

In contrast to those of Descartes or Spinoza, Leibniz's perspective is diaphanic. Each of the infinite series of monads reflects directly God's moral vision of the whole—a variation on a long-standing theme in theological and mystical traditions. In a key passage in his *Discourse on Metaphysics* Leibniz cites Plato's doctrine of the soul's reminiscence that the divine ideas are all stored up within us.[41] It is a bad habit, Leibniz insists, to think that our minds receive messengers, as it were, or that they have doors or windows. He continues, "The only immediate object of our perceptions which exists outside of us is God, and in him alone is our light."[42] Accordingly, it is God, who by his continual concurrence determines our thinking. "God is the sun and light of souls, *lumen illuminans omnem hominem venientem in hunc mundum,* although it is not the current conception"; and God is "the light of the soul, *intellectus agens animae rationalis.*"[43] Leibniz's doctrines of antecedent grace and of the excellence of spirits, which directly express God rather than the world, are grounded in the diaphanic perspective of his text.

Leibniz concludes the *Monadology* with a vision of the kingdom of grace, the community of spirit monads whose reflection of God's love constitutes the glory of God. This passage forms a variation on the theme of God's glory to be found at the end of Spinoza's *Ethics*. Here too Leibniz gives precedence to a comprehensive principle as opposed to the reflexive principle of Spinoza's *amor Dei intellectualis*. The same passage also exhibits Leibniz's diaphanic perspective, which colors his conception of spirit monads in the kingdom of grace.[44]

We have now analyzed the three Continental rationalists. In perspective, Descartes's, Spinoza's, and Leibniz's texts are personal, objective, and diaphanic, respectively. Descartes's is essentialist in ontological focus, while Spinoza's and Leibniz's stress noumenal realities. Descartes's and Spinoza's texts are governed by reflexive principles, whereas Leibniz's employs a comprehensive principle. All three are logistic in method.

Descartes sought to place the scientific disciplines and the social order of his time on a new foundation of personal, autonomous reflection. Spinoza set out to reorder Descartes's metaphysical priorities in order to achieve an ethics of human blessedness based on the objective identity of the divine and human mind. Leibniz attempted to reconcile Descartes's philosophical project with Spinoza's, and with all the principles of human science and conduct. Each of these texts represents a different form of discourse. Each establishes laws of human reason and stands as an "eternal contemporary" to any other philosophical project of similar scope in the history of ideas.

Newton, Locke, and Adam Smith

In their quest for the quintessential materialistic text of early modern philosophy, some critics have mistakenly pointed to the work of Spinoza. Others have dwelled on Descartes's dualism of *res inextensa* and *res extensae,* separating this alleged "ghost in the machine" from the reflexive essentialism of his text, in order to deconstruct his mechanistic theory of the body. These critics should have consulted first Machiavelli and then the thinkers of the British tradition.

The principal works of the British materialist tradition are those of Bacon, Hobbes, Newton, Locke, and Adam Smith, the last three of whom are identical in their semantic assumptions.

In the seventeenth century, the materialistic worldview resurfaced in Hobbes's masterpiece of worldly political theory, *Leviathan* (1651). Hobbes transformed Descartes's metaphysical reflections on the three kinds of *res verae* into a unitary ontology of material bodies in motion.[45] He combined this substrative sense of reality with a creative principle and logistic method in the first words of the text:

> Nature (the Art whereby God hath made and governes the World) is by the Art of man as in many other things, so in this also imitated, that it can make an Artificial Animal. For seeing life is but a motion of Limbs, the beginning whereof is in some principall part within; why may we not say, that all Automata (Engines that move themselves by springs and wheeles as doth a watch) have an artificiall life? For what is the Heart, but a Spring; and the Nerves, but so many Strings; and the Joynts, but so many Wheels, giving motion to the whole Body, such as was intended by the Artificer?[46]

Extending the analogy to the creation of the commonwealth, or state, Hobbes continues:

> Art goes yet further, imitating that Rationall and most excellent worke of Nature, Man. For by Art is created that great LEVIATHAN called a COMMON-WEALTH, or STATE (in latine CIVITAS), which is but an Artificiall Man; though of greater stature and strength than the Naturall, for whose protection and defence it was intended; and in which, the Soveraignty is an Artificial Soul, as giving life and motion to the whole body; the Magistrates, and other Officers of judicature and execution, artificiall Joynts; Reward and Punishment . . . are the Nerves, that do the same in the Body Naturall; the Wealth and Riches of all the particular members, are the Strength; etc.[47]

Hobbes then describes the great Leviathan's provisions for the peoples' safety, the duties of its counsellors, its laws, and its response to sedition and civil war according to the same metaphor. He concludes the first paragraph of his text with the statement that the "Body Politique" is made by "Man, the human Artificer," after the model of that fiat pronounced by God in the first creation.

Hobbes, like Descartes, employs a personal perspective. This produces a unique combination of archic elements underlying Hobbes's views on the vagaries of human passion and man's warlike character in the state of nature, and his insistence that without the commonwealth there would be only continual fear and danger of violent death, and the life of man would be nasty, mean, brutish, and short.[48]

The sovereign or sovereign body of such a commonwealth also wields an absolutely subjective power of will, or of command and execution. In Hobbes's version of the social contract, the personal perspective is authoritative: "I authorize and give up my right of governing myself, to this man, or this assembly of men, on this condition, that thou give up thy right to him, and authorize all his actions in like manner."[49]

Thus, in the first three paragraphs of the introduction to *Leviathan*, Hobbes's archic profile is clearly outlined. He gives precedence to a personal perspective, substrative reality, logistic method, and creative principle—elements that appear in his other works as well.[50]

Much of early modern Western philosophy, however, flows not from the personalistic materialism of Hobbes, but from the objective naturalism of Newton. Newton's resolution of the problems of Renaissance mechanics gave the major impetus to the physics of his day; the implications of his formulations remained an essential point of reference for all thinkers of the European Enlightenment and beyond. The Newtonian worldview, expanding with Europe's scientific and technological progress in the nineteenth century, set the stage for Darwin's revolution in biological theory, and served as a negative foil to most of the Romantic thinkers who strove mightily against Newton's assumptions.

Newton's objective perspective gave his work a significant advantage over Hobbes's. Concomitantly, it made perhaps the greatest contribution to the materialistic conception of physical bodies in motion on which Hobbes's own treatise was predicated.

Newton's physics is directly descended from the revolutionary theories of Copernicus, Gassendi, Kepler, Galileo, Bacon, and Descartes, among others, yet radically transforms them. (In particular, Newton converted Bacon's reflexive principle into a creative one.) His writings provide a prime example of a complex set of heteroarchic transferences in the historical transmission of ideas. Although brilliantly modern for its day, Newton's theories also indirectly draw on an ancient configuration of archic variables.

Newton explicitly revived what he called "the mechanical theory of the ancients." With it he also adopted Bacon's objective perspective. In a typical passage, he writes:

> But I consider philosophy rather than the arts, and write not concerning manual but natural powers, and consider chiefly those things which relate to gravity, levity, elastic force, the resistance of fluids, and the like forces, whether attractive or impulsive; and therefore I offer this work as the mathematical principles of philosophy, for the whole burden of philosophy seems to consist in this: from the phenomena of motions to investigate the forces of nature, and then from these forces to demonstrate the other phenomena."[51]

As this passage makes clear, Newton espoused the Baconian and Cartesian method of mathematical—that is, axiomatic—reasoning and demonstration. He differed from Descartes in perspective and ontological focus, and from Descartes and Bacon in grounding principle. Newton makes it abundantly clear that his inspiration is biblical. God, the universal ruler, is portrayed in his sheer power of will as the author of creation, who in the beginning formed matter into solid, impenetrable, movable particles, set them in motion, and ensured that they should not wear away or break into pieces, lest the nature of things depending on them be changed.[52] God in his almighty will continues to exercise absolute dominion over the forces of nature. In this way, therefore, Newton reinforces Hobbes's view that physical nature is the art by which God makes and governs the world and in its mechanistic causation provides the master analogy for all its works, including man himself and his artifices.

In terms of our comparative hermeneutic, Newton is a naturalist with a creative principle. Although he drew criticism from Leibniz,

Newton systematically displaced the comprehensive principles of Copernicus, Kepler, and Galileo, and the reflexive principles of Bacon, Descartes, and Spinoza. He discarded the dialectical methods of Copernicus and Kepler and transformed the agonistic method of Galileo, which was based on a conflict between the old and new sciences. Newton's naturalistic theories superseded the noumenal ontologies of Copernicus, Galileo, and Spinoza, and the essentialist ontology of Descartes.[53]

From our analyses of these early modern figures we can see that many of the great texts have in common a set of archic assumptions. John Locke, for instance, conceived it as one of his many missions to provide the epistemology for the physics of "the incomparable Mr. Newton."

Locke's semantic profile proves to be identical to that of his illustrious contemporary, Newton, as do Adam Smith's a century later and Charles Darwin's two centuries later. In examining these interrelationships it becomes apparent that Newton's theories triggered revolutions in physics, biology, political philosophy, economics, and epistemology in the modern West.

Locke's writings cover many subjects, but of special importance are works in which he elucidated the epistemological foundation of Newton's physics and applied these principles to political theory. He writes from the perspective of the objective observer who seeks to examine human abilities and thus "to see what objects our understanding were, or were not, fitted to deal with."[54] Like the "experimentalist" Hume after him, Locke claims to use the "historical, plain method" of observing the human mind and the springs of human action. Like Bacon and Hume, Locke the logicist relishes the clarity and distinctiveness of direct observation. Thus Locke writes: "If any one asks me, What solidity is, I send him to his senses to inform him. Let him put a flint or a football between his hands, and then endeavor to join them, and he will know."[55]

But in propounding the doctrine of the direct experience of objective phenomena, Locke consciously echoed Newton. Furthermore, both Newton and Locke have Epicurean semantic profiles. Unlike Hume the existentialist observer, therefore, Newton and Locke adopted substrative ontologies, in which invisible bodies in motion underlie and cause the "appearances" of our senses. In Locke's words: "I cannot conceive how bodies without us can anyway affect our senses, but by the immediate contact of the sensible bodies themselves, as in tasting and feeling, or the impulse of some sensible particles coming from them, as in seeing, hearing, and smelling; by the different impulses of which parts, caused by their different size, figure, and motion, the variety of sensations is produced in us."[56]

What is distinctive in this doctrine is that the material causes of the impulses that result in our phenomenal perceptions are properties of the unobservable particles postulated by Newton's physics, whose roots can be traced back to the philosophies of Democritus and Epicurus. To Locke these bodies in motion comprise the "real essences," as distinguished from the "nominal essences" of scientific classifications of useful ideas about them.[57]

Locke's political theory provides further illustrations of these semantic features. In his *Second Treatise of Government,* Locke continues to write as the "plain, historical" spectator of life, devoid of Hobbes's subjectivity. Crucial to this perspective is Locke's insistence on the common, God-given rationality of men, which enters into his concept of the impartiality of magistrates in a civil society.

In the same work, Locke's substrative sense of reality emerges wherever he describes the vital self-interests of men in the state of nature. To Locke, no less than to Machiavelli or Hobbes, men are motivated by their instincts and passions—a view that achieves full expression in Locke's concept of private property.[58]

Locke's views on private property involve a materialistic sense of reality and a logistic method. His concept of the executive power of individuals in the state of nature, of political rights and obligations in civil society, and of the voting force of the consenting majority are further instances of these semantic assumptions.

In Locke's words: "It is necessary the body should move that way whither the greater force carries it, which is the consent of the majority; or else it is impossible it should act or continue one body, one community, which the consent of every individual that united into it, agreed that it should."[59] Close examination of Locke's *Second Treatise* reveals that all its major concepts—executive rights; political privileges; consent of the majority; the appropriation of property through individual industry; private wealth and inheritance; and the increase of material value through labor—are functionally related to his semantic assumptions.

Locke assimilated Newton's creative principle in formulating his political theory. This is already apparent in the second chapter, on the state of nature, where he argues that men are all equal and independent, such that "no one ought to harm another in his life, health, liberty, or possessions; for men being all the workmanship of one omnipotent, and infinitely wise maker; all the servants of one sovereign master, sent into the world by his order, and about his business; they are his property, whose workmanship they are, made to last during his, not one another's pleasure: and being furnished with like faculties, sharing all in one community of nature, there cannot be supposed any such subordination among us, that may authorize us to destroy one another, as if we were made for one another's uses, as the inferior ranks of creatures are for ours."[60]

This voluntary principle merges with Locke's other semantic assumptions in his justification of private industry and therefore of the production of human wealth or property. "God, who hath given the world to men in common, hath also given them reason to make use of it to the best advantage of life, and convenience."[61] Locke goes on to say that the earth, and all inferior creatures, are common to all men. Yet every man has a property in his own person: the labor of his body, and the work of his hands, are properly his.[62] Therefore he who takes pains about it, begins to extend his bodily property.[63]

Locke's ultimate justification of private property centers on a voluntary principle as well. "God, when he gave the world in common to all mankind, commanded man also to labour, and the penury of his condition required it of him. God and his reason commanded him to subdue the earth. . . . He that in obedience to this command of God, subdued, tilled and sowed any part of it, thereby annexed to it something that was his property, which another had no title to, nor could without injury take from him."[64]

Locke voices other versions of the divine authorization of private appropriation and the production of wealth in his *Second Treatise.* Labor, industry, and work, are themselves variations on Newton's concept of force through a distance. Other Lockean concepts involving the voluntary principle are the invention of money by mutual agreement of men, the consentual basis of political and marriage contracts, and the inalienable freedom of men from the absolute, arbitrary power of others. In short, a creative (or voluntary) principle informs Locke's multifaceted concept of freedom and liberty. In these essential aspects of his political theory Locke remained faithful to the Newtonian paradigm.

If Locke can be said to have written his *Essay* and *Treatises of Government* within the framework of Newton's philosophy, so too Adam Smith wrote his influential *Inquiry into the Nature and Causes of The Wealth of Nations* (1776) within the framework of Newton's and Locke's theories.[65]

The social context for the great works of modern European philosophy derives not merely from the individual thinker's career but from the history of his era, with its complex institutional changes. Nonetheless, the great texts are individual in their formulations. *The Wealth of Nations,* which lays the foundation of modern economic thought in the non-Marxist West, is one of these. In the words of Max Lerner, it simultaneously spelled the death of medieval economic institutions and provided justification for the rising class of modern businessmen, their political executive committees in the parliaments of the world, and their intellectual executive committees in the academies.[66]

For our comparative hermeneutic the interesting point is that the archic presuppositions of Adam Smith, the philosopher of the capitalist revolution, have their precedents in the texts of Thales and Epicurus. In his eighteenth-century version, Adam Smith applied the principles of Newton and Locke to the subject matter of political economy. In his central concept of laissez-faire economic liberalism, he emphasized a principle of competition based on materialistic self-interest, which works both to maximize the available capital of a given economic class and to reinvest that capital to a maximum degree.

Adam Smith therefore championed a principle of liberty against the surviving feudal and mercantilist restrictions on individual initiative. His notion of competitive self-interest is a specific application of Locke's general concept of vital, appropriating instincts in the state of nature and in civil society. His concept of individual and corporate productivity is entirely logistic in formulation.

This well-known passage from *The Wealth of Nations* illustrates Adam Smith's objective perspective, substrative sense of reality, logistic method, and creative principle:

> Every individual necessarily labours to render the annual revenue of the society as great as he can. He generally, indeed, neither intends to promote the public interest, nor knows how much he is promoting it. By preferring the support of domestic to that of foreign industry, he intends only his own security; and by directing that industry in such a manner as its produce may be of the greatest value, he intends only his own gain, and he is in this, as in many other cases, led by an invisible hand to promote an end which was no part of his intention. Nor is it always the worse for society that it was no part of it. By pursuing his own interest he frequently promotes that of the society more effectually than when he really intends to promote it.[67]

Smith's notion of "an invisible hand" reveals the two essential components of the substrative ontological focus, namely, the deceptive appearance of the surface and the deep causation of the substrate. Marx introduces a different version of Smith's "invisible hand" in his concept of the underlying "forces of production."

The same passage from the *Wealth of Nations,* incidentally, rehabilitates the concept of "annual revenue" developed by the French Physiocrats, and presupposes Locke's understanding of the production of wealth. The imprint of Adam Smith's mind, however, is evident from the opening chapter of the first book of his monumental work. His classic description of the division of labor in a pin factory deserves further recognition as assertion and demonstration of the logistic method.[68]

It is important to observe that Newton's basic assumptions survived in the texts of Locke, Adam Smith, and Darwin, among others.[69] To reiterate, Newton elaborated a materialistic concept of nature through an objective perspective, a logistic method, and a creative principle—a powerful configuration of archic variables that has helped to shape modern Western institutions. But it is neither a pure nor a unique configuration of archic variables. It differs in its creative principle from the pure materialistic texts of Anaximenes and Democritus (or later of Santayana), reinterpreting the archic elements of the texts of Thales, Epicurus, and Lucretius.

Berkeley, Hume, and Kant

Well versed in Greek and Roman literature, English history, philosophy, and social customs, Hume also had a genius for posing foundational questions. Hume called this his "sifting humour," and with it he probed the principles of human nature.[70] Kant said that the power of Hume's mind had awakened him from his dogmatic slumbers.

Like every other philosopher, Hume reached his greatest insights through stages of refinement and consolidation. He formulated the paradigm of logical empiricism, whose influence is still broadly felt in the human sciences and whose contemporary exponents include such thinkers as G. E. Moore, Bertrand Russell, Carnap, and early Wittgensteinians.

For our comparative hermeneutic, this is a crucial point. The major philosophers produce the paradigms of future discourses. They contribute more fundamentally to the growth of mind than do secondary figures. Although the careers of minor figures sometimes prepare the way for a major figure, often enough it is the other way around. The innovative mind, in its fresh grasp of some dimension of the world, is often the decisive factor in the emergence of an essential form of thought and discourse.

In analyzing Hume's writings, we see he is an existential Democritean. In contrast to the Epicurean tendencies of Newton, Locke, and Adam Smith, Hume claimed that he had stormed the citadel of human nature and thus invalidated the premises of the natural philosophers of the British and Continental traditions.[71]

In passing, it is interesting to observe that the historian Edward Gibbon (1737–94), produced a classic with the same archic profile as that of his contemporary, David Hume (1711–76). Gibbon's *The Decline and Fall of the Roman Empire* remains the definitive treatment of the subject to this day. It is reminiscent of Hume in its rare brilliance of style and accuracy of statement.[72] Two of the world's musical geniuses, Franz Josef Haydn

(1732–1809) and Wolfgang Amadeus Mozart (1756–91), flourished at this time as well.

Hume adopted Berkeley's existential ontological focus, rejecting his other semantic elements.[73]

	PERSPECTIVE	REALITY	METHOD	PRINCIPLE
Berkeley	*diaphanic*	*existential*	*agonistic*	*creative*
Hume	*objective*	*existential*	*logistic*	*elemental*

In espousing Berkeley's existential reality, Hume aimed to refute the works of all materialists. Although he was a Democritean in most respects, he rejected the entire philosophy of substrative bodies developed by such philosophers as Bacon, Hobbes, Newton, and Locke. Hume prided himself on having invented the philosophical equivalent of the concept of gravity—the doctrine of the mind's association of simple ideas, which correspond to the simple elements of our sense impressions, united by a principle of habit, or custom.[74]

The immediate precedent for Hume's existential focus is Berkeley's. Because of the irreducible particularity of our sense impressions, Berkeley argues, an object under the microscope is not the same as the object seen by the naked eye. Perceptions of distance through sight and touch do not provide us with two different references to a common reality, distance. The "primary qualities"—extension and figure and the like—of Hobbes's, Newton's, and Locke's substrative bodies in motion are no more objective than the "secondary qualities" of our immediate perceptions. Visual, tactile, and other sensory experiences only provide mutually referent signs of what we may expect among our perceptual effects. Our perceptions in turn are grounded in God's perception, and their commonality of reference, in God's will.[75]

For Berkeley's theory of vision, to be means ultimately to be perceived in both human and divine perception. The creative acts of God are central to this view, which combines sophistical elements with a diaphanic perspective.

Jaspers propounded another version of this doctrine in his account of the irreducible variety of perspectival methods, all of which founder in the face of transcendence. Like Berkeley, Jaspers reorients philosophical discourse to the revelatory language of being, which takes place within our existential world-being.[76] Jaspers's text is identical to Berkeley's in archic profile—diaphanic in perspective, existential in ontological focus, agonistic in method, and creative in principle. In Berkeley's view, one has only to take a walk through the woods to see God revealed in the iridescent book of nature. For Jaspers, history itself is the book of transcendence, which breaks through the cracks and fissures of great epochs, with their cipher-texts.[77] Berkeley and Jaspers direct our thinking to creative theophanies. One can imagine their God as an inexhaustibly eloquent rhetorician who speaks through an irreducible multiplicity of existential shapes and forms, tongues and tropes.

One of Hume's goals was to show that Berkeley's position was largely Sophistical and a form of religious Pyrrhonism as well.[78] His quarrel with Berkeley proceeds from the perspectives, methods, and grounding principles of their respective texts. Hume's text epitomizes the objective perspective. An experimentalist in the tradition of Bacon, Newton, and Locke, he explicitly bases philosophical thinking on the study of human nature. He agrees with Locke that the mind has no innate ideas and holds that all ideas derive from vivid sense impressions. The epistemological attitude of Hume's *Treatise* and first *Enquiry* resurfaces in his second *Enquiry* in the form of the "spectator" of manners and morals.

Hume undermined Berkeley's position by abandoning his creative principle, his diaphanic perspective, and his methodological form. He stated that the creative power of the mind or spirit "amounts to no more than the faculty of compounding, transposing, augmenting, or diminishing the materials afforded by the senses of experience."[79] Hume combines this logistic doctrine with an emphasis on present states of consciousness. "But consciousness never deceives"—that is to say, it is always vivid and intense in its concrete, existential immediacy.[80] Berkeley, of course, had enunciated a doctrine of the immediacy of perceptions. But he blurred the distinction between sense perceptions and divine perception, producing a version of "presence and absence," which has its diaphanic analogues in some of the world religions (and in some postmodern religious discourses).

Hume's text refutes those of his immediate precedessors. Hume is consciously foundational in intent when he says in *A Treatise of Human Nature:* "I may venture to affirm of the rest of mankind, that they are nothing but a bundle or collection of different perceptions, which succeed each other with an inconceivable rapidity, and are in a perpetual flux and movement."[81] Here, indeed, Hume appears to take the position ascribed to the Sophists by Plato in his *Theaetetus* and other writings—the doctrine of the existential flux of sense perceptions. Hume, however, combined the Sophistic existential focus with the Democritean assumption as to the discrete character of the objective elements of the flux. Thus his vivid sense perceptions are the nonrecurrent Archimedean points, the "places" of lived experience in its pristine originality. But experience is compounded, forward-moving, and habitual, so these qualities associate at the level of ideas. Our probable, or moral, reasonings consist of cause-and-effect relations of ideas, which derive from and reduce to their corresponding sense perceptions. The constant conjunction of such ideas provides our sense of the regularity of experience, which cannot be understood otherwise.

Hume examined the pattern of experience to discover an adequate principle of human knowing and doing. In custom, or habit, he found such a principle. Custom is the instinctual tendency of our nature that provides for the sense of ongoing experience. In numerous passages Hume identified the propensity of human nature to repeat itself and to expect repetition in the flow of life as the source of all connected experiences.[82] He therefore espoused an elemental principle of the antecedent mechanism of human nature, which is innately conservative.

With these ideas, Hume parted company with the major philosophers of his day. His famous arguments against miracles and all forms of a priori and a posteriori theisms, as well as his attack on the foundations of the rationalistic systems of science, metaphysics, and theology in his *Dialogues Concerning Natural Religion* and other works, have their source in this elemental principle.[83]

Hume's Democritean principle reveals itself in his arguments for innate moral sentiment, taste, and feeling. "The quick sensibility, which, on this head, is so universal among mankind," he writes, "gives a philosopher sufficient assurance, that can never be considerably mistaken in framing the catalogue" of moral virtues and vices, if he will only observe the instinctual reponses of men in their concrete circumstances of behavior.[84]

Social utility is another concept derived from the elemental principle in Hume's account of the origin of morals. In one passage in which Hume renounces the theory of self-love in favor of "a more public affection," he argues for benevolent feeling as its own innate principle of morals.

> It is needless to push our researches so far as to ask, why we have humanity or a fellow-feeling with others. It is sufficient, that this is experienced to be a principle of human nature. We must stop somewhere in our examination of causes; and there are, in every science, some general principles, beyond which we cannot hope to find any principle more general. No man is absolutely indifferent to the happiness and misery of others. The first has a natural tendency to give pleasure; the second, pain. This every one may find in himself. It is not probable, that these principles can be resolved into principles more simple and universal. . . .[85]

Hume's concepts of fellow-feeling, justice, social utility, and the like all stem from the fundamental Democritean axiom that "like attracts like," as does the principle of the association of ideas.

Hume produced a version of the Democritean ethics of cheerfulness in his catalogue of the bright, affable, agreeable virtues, to which he contrasted those of monkish asceticism. "A gloomy, hair-brained enthusiast, after his death, may have a place in the calendar," he wrote, "but will scarcely ever be admitted, when alive, into intimacy and society, except by those who are as delirious and dismal as himself."[86] Here Hume's argument rests on an appeal to the commonality (and, therefore, the normality) of human nature. His autobiography, written just before his death,[87] clearly illustrates the agreeable virtues.

Rousseau and Voltaire also developed elemental principles. The difference between Hume and Voltaire is that the latter's text was personal in perspective and agonistic in method. Rousseau's career-text proved to be the *magna carta* of political, educational, and aesthetical Romanticism. It differed from Hume's in perspective, sense of reality, and method.[88]

French philosophy is noted for its many practitioners of the personal perspective—Montaigne, Descartes, Voltaire, Rousseau, Sartre, and Merleau-Ponty.[89] British philosophers, by contrast, tend to favor the objective perspective. Bacon, Newton, Locke, Hume, John Stuart Mill, and Bertrand Russell come to mind.

Through his objective perspective and principle of innate nature Hume can be linked with some of the Greek and Roman classics he loved. He employed a Democritean principle in his discourses against the reflexive principles of Bacon, Descartes, and Spinoza, the comprehensive principle of Leibniz, and the creative principles of Hobbes, Newton, Locke, and Berkeley. If, as I have argued, we must study the great philosophical texts to see how meanings are formed, then Hume's writings must be considered one of our richest resources.

Immanuel Kant was another giant of Western philosophy. With his three *Critiques* and ancillary writings, we can say that Kant responded fully to Hume's attack on all forms of rationalistic and naturalistic philosophy.[90] Kant's text disagrees with Hume's in every respect:

	PERSPECTIVE	REALITY	METHOD	PRINCIPLE
Hume	*objective*	*existential*	*logistic*	*elemental*
Kant	*disciplinary*	*noumenal*	*synoptic*	*reflexive*

Through the concept of "critical" thinking, which this intertextual profile represents, Kant also revived the strains of architectonic theory that originated with Bacon and Descartes.

The three *Critiques* were designed to lay the theoretical groundwork for the general and special sciences. Kant's critical text is a theory of theories *par excellence*. Kant set himself the goal of reconstructing a "metaphysics as science," which would establish valid concepts in all the sciences. His disciplinary perspective manifests itself in his intent to redefine these forms of "consciousness in general." The *Critiques* are accordingly addressed to an idealized group of thinkers who share this orientation.

Kant's first *Critique* defines the complete set of transcendental conditions for the two forms of pure sensibility (space and time), the twelve categories of the understanding, and the three ideas of pure reason. These universal cognitive forms are mirrored by the universal moral law, which forms the subject matter of the second *Critique*.

Kant's reflexive principle of pure reason combines with his disciplinary perspective to produce the various meanings of his text. The morality of our actions, their worth and dignity, require a commitment to reason. A moral agent, in Kant's view, always acts as a "representative of mankind." Similarly, a philosopher occupies himself with "cosmical concepts"—fundamental concept of human knowing, doing, and making.[91]

Kant's text is a paradigm of the synoptic method, which examines a subject through the interrelationships of the whole to its parts. The analysis of the transcendental categories of pure reason was Kant's special philosophical project. The principle of pure reason, which reflexively brings to completion the self-examination of its essential properties, supplies the driving force for Kant's monumental undertaking.

Kant's reflexive principle accounts for the essential variety of the faculties of reason—the cognitive, practical, and productive—and for their self-sufficiency and self-completion in his architectonic set. In contrast to Hume's principle of custom, or habit, or of innate moral sentiment, therefore, Kant always grounds his discourse in the principle of the autonomy of reason.

From the perspective of our comparative hermeneutic we see that Kant reinterpreted Aristotle's critique of Democritus's elemental principle, as well as Aristotle's rejection of Anaxagoras's or Democritus's logistic method which evolved into the "aggregational and segregational method" of epistemological, physical, and metaphysical theories after Bacon and Descartes.

Kant is the only major philosopher of the eighteenth century to use a reflexive principle and synoptic method. Together with his disciplinary perspective, which was equally unusual for its time, this configuration of semantic variables accounts for Kant's unique status as a "critical" philosopher. From a distance, Kant's work stands alone, separated on the one hand from the various logistic philosophies of the seventeenth and eighteenth centuries, and on the other from the prevailing dialectical and agonistic theories of the nineteenth century. Kant's archic profile, however, is identical to that of Thomas Aquinas.

Since Kant's alleged antimetaphysical stance has come under attack from Thomists, it is advisable that we examine their archic correspondence. Kant's text is "dogmatical" in its main concepts and arguments, including those against the possiblity of metaphysical knowledge. At the same time, however, he produced a "metaphysics as science," with its own presuppositions. It is this "archic text" I am comparing with that of Aquinas. The key to it is Kant's noumenal sense of reality, which he shared with Aquinas, Spinoza, and Leibniz.

The volumes of commentary focusing on Kant's first *Critique* will not help us here unless they can establish the importance of Kant's noumenal sense of reality, which becomes prominent only in the second *Critique*. Logical empiricists who concentrate on epistemological problems in Kant fail to appreciate Kant's synoptic method, which encompassed questions of noumenal freedom and related questions of religion. Pragmatists and more recent philosophers have directly altered the ontology of Kant's moral discourse, as well.

Berkeley, Hume, and Kant produced alternatives to the materialistic theories of Hobbes, Newton, Locke, and Adam Smith, even though they differed radically from one another. Berkeley's "new theory of vision" proved to be the worldview of a diaphanic Sophist; Hume's "moderate skepticism," that of an existential Democritean; and Kant's "critical philosophy," that of a noumenal Aristotelian.

Most of these philosophers were well aware of their antecedents in Greek philosophy. They studied the ancients and in some cases deliberately strove to reinterpret their principles of thought and conduct. Following Leibniz's example, the eighteenth-century French *philosophes* and Adam Smith, among others, became interested in the accounts of Chinese philosophy that reached Europe through the letters of Jesuit missionaries and other travelers. These instances illustrate the global and historical interconnections of ideas.

8

The Changes of the Books in Nineteenth- and Twentieth-Century Thought

Philosophical Trends after Kant

Kant's text marks a watershed in philosophy, because it undertook the analysis of theories themselves. Following Aristotle in this respect, Kant attempted to establish the possibilities of reason as a complete set.[1] He condemned as merely dogmatical all the precritical theories before Hume. The need to distinguish "dogmatical" from "critical" philosophy occupied Kant's immediate successor, Fichte, as well.[2] Such philosophers as Hegel, Schopenhauer, and Peirce maintained Kant's emphasis on a critical philosophy.

With regard to discursive method, nineteenth-century continental European philosophy can be generally divided into dialectical and agonistic groups. I refer here to the new philosophies of Fichte, Schelling, Hegel, Marx, Kierkegaard, Schopenhauer, and Nietzsche, recognizing that the seventeenth- and eighteenth-century styles continued to have an important cultural impact.

The older, predominantly logistic methods were the legacy of Bacon's and Descartes's methodological revolutions, as we have traced them through the major rationalistic and materialistic systems up to the time of Kant. In particular, the logistic method embedded in Newtonian science and industrial liberalism provided the impetus for a variety of scientific, technological, and social developments. Some nineteenth-century philosophers continued to use logistic methods—notably such British philosophers as John Stuart Mill, Malthus, and Darwin.

By contrast, the nineteenth-century German philosophers, who venerated Kant even as they sought to go beyond him, appear to have assimilated Kant's devastating critique of the logistic method in seventeenth- and eighteenth-century philosophy and science. Fichte, Schelling, Hegel, Marx, and even Comte were all dialectical thinkers, as was Bergson later. Kierkegaard, Nietzsche, and later Freud were agonists.

Only Schopenhauer deviates from this pattern. While it exhibits strong agonistic tendencies in its descriptions of the primordial will, Schopenhauer's text is ultimately synoptic in its discussions of the world as representation and as will. Nietzsche understood these categories in agonistic terms, but Schopenhauer, as Kant before him, did not.[3] Schopenhauer rejected the Sophistic method, as well as the dialectical methods of Fichte and Hegel.[4] (Schopenhauer's text—with its diaphanic perspective, substrative reality, synoptic method, and elemental principle—appears to have no archic parallels in the history of philosophy.)

Perhaps more important, Kant's synoptic method entered the American tradition through Peirce, who bequeathed it in turn to James, Dewey, Mead, and Buchler, and others down to the present.[5] These philosophers have produced a series of variations on Kant's critique of logistic, associationist theories of ideas. With the exception of the Hegelian Royce, the major American philosophers, headed by Peirce, have also tended to reject the dialectical method.

Among post-Kantian philosophers who reassert the primacy of logistic methods, Husserl's text is consciously Neo-Cartesian.[6] Its cardinal doctrine of eidetic intuition performed through Husserl's *epoché*—that is, the bracketing out of the naturalistic attitude in the service of achieving a transcendental analysis—is brilliantly logistic in form. Husserl's text also adopted Descartes's essentialist reality and reflexive principle. However, it displaces Descartes's personal perspective with a disciplinary one.[7]

Husserl's essences, incidentally, function as semantic principles of organization of concepts and of conduct, analogous to Peirce's semiological doctrine of thirds, which are real generals or universals. Both Husserl and Peirce describe themselves as phenomenologists.

Husserl's sense of reality is essentialist, and his text is Aristotelian in this respect. Moreover, his perspective is disciplinary, in the tradition of Aristotle and Kant. Husserl's text uses the reflexive, self-determining *cogito* as its grounding principle, in the tradition of Aristotle, Descartes, and Kant.

Peirce, by contrast, liked to call himself a "phaneroscopist"—one who objectively observes what appears in the mind.[8] The differences between Peirce and Husserl are represented in the following schematic set:

	PERSPECTIVE	REALITY	METHOD	PRINCIPLE
Peirce	*objective*	*essentialist*	*synoptic*	*reflexive*
Husserl	*disciplinary*	*essentialist*	*logistic*	*reflexive*

Although each philosopher departs from the pure Aristotelian model in only one respect, the distribution of these variables produces profoundly different kinds of philosophical discourses.

In further contrast, such philosophers as Carnap, Frege, G. E. Moore, and Russell employ logistic methods, but their senses of reality are existential. They are logistic in their concern for reducing the complexities of philosophy to a grammar of elemental propositions, to say nothing of their penchant for precisely constructed arguments. Thinkers who have been called logical empiricists and ordinary language philosophers tend to have objective perspectives and elemental principles and to pursue logico-semantic analyses with an existential focus. They belong to a tradition that derives from Hume, as does the younger Wittgenstein. But Wittgenstein gradually freed himself from this tradition and began—to the chagrin of his colleague Russell—to use an agonistic method in the closing pages of his *Tractatus Logico-Philosophicus*.[9]

Santayana's writings appear to be unique. His doctrine of essences, each of which is a perfectly definite and final form of the animal good,[10] is based on a logistic method. His text is objective in perspective, substrative in reality, and elemental in principle. Santayana therefore developed, in contrast to the "youthful materialism" of the American Pragmatists, what he called "a materialism of old age."[11] In its fundamental assumptions, his text is entirely Democritean. This becomes especially clear in his *Dialogues in Limbo*, where the Greek materialist is the main exponent for Santayana's own position.[12]

Nineteenth-Century Philosophies

Returning to the German philosophers who followed Kant, our task is to analyze the career-texts of a number of major thinkers whose lives and theories overlap in many ways, without overemphasizing their similarities or misinterpreting their areas of disagreement. Judging from the literature on these subjects, it is easier to adopt Hegelian, Marxist, or Nietzschean dogmas than it is to attempt to balance their historical significance. In actual practice, the nineteenth-century philosophers tend to displace one another along the following lines.

In perspective, Fichte was a Kantian, with a disciplinary attitude to "universal science,"[13] which inquires, first, into how spatiotemporal objects are possible and, second, into the universally valid forms of our cognitive and moral faculties. In this basic philosophical orientation Fichte retained both Kant's noumenal sense of reality and his reflexive principle—both of which underlie his doctrine of the transcendental ego as will. He departed radically from Kant, however, in his dialectical concept of the self-positioning of the transcendental will. Fichte's cardinal doctrine of "activity" (*Tathandlung*, that is, the pure noumenal will's own self-activity) also derives from that configuration of archic variables.[14]

By contrast, Schelling, Hegel, and Schopenhauer used diaphanic perspectives and produced theories of "absolute knowledge" (as did later Bergson, Jaspers, Heidegger, and Nishida). Marx, Comte, John Stuart Mill, Darwin, and Malthus used objective perspectives (as did later Peirce, Max Weber, Freud, Einstein, Santayana, Russell, Wittgenstein). On the other hand, Kierkegaard, Nietzsche, and James preferred the personal perspective (as did later Scheler, Sartre, Unamuno, and Merleau-Ponty).

In their sense of primary reality, the texts of Fichte, Schelling, and Kierkegaard are noumenal. Indeed, Kierkegaard appears to be the last major philosopher to give precedence to a noumenal reality, although Neo-Thomists and some other traditionalists have reverted to the noumenal ontologies of their founding fathers. This ontological focus contrasts with the essentialist realities of Hegel or Peirce (and later of Dewey, Whitehead, Scheler, and Heidegger); with the substrative realities of Marx, Darwin, Freud, Unamuno, or Santayana; and with the existential realities of John Stuart Mill or James (and later of Russell, Wittgenstein, Sartre, Jaspers, and Merleau-Ponty).

But in their integrative principles, the texts of Fichte, Hegel, and Peirce are reflexive; those of Marx, Kierkegaard, James, Bergson, Dewey, Whitehead, Sartre, Unamuno, Heidegger, Jaspers, and Merleau-Ponty are creative; while those of Schelling, Schopenhauer, Nietzsche, Freud, Scheler, Russell, Wittgenstein, and Santayana are elemental.

Among the post-Kantian philosophers, F. H. Bradley employs a comprehensive principle, which informs his Platonic doctrine of "degrees of truth and reality" and of "my station and its duties."[15] Comprehensive principles also underlie the scientific theories of Louis Ampere and Albert Einstein. Einstein, like F. H. Bradley, was an existentialist, but with an objective perspective and agonistic method.[16]

While only summarily sketched here, these readings purport to specify the archic variables at work in the texts of the major post-Kantian philosophers. They are of course subject to changes from new textual evidence and better insight. To the extent these readings hold up, it should be possible to compare the teachings of individual philosophers to each other. Marx displaces Hegel's perspective, reality, and principle;

Freud displaces Nietzsche's perspective; Dewey subordinates James's perspective and reality; Russell rejects Wittgenstein's agonistic method; and so on. We should also be able to see how the lesser texts agree or disagree with the great works, depending on their grounding principles, scholastic affiliations, and other characteristics. The principles of interpretation practiced by contemporary Deconstructionists and other postmoderns should also be illuminated through such readings.

Since a more extended reading of the post-Kantian philosophers mentioned is beyond the scope of this work, I simply summarize their archic profiles. These summaries are intended to moderate the truth claims of their theories according to the rules of our comparative hermeneutic. The archic profiles of Fichte, Schelling, and Hegel distribute themselves in the following way:

	PERSPECTIVE	REALITY	METHOD	PRINCIPLE
Fichte	*disciplinary*	*noumenal*	*dialectical*	*reflexive*
Schelling	*diaphanic*	*noumenal*	*dialectical*	*elemental*
Hegel	*diaphanic*	*essentialist*	*dialectical*	*reflexive*

This set of archic elements should account for the points of agreement or disagreement among their texts, each one of which presents a compelling worldview, yet draws severe criticism from the others. Such a trenchant critic as Santayana would call them the texts of transcendental egotists.[17] But Santayana's criticism presupposes the archic assumptions of his own text.

Fichte's and Hegel's philosophies each combine two Platonic and two Aristotelian values, although they are differently distributed.[18] Schelling's has three Platonic elements, along with a Democritean principle of identity, or indifference. In terms of its antecedents, Schelling's philosophy represents a purer configuration of archic elements and is also more deeply rooted in the spiritual traditions. But Hegel's is remarkable for its Aristotelian sense of reality, which relates Schelling's thought to the historical traditions.[19]

Marx's archic profile, of course, has a special relation to Hegel's, which the following schema reveals:

	PERSPECTIVE	REALITY	METHOD	PRINCIPLE
Hegel	*diaphanic*	*essentialist*	*dialectical*	*reflexive*
Marx	*objective*	*substrative*	*dialectical*	*creative*

Marx's text displays two Democritean values, combined with a Sophistic principle and Platonic method. His dialectical method comes from

Hegel, as he acknowledges. His objective perspective and substrative ontology come from Feuerbach. These appear prominently in Marx's doctrine that ideology is determined by the impersonal forces of production. His creative principle takes the form of the teaching that human work, dedicated to the revolutionary goals, can change the world.[20]

Schopenhauer's text also displays mixed semantic variables, as noted above. Comparing it with that of his archrival, Hegel, we see a pattern of fundamental disagreements:

	PERSPECTIVE	REALITY	METHOD	PRINCIPLE
Hegel	*diaphanic*	*essentialist*	*dialectical*	*reflexive*
Schopenhauer	*diaphanic*	*substrative*	*synoptic*	*elemental*

We see also that Schopenhauer's text anticipates Nietzsche's and Freud's in ontological focus and integrative principle.

By comparison, the Kierkegaard's text differs from Hegel's in the following way:

	PERSPECTIVE	REALITY	METHOD	PRINCIPLE
Hegel	*diaphanic*	*essentialist*	*dialectical*	*reflexive*
Kierkegaard	*personal*	*noumenal*	*agonistic*	*creative*

Kierkegaard's is the text of a noumenal Sophist. Religious faith is the creative work, the life's task, of an incommensurable person. He repudiates the dialectical system of Hegel's absolute subject through a series of paradoxical statements that express the ambiguous relation between persons, and the absolute gap between the sinful self and the infinite purity of God. Christ, the God-man, is the ultimate paradox in Kierkegaard's discourse.[21]

Nietzsche's text shares two archic variables with Schopenhauer's, on the one hand, and three with Freud's, on the other:

	PERSPECTIVE	REALITY	METHOD	PRINCIPLE
Schopenhauer	*diaphanic*	*substrative*	*synoptic*	*elemental*
Nietzsche	*personal*	*substrative*	*agonistic*	*elemental*
Freud	*objective*	*substrative*	*agonistic*	*elemental*

Schopenhauer's elemental principle of the blind, primordial will is transformed by Nietzsche into his doctrines of the eternal return, of the inevitable ascendancy of the instincts, of the deep-seated power of the species, and the like.[22] But in contrast to Schopenhauer's final negation of the will through the "pure perception" attained in art and in religious enlightenment, Nietzsche's *gaya scienzia* reaffirms the individual's will to power.[23] Nietzsche attacked objective and disciplinary perspectives as well.

Freud's text is closer to the materialistic paradigm of Democritus (or of Santayana), differing only in its agonistic method. He shares his methodological form with Nietzsche, although he rejects his personal perspective for an objective one. The concepts of repression, conflict, resistance, and defense mechanism are ubiquitous in Freud's analyses of the etiology of the neuroses. He considers ambivalence to be a general characteristic of all mental life and a special feature of the psychology of neurotics. The Oedipal complex, the keystone of Freud's mature system, turns out to be a doubly bisexual concept. Pleasure and reality principles, id and ego, civilization and its discontents, life and death instincts, in various interrelationships, emerge in Freud's writings on the Oedipal complex. Moreover, Freud viewed these psychodynamic tensions as having no end. Analysis itself has no end, because unconscious desires evolve throughout a person's life and therefore the process of relating the surface of consciousness to its hidden depth never reaches completion.

In *Civilization and Its Discontents,* among other works, Freud rejects, as did Nietzsche before him, various idealistic solutions to the individual and cultural tensions of human life offered by Christianity, Marxism, and other "psychological illusions."[24] But with his central distinction between the pleasure and reality principles he distances himself once again from the personal perspective of Nietzsche's text.

We are not so much concerned here with the details of Freud's thought as with the semantic variables of his text. Freud clearly based his theories on an elemental principle. In *An Autobiographical Study* Freud reflects on his own theoretical concepts in the following words:

> I have combined the instincts of self-preservation and for the preservation of the species under the concept of Eros and have contrasted with it an instinct of death or destruction which works in silence. Instinct in general is regarded as a kind of elasticity of living things, an impulsion toward the restoration of a situation which once existed but was brought to an end by some external disturbance. This essentially conservative character of instincts is exemplified by the phenomenon of the compulsion to repeat. The picture which life presents to us is the result of the working of Eros and the death-instinct together and against each other.[25]

In the broader perspective, we see that Freud's archic profile resembles Homer's or Empedocles' (and Chuang Tzu's), except for its objective perspective. Furthermore, Freud's archic profile is identical to that of the Han dynasty skeptic, Wang Ch'ung! In the psychological language of his own text, Freud adopted Wang Ch'ung's "hermeneutics of suspicion" in relation to various idealistic philosophies. His text not only perpetuates that outlook, which originates with Marx and endures in Foucault and Derrida, it is also a great theory in its own right.

Contemporary Philosophical Differences and the Growth of Mind

In examining contemporary trends in philosophy, we will begin with the Neo-Nietzschean groups, which include deconstructionism and postmodernism. As an example, Derrida's theory—and it is a theory—consistently exhibits semantic elements that overlap with Nietzsche's and Freud's:

	PERSPECTIVE	REALITY	METHOD	PRINCIPLE
Nietzsche	*personal*	*substrative*	*agonistic*	*elemental*
Freud	*objective*	*substrative*	*agonistic*	*elemental*
Derrida	*objective*	*substrative*	*agonistic*	*creative*

Derrida's text therefore has two Nietzschean, or three Freudian, elements; we may say that it is half-Democritean and half-Sophistic. Derrida's text is Democritean in its relentless tracing of "writing" to an impersonal substrate, which, like Freud's death instinct, operates in silence.[26] It is Sophistic in its emphasis on the "play of differences," that is, the endless proliferation of adversative supplements that presuppose Derrida's creative principle and agonistic method.[27]

Although they have all been labeled "postmodern," Derrida's text differs radically from those of Wittgenstein and so-called later-phase Wittgensteinians:

	PERSPECTIVE	REALITY	METHOD	PRINCIPLE
Derrida	*objective*	*substrative*	*agonistic*	*creative*
Wittgenstein et al.	*objective*	*existential*	*agonistic*	*elemental*

Wittgenstein's sense of reality agrees with that of Russell and other logical empiricists, who follow in Hume's footsteps. This is very different from Derrida, who asserts that a perception "can never be booked in the present." In method, however, Wittgenstein's "language-games" and "forms of life" show a family resemblance to Derrida's logical operator—the agonistically polarized form of presence and absence.[28] This method carries over into the post-Wittgensteinian position on the indeterminacy of translation. Wittgenstein's profile is identical with that of the Hellenistic Skeptics.[29]

Husserl's text, we have noted, is that of a logistic Aristotelian. Very different are the texts of Sartre, Merleau-Ponty, Jaspers, and Heidegger, all of whom reject Husserl's Neo-Cartesian project:

	PERSPECTIVE	REALITY	METHOD	PRINCIPLE
Sartre	*personal*	*existential*	*dialectical*	*creative*
Merleau-Ponty	*personal*	*existential*	*dialectical*	*creative*
Jaspers	*diaphanic*	*existential*	*agonistic*	*creative*
Heidegger	*diaphanic*	*essentialist*	*dialectical*	*creative*

Sartre and Merleau-Ponty share the archic profile of dialectical Sophists. Jaspers's is that of a diaphanic Sophist, like Berkeley's.[30] Heidegger's, as noted elsewhere, is that of an Old Testament prophet.[31]

Among British philosophers, Russell's profile agrees in all respects with Hume's. How does it compare to such philosophies as those of F. H. Bradley and Whitehead?

	PERSPECTIVE	REALITY	METHOD	PRINCIPLE
Russell	*objective*	*existential*	*logistic*	*elemental*
Bradley	*disciplinary*	*existential*	*dialectical*	*comprehensive*
Whitehead	*disciplinary*	*essentialist*	*dialectical*	*creative*

Russell was an existential Democritean, but Bradley and Whitehead have more mixed profiles. Bradley was more of a Platonist, and Whitehead more of an Aristotelian, but each had Sophistic elements as well, although not the same ones.[32]

Whitehead's creative principle established his affinity with the "process" philosophies of Bergson, James, and Dewey, as he himself announced in the opening paragraphs of *Process and Reality*.[33] The full intertextual relation among the latter thinkers is as follows:

	PERSPECTIVE	REALITY	METHOD	PRINCIPLE
Bergson	*diaphanic*	*substrative*	*dialectical*	*creative*
James	*personal*	*existential*	*problematic or synoptic*	*creative*
Dewey	*disciplinary*	*essentialist*	*problematic*	*creative*
Whitehead	*disciplinary*	*essentialist*	*dialectical*	*creative*

These archic profiles shed some light on the attacks that Whitehead, Dewey, and James directed against Bradley, whose philosophy, as developed in such works as *Appearance and Reality* and *Essays on Truth and Reality*, served as a critical foil to the development of the "process" philosophies.[34] We can retrace the polemical differences between Bradley and Russell in a similar fashion.

Such analyses will account for the diversity of styles and schools that form contemporary philosophical culture and will deepen our understanding of the great traditions of philosophy. To define the relationships among the major tendencies in contemporary philosophy calls for the collaboration of competent researchers sharing a common approach.

Philosophy, however, tends to become specialized, and with specialization comes the need to assert minor differences, as Peirce and Freud observed. Peirce noted that mental life seeks to fill up all the available niches in a cultural landscape. Freud described the process through which mental cultures become narcissistic and thereby assume adversarial forms.

The tendencies toward specialization and differentiation may be phases of what Peirce calls synechism—the process of generalization through which mental cultures grow. Good ideas, like good houses, last. They are inhabited by many generations, each of which adds to their value. Time refines their textures and sets off their lines. To Peirce's way of thinking, the synechistic pattern of continuity and growth, ramification and generalization illustrates the law of mind governing the natural and human orders.[35] The human mind tends to generalize because the natural universe does. Works of philosophy, science, and art are the ultimate generalizations, clarifying the lines of a culture's evolution. They *are* the world's lines, or views, synechistically forming.[36]

Nietzsche developed an analogous thought when he wrote, "That individual philosophical concepts are not anything capricious or autonomously evolving, but grow up in connection and relationship with each other: that, however suddenly and arbitrarily they seem to appear in the history of thought, they nevertheless belong just as much to a system as all the members of the fauna of a continent—is betrayed by the fact that the most diverse philosophers keep filling in a definite scheme of possible philosophies. . . ."[37] Philosophies live, and move, and have their being within certain enduring principles of design.

Some contemporary philosophers are at work deconstructing so-called representational, logocentric discourses. Others are reviving traditional antinomies between philosophy or religion and science, or between East and West. In contrast to them, Peirce's philosophical intuitions grew out of a first-hand knowledge of the sciences. He went on to develop teleological concepts of human agency, the growth of personality and institutions, and the functioning of mind in guiding the energies of life through rational prediction. Peirce also pursued the theological implications of his own theory, insisting that "the one intelligible theory of the universe is that of objective idealism," which envisions a progressively mental creation.[38]

Compared to Peirce, Nietzsche was still a romantic, and an irrationalist, as are the various postmoderns who proclaim the "end of philosophy," the "closure of metaphysics," or the disintegration of mental cultures.

Thus Heidegger solemnly declares the end of "representational thinking," which he considers to extend from Plato to Nietzsche.[39] Derrida et al. accuse even Heidegger of another kind of representational thinking—namely, diaphanic thinking, a form of theological regality, that represents the appropriation of a sovereign in the event of *Ereignis.*[40] Jaspers, another agonist, strives to reinstate the notion of Transcendence, which functions in his *Existenz*-philosophy to "shipwreck" all the principles and methods in the cipher-texts of history.[41] Although the postmoderns form opposing groups in their assaults on the great traditions,[42] they nonetheless contribute to Peirce's generalizing movement of ideas.

If we compare the postmodern philosophies with Peirce's as potential instruments of historical research and interpretation, Peirce's proves to be the more comprehensive, flexible, and fair-minded. It is "laboratory-minded" and deeply thought through. Peirce's reflexive principle of mind, which synoptically organizes generalities of natural and human cultures, provides clearer insights into the history of ideas and can moderate the more extreme claims of the others.

Peirce also rejected the merely logistic conceptions of the materialist and mental atomists. In a typical passage he writes:

> To be a nominalist consists in the undeveloped state of one's mind of the apprehension of Thirdness as Thirdness. The remedy for it consists in allowing ideas of human life a greater part in one's philosophy. Metaphysics is the science of Reality. Reality consists in regularity. Real regularity is active law. Active law is efficient reasonableness, or in other words, is truly reasonable reasonableness. Reasonable reasonableness is Thirdness as Thirdness.[43]

The direction of Peirce's thinking can be seen from his first reaction to Darwin's *Origin of Species.* Off surveying in the wilds of Louisiana, the twenty-one-year-old Peirce wrote to Chauncey Wright that Darwinism spelled the death of associationism in the traditional empirical account, and of Spencer's mechanistic associationism as well.[44] In his career-text, Peirce took the lead in reinterpreting Darwin's text, with its background in Newtonian physics and Lockean epistemology, in a synoptic fashion. The American philosophers James, Dewey, and Buchler followed Peirce in this respect.

The Classical American Philosophers

In concluding this chapter on philosophical tendencies after Kant, let us briefly examine the classical American philosophers. Of the five most prominent figures, James and Dewey employ creative principles, which represent the dominant strain of the classical American traditions. The texts of Peirce and Royce reveal reflexive principles; that of Santayana, an elemental one. Their writings exhibit the following intertextual relationships:

	PERSPECTIVE	REALITY	METHOD	PRINCIPLE
Peirce	*objective*	*essentialist*	*synoptic*	*reflexive*
James	*personal*	*existential*	*synoptic*	*creative*
Dewey	*disciplinary*	*essentialist*	*synoptic*	*creative*
Royce	*diaphanic*	*essentialist*	*dialectical*	*reflexive*
Santayana	*objective*	*substrative*	*logistic*	*elemental*

Royce was a Hegelian; Santayana, as indicated above, was a Democritean. The career-text of James proves to be Sophistic, but with an Aristotelian method. Peirce's is an Aristotelian text with a Democritean perspective. Dewey's text is Aristotelian, with a Sophistic principle.

Royce's is the most mixed of these texts, with two Platonic and two Aristotelian elements. Peirce, James, and Dewey have texts that show three natural affinities, and Santayana's is a "pure" text. Indeed, Santayana's text appears to be the only pure text in the more recent history of Western philosophy. This may account for the cogency of Santayana's writings, among the changing books of modern and postmodern philosophy.[45]

If James and Dewey, with their creative principles, represent the central strain of American philosophy, Peirce and Santayana can be considered to occupy positions to the left and right of it. In his personal influence, James can be viewed as the major figure in this configuration, and in fact James's personal perspective is remarkable not only in American philosophy, but also in the wider history of thought.[46] James asserts that the source of ontological activity lies in the push and pull of our personal lives—here and now, and not in some long run. As a result of this perspective, he distinguishes among types of personalities—

between tough-minded and tender-minded philosophers, for example. He celebrates this human perspective in the warmest, most uplifting terms. Under steady criticism from Bradley, Royce, Peirce, and Dewey, he continued to advocate a doctrine of the personal meaning of truth, based on the "each form" of pure experience, which includes subjective varieties of religious experience.

In his own life and writing, James, with characteristic generosity of spirit, promoted the careers of both Peirce and Santayana. They responded to him with sincere appreciation and esteem, but differed on fundamental points. Each framed a worldview that assimilated and reinterpreted the principal elements of the others.

While playing an exhortatory, Emersonian role in American philosophy, James defended a "radically empiricist"—that is, personalistic, existential, and voluntaristic—worldview.[47] Peirce responded with a teleological model, based on a principle of "the growth of mind" in the person, in human civilizations and particularly their rational institutions, and in the habit-forming universe at large. Santayana developed what he called an "old" materialism, somewhat at the expense of James's and Dewey's views.[48]

Peirce interpreted James's doctrine of "pure experience" as pertaining to his category of firstness, whereas thirds, or generals, were central to his system.[49] Santayana not only attacked James and Dewey head on, he obliquely attacked Peirce as well.[50] Santayana's last work, *Dominations and Powers*, is organized in three parts: the generative, militant, and rational orders.[51] These correspond to Peirce's three categories, except that Santayana reverses the priority Peirce assigned to them. Thus contrary to both James and Peirce, Santayana asserted that the naturally generative and militant orders underlie any spiritual life.

Nevertheless, for our comparative hermeneutic, Peirce's is the most significant text since Hegel's in formulating a sense of the development of human understanding as embodied in the great works of philosophy, science, and the arts. Peirce's synoptic method is more flexible than Hegel's dialectical sublations; its objective perspective avoids the absolutistic orientation of Hegel's diaphanic perspective.[52]

Of the many post-Kantian philosophers, Peirce alone formulated a universal semiology that permits limitless generalizations and continuities of ideas. In this way, he suggests the possibility of our comparative hermeneutic, which is a theory that moderates the claims of theories, including those which disclaim the possibility of systematic analysis.

The essential difference between Peirce's universal semiology and this comparative hermeneutic lies in their perspective. While Peirce's text is objective, transcending the claims of individuals in favor of a concept of truth and reality "in the long run," I seek to establish a generically normative theory in this architecture of theories. Therefore, a discussion of first principles can no longer be postponed.[53]

Like Peirce's, my classifications of the sciences and arts are drawn from the history of ideas, and particularly from the major works of philosophy (indeed, they cannot be acquired in any other way). But I argue that such texts, being the fullest expressions of a worldview, are already enduring monuments of mind. In their amplitude they give us sufficient evidence to form an encompassing intuition of the architecture of theories.

This comparative hermeneutic differs in approach from the text of Santayana, for whom (as again for Nietzsche) the appearance of essences is as epiphenomenal as it is natural for the human spirit. In terms of this hermeneutic, Santayana does not adequately explain the consummatory quality of his own text and its essential continuity with those of Anaximenes, Democritus, and other pure materialists in the world traditions.

Santayana nonetheless was one of the most literate and cosmopolitan of the modern philosophers, as one can see in the following passage, which he wrote at the age of eighty-eight:

> Circumstances from the beginning had prepared me to feel this limitation of all moral dogmatism. My lot had been cast in different moral climates, amidst people of more than one language and religion, with contrary habits and assumptions of their political life. I was not bound to any type of society by ideal loyalty nor estranged from any by resentment. In my personal contacts I found them all tolerable when seen from the inside and not judged by some standard unintelligible to those born and bred under that influence. Personally I might have my instinctive preference; but speculatively and romantically I should have been glad to find an even greater diversity; and if one political tendency kindled my wrath, it was precisely the tendency of industrial liberalism to level down all civilizations to a single cheap and dreary pattern. I was happy to have been at home both in Spain and in New England and later to have lived pleasantly in England and in various countries frequented by tourists; even happier to have breathed intellectually the air of Greece and Rome, and of that Catholic Church in which the world and its wisdom, without being distorted, were imaginatively enveloped in another world revealed by inspiration. All this was enlightening, if you could escape from it; and I should have been glad to have been at home also in China and in Carthage, in Bagdad and in Byzantium. Had that been possible, this book could have been written with more elasticity. It is a hindrance to the free movement of spirit to be lodged in one point of space rather than

> another, or in one point of time: that is a physical necessity which intelligence endeavours to discount, since it cannot be eluded. Seen under the form of eternity, all ages are equally past and equally future; and it is impossible to take quite seriously the tastes and ambitions of our contemporaries. Everything gently impels us to view human affairs scientifically, realistically, biologically, as events that arise, with all their spiritual overtones, in the realm of matter.[54]

Santayana transcended the chauvinistic claims of the American tradition. Contrary to his own philosophical protestations, he produced a text for all ages and cultures by realizing an essential possibility of thought.

9

The World Religions

The major contemporary and future philosophies will reflect the influence of past achievements, and will accordingly confirm our sense of the growth of philosophical mind within a realm of possible forms. The great religions represent some of the most enduring forms of world-perception, and it is to them we now turn.

Most of us can attest to the fact that our first worldviews, and particularly our religious beliefs, were acquired through our families. For many of us, such primal beliefs are the precondition for our acceptance and understanding of the worldviews of our adult lives. In some cultural contexts, secularization never occurs; in others, a public education gradually introduces other systems of thought.

The great world religions continue to govern the ways in which the majority of human beings interpret the world. They also show their resiliency by adapting contemporary styles of philosophy to their fundamental doctrines. Except in certain cases, the rule seems to be that secularization involves replacing a diaphanic perspective with some other perspective, while conversion, in the religious sense, presupposes a metanoesis to a diaphanic perspective. Conversion from one religion to another obviously entails a more complex transformation in the archic values in an individual's experience. Such transferences may be more or less complete, but this is also true of the transmission of sacred doctrine within traditions as well as across them.

All metanoetic passages in religious or secular writing reveal mental growth, as a person evolves into a more mature understanding of life. This topic is amply documented in biography, autobiography, and other historiographical studies. It is nonetheless a proper topic for philosophical reflection. Many people retain their childhood religious or secular beliefs—some professional theologians and philosophers are no exception to this rule. Others either abandon their former beliefs or subordinate them to their more mature worldviews.

I will discuss this topic further in chapter 10, which explicitly addresses the question of the gradations of possible worldviews. For now I propose to review the theoretical claims embedded in the religious texts, and particularly in the texts of the world religions.

Freud took very seriously the relationship between civilization and religion. Indeed, in his framework the two terms are synonymous. The parallels between them emerge in his theory of "totemic culture," which describes the dynamics of the Oedipus complex on a civilizational scale (borrowing prominent concepts of Greek tragedy and pre-Socratic philosophy).[1] Our comparative hermeneutic, however, shows us that Freud's text grants precedence to a particular set of archic values and therefore makes possible only one interpretation of the world religions. We clearly need a broader set of heuristic concepts to do justice to the plurality of world religions and their interrelations.

A local version of the problem of religious orthodoxy has already surfaced in our discussion of the Neo-Confucian texts of China. Analogous claims of orthodoxy recur in every known historical and cultural context. The neo-Confucian texts draw on the epistemological authority of the Confucian classics and the I Ching. The latter is perhaps the paradigmatic divination text in the history of philosophy. In our comparative hermeneutic, however, every text that is diaphanic in perspective is a kind of divination text. Every such text represents itself as the vehicle of a higher, superhuman revelation and presence. Texts are diaphanic when they "testify" and "bear witness" to the truth of their own utterance as issuing from some higher authority.

Plato describes all diaphanic perspectives when he has Socrates say in the *Phaedrus* that "the mind itself has a kind of divining power."[2] In the *Apology, Crito, Symposium,* and other Dialogues Socrates bears witness to this higher epistemic horizon. A divine voice or viewpoint is also a semantical feature of the works of Homer, Hesiod, and many of the world's poets. This standpoint recurs in several pre-Socratic texts, particularly those of Pythagoras, Heraclitus, Parmenides, and Empedocles.

A diaphanic perspective, however, can function as a semantic factor even in texts that appear to distance themselves from the "mythic" by virtue of their strongly "scientific" character. Thus, while Hegel's *Phenomenology of Mind* subordinates the mythological and revealed religions to philosophical science, it culminates in a notion of philosophy as absolute knowledge, the highest form of the self-manifestation of spirit.[3] In that respect, Hegel's text reinterprets Plato's concept of philosophy as "a divining power."

Among more recent Western philosophers, two thinkers are conspicuous for writing with diaphanic perspectives. Cultivating a poetic and mythic authority in his later writings, Heidegger bases his reflections on a creative temporality in the concept of *Ereignis*—the event of divine appropriation.[4] Jaspers developed another such diaphanic discourse in his *Existenz*-philosophy, which hinges on a transcendent encompassing.[5]

Heidegger and Jaspers shares this perspective with the Upanishads, the Tao Te Ching, the Confucian and Neo-Confucian classics (with the exception of the text of Hsün Tzu), and most of the forms of Western religious discourse that center on the divine word, grace, or illumination. Such connections tend to underlie the work of scholars who favor the theories of Heidegger or Jaspers or those of theologians working with their categories. In Jaspers's words, while we may adhere to different faiths, we can understand each other as adhering to a faith; and as we bring to mind the modes of the transcendent encompassing we illuminate the space common to us as human beings.[6] Quite clearly, texts that speak of and for God or the absolute differ in semantic intention from texts that do not. Thus texts with objective perspectives—as in Democritus, Hsün Tzu, Han Fei Tzu, Spinoza, Hume, or Freud—represent shifts in paradigm for this archic variable. Their objective perspective alters the light in which sacred, divination, or other kinds of diaphanic texts are to be interpreted. In such texts, the divine illumination may degenerate into the voice of anthropocentric superstition, manic fear, or infantile fantasy.

Texts with subjective perspectives—such as Nietzsche's "all too human" and vividly personal writing, or Sartre's version of a personal atheistic humanism—also reject the diaphanic perspective. But it is possible to be personal in perspective and yet religious in orientation, as were Kierkegaard and James. By comparison, Dante's *Divine Comedy* is religious, but not archically personal.[7]

It is also possible for a text to be religious from an objective perspective, as are those of Spinoza or Einstein; or from a disciplinary perspective, as are those of Aristotle, Kant, and Dewey.[8] As the archic perspective changes, however, so does a text's sense of religion and what is religious. Similarly, as we agree or disagree with another's religious text, we put into play the governing assumptions of our own.

With our comparative hermeneutic, it becomes possible to analyze the variety of world religions in their regular and irregular conjugations. Discussion of this topic inevitably includes the texts of the Old and New Testaments, the Koran, Hinduism, Buddhism, Jainism, Taoism, Confucianism, Neo-Confucianism, and other world religions. We will limit ourselves, however, to an analysis of the classical texts of Hinduism, Buddhism, and the major Western religions.

The Text of Hinduism

Let us first turn to the text of Hinduism, with its pristine expression of an elemental principle. This oldest of texts is still perfectly contemporary and vigorous among the world's religions. Hinduism is at once a cultural manifestation of a religious form of life, and an example of certain universal conditions of discourse. For our comparative hermeneutic, it is noteworthy that the basic text of Hinduism shares archic semantic features with such diverse texts as those of the Sufi mystics, Plotinus, the "unorthodox" Christian Neoplatonists of the Middle Ages, and the prince of the Romantics, F. W. J. Schelling.

Interpretive methods that merely separate these related texts according to their linguistic and other cultural traits succeed in trivializing them. (The result of this methodic narrowness is effectively to eliminate them from philosophical curricula, where they truly belong.)

In referring to the basic text of Hinduism, we acknowledge that we may encounter various irregular patterns within the traditions that trace their spiritual ancestry back to the Vedas and Upanishads. If we find correspondences among Neoplatonic, Sufi, and Schelling's concepts, we should not neglect the different social and historical contexts of those works. The texts of the Sufi mystics, Plotinus, and the Neoplatonists are products of their own time and place. Still, the texts of the Bhagavad Gita, the Sufi mystics, Plotinus, Erigena, Eckhart, Boehme, Cusanus, and Schelling form complex intertextual relationships of their own, which can be characterized as a set of cross-cultural but essentially similar discourses.

The Bhagavad Gita, a subtext of the *Mahabharata,* is a sprawling description of the cultural dynamics of ancient India. As with the texts of Homer or Confucius, it took a millennium of civilization to produce such a classic. Although it can be reinterpreted in many ways, it has only one archic profile.

In an archic analysis, the Bhagavad Gita's doctrines of heavenly manifestations and of social stratifications and duties are all functions of its diaphanic perspective, elemental principle, and dialectical method. Its avatar theology and dharmic ethics represent models of dialectically theophanic thought. Tolerant of all religions, it incorporates all theologies and their special social cultures into the higher identity of the inexpressible absolute, which is Brahman.

Thus the Gita expresses an ancient tradition of Vedic and Upanishadic thought in the perfect dialectical expression:

> From the unmanifest all manifestations
> Come forth at the coming of (Brahman's) day,
> And dissolve at the coming of night,
> In that same One, known as the unmanifest.[9]

The religious subtleties of the Gita always return to this dialectical assertion. Without it, the principal element of the text is lost. Some scholars depict the Hindu concept of Brahman as "static" in a pejorative sense, misreading the dialectical movement of the text. The Brahman is infinitely creative and thus "comes forth," even while maintaining its eternal identity.

That the absolute eternally manifests itself in its own magical appearances (*maya*), material embodiments (*prakrti*), and fields (*gunas*), and eternally returns to itself in its absolutely unconditioned immediacy, is the fundamental teaching of the Gita. We need only switch vocabularies of manifestation—however different and complicated these are—and we have the basic doctrine of the Sufis, Neoplatonists, and Schelling as well. The same set of archic assumptions generates their respective senses of the necessity and the spontaneity of the myriad divine, human, and world manifestations.

Hegel can be considered to have understood this configuration of archic variables in the texts of Hinduism, Sufism, the Neoplatonists, and Schelling. Hegel sought to replace their noumenal realities and elemental principles with his own essential sense of reality and reflexive principle. In a well-known quip Hegel satirized Schelling's system "as the infinite night in which all cows are black"[10]—and continued his attack throughout the preface and main body of his *Phenomenology of Mind* (published 1807). In archic analysis, Hegel's criticism extends to the other texts as well.

This did not prevent Schelling from writing in his *Inquiries into the Nature of Human Freedom* (published 1809) as follows:

> The unruly (*das Regellose*) lies ever in the depths. . . . This is the incomprehensible basis of reality in things, the irreducible remainder which cannot be resolved into reason by the greatest exertion but always remains in the depths. Out of this which is unreasonable, reason in the true sense is born. Without this preceding gloom, creation would have no reality; darkness is its necessary heritage. . . . Nevertheless we can think of nothing better fitted to drive man to strive towards the light with all energy, than the consciousness of the deep night out of which he was raised into existence. . . . All birth is a birth out of darkness into light; the seed must be buried in the earth and die in darkness in order that the lovelier creature of light should rise and unfold itself in the rays of the sun.[11]

In other words, Schelling responded to Hegel by undermining his rationally reflexive principle. Like those of the Bhagavad Gita, Plotinus, the Sufi or the Christian mystics, Schelling's text reaffirms a principle of elemental darkness—the principle of absolute identity.[12]

For our comparative hermeneutic, there is no arguing with this kind of passage, which masterfully controls its intertextual relation with Hegel. Of course, Hegel's condemnation of Schelling's "infinite night" remains historically significant. But what is more significant for us is the broader paradigm that Schelling's thought clearly represents. Schelling imagines the "primal longing" of creation through to its "transmuted" spiritual completion in vividly trinitarian imagery. His text accomplishes in principle the conversion of the dark, unruly, spontaneous, magical Maya of nature and human life into the triumphant spiritual personality of God. Schelling's text is no less brilliant than the Bhagavad Gita in the dialectical movement of its noumenal reality.

Drawing upon Plato, Spinoza, and Leibniz, Schelling repeatedly postulates the entire unfolding and breadth of the divine personality—which includes the darkest, most destructive tendencies of natural and human life—as having an eternal, "intelligible reality."[13] Numerous passages assert the eternal, noumenal identity in Schelling's writings.[14]

Schelling's writings are as far-ranging and diverse as the avatar theology of the Bhagavad Gita. The difference between them is that Schelling addresses the post-Kantian question of the phenomenality of being in his own vocabulary of manifestation, as this was influenced by his cultural milieu.

Schelling's text disagrees with those of Spinoza and Leibniz, which it tends otherwise to assimilate into itself. It differs from both Fichte's and Hegel's in two semantic variables, and from Kant's in three. We can pursue such analyses across a range of other cultures and historic periods, but our purpose here is to outline the similarities between the texts of the Gita, the Sufi mystics, the Neoplatonists, and Schelling.

Plotinus clearly subordinated Plato's comprehensive principle and Aristotle's and the Stoics' reflexive principles to his own principle of absolute oneness, or identity. To Plotinus, "The One is all things and not a single one of them."[15] Accordingly, the human soul, when it brakes its downward plunge into multiplicity and evil and succeeds in returning to its own true reality, must not rest at the levels of world-soul or even of nous, but "strike forward yet a step" into mystical reabsorption in the One.[16] The Christian Neoplatonists—Dionysius the Areopagite, Erigena, Eckhart, Boehme, Cusanus, and so on down to Thomas à Kempis and the Brothers of the Common Life—all produced versions of this mystical text, which is diaphanic in perspective, noumenal in reality, dialectical in method, and elemental in principle.

We can see that this paradigm underlies the texts of monastic inwardness, as in the case of Eckhart, Thomas à Kempis, and many other mystical writers of the West. Notwithstanding, it is a deeply pagan text, with its origins in the doctrines of Plotinus. Without sacrificing its spiritual inwardness, it can provide the model for universal theophanies of any culture. The Bhagavad Gita demonstrates such a semantic function, to which we now return.

The Gita, no less than the great dialectical texts of the West, exhibits

its own version of "the labor of the negative" in its doctrine of the necessary outpouring of the absolutely undifferentiated One into its magical manifestations (maya), which are its appearances. This absolute oneness gathers back the myriad appearances of its unfolding into itself, coming around full circle to complete itself.

Every critique of this basic Hindu text elevates its own semantic assumptions. A long tradition of such critiques exists in the Carvaka, Buddhist, Jain, and Neo-Confucian texts of Asia. But on its own terms, the Bhagavad Gita is one of the great works of religious inspiration. It has three Platonic (diaphanic, noumenal, and dialectical) and one Democritean (elemental) values, a combination that recurs in other religions and philosophies and endures in today's civilizations.

The Text of Buddhism

The modern Japanese philosopher Nishida Kitarō became interested in the structural affinity between the Christian logic of Kierkegaard and the Mahayana logic of Lin-chi, Dōgen, and Shinran. Nishida's own "logic of contradictory identity" seemed to resemble Kierkegaard's and that of the ancient Buddhist figures.

Nishida also considered his and Kierkegaard's paradoxical logics to be consistent in form with the Madhyamika logic of Nagarjuna, in contrast to the Hegelian logic of the absolute subject.[17] Nishitani Keiji, a disciple of Nishida, produced another Buddhist text, which clarifies the similarities of the agonistic method in its cross-cultural forms.[18]

In our analysis, the Sophists' method is a common thread linking the Mahayana sutra literature, the writings of Nagarjuna, and all the East Asian Mahayana traditions, down to Nishida's and Nishitani's modern interpretations of those texts in their philosophical encounter with the West. The profile of this standard Buddhist text is diaphanic, existential, agonistic, and elemental.

The relation between the archic texts of Hinduism and Buddhism is as follows:

	PERSPECTIVE	REALITY	METHOD	PRINCIPLE
Hinduism	*diaphanic*	*noumenal*	*dialectical*	*elemental*
Buddhism	*diaphanic*	*existential*	*agonistic*	*elemental*

While they share two archic elements, Buddhism's two Sophistic elements diverge radically from the Hindu text.[19]

The Indian pre-Mahayana forms of Buddhism appear to conform to the profile outlined above. From the Indian Abhidharma treatises to the

Indian Mahayana sutras and sastras, and from the Chinese Mahayana schools to the Japanese texts of Kūkai, Dōgen, and Hakuin, the same archic profile seems to recur in different forms. This does not preclude our discovering some irregular forms within the mainstreams of Buddhist thought.

The one clear difference among the branches of Buddhist theory appears to be the noumenal ontology of the Pure Land schools. This tradition, which stems from the Indian Pure Land sutras, encompasses the Chinese and Japanese schools that emphasized Amida's Pure Land, a kingdom not of this world, and taught that perfect enlightenment would be attained in the life to come. Zen Buddhism often clashed with Pure Land teachings on this point. The relationship between these two schools can be represented as follows:

	PERSPECTIVE	REALITY	METHOD	PRINCIPLE
Zen	*diaphanic*	*existential*	*agonistic*	*elemental*
Pure Land	*diaphanic*	*noumenal*	*agonistic*	*elemental*

It will be necessary to study the individual classics in these traditions, particularly those of the Pure Land, to verify this generalization.[20]

The perspective of all Buddhist texts is diaphanic. Kūkai's version of "the Dharmakaya preaches the Dharma" exemplifies the innumerable variations on the theme of the immanence of the absolute. The Ch'an theme of awakening to one's original face also relies on a diaphanic perspective. In Pure Land teaching, all saving graces come from the compassionate Buddha. All Buddhist texts "take refuge in the Enlightened One"—whether in Gautama, Amida, or Vairocana Buddha.

This diaphanic spirituality of the Buddhist text is governed by the principle of *sunyata*. Voidness—or Nothingness, Dharmakaya, Buddha-nature, Buddha-mind, Suchness, Tathata, Tathatagarbha, or Dharmadhatu, with all their mystical and poetical variants—is the key to the Buddhist text. *Sunyata* describes the ultimate purpose of all Buddhist literature.

As Richard Robinson and other commentators have pointed out, the concept of *sunyata* is a generalization of the three original marks, or predicates, attributed to existence by early Buddhism—namely, suffering, impermanence, and no-self.[21] *Sunyata* is an elemental principle of absolute identity, sameness, and synchronity. It is the perfection of wisdom (*prajna*), the insight into the emptiness of all differentiated dharmas. In ethical terms it becomes the principle of absolute compassion (*karuna*). It is also the principle of absolute existential indifference underlying the prominent theme of "expedient means" (*upaya*), the stock-in-trade of the bodhisattvas of the Mahayana sutra literature.

The Ch'an masters, as one example, have invested heavily in the principle of *upaya,* which controls the sense (or non-sense) of their religious paradoxes. The Ch'an masters also produced a variety of inventive images to describe existential reality, which, because of their elemental principle, they equate with the absolute reality. Japanese Tendai and Tantric masters also expounded this equation in their respective doctrines of "becoming Buddha in this very body."

Both the Chinese and the Japanese schools trace the lineage of this theme to the "bliss body" (*sambhogakaya*) concept of the "three bodies" doctrine of the earlier Mahayana traditions.[22] Tendai, Tantric, and Zen schools interpreted it existentially, while the Pure Land schools interpreted it noumenally.

In comparative analysis, these teachings all show similarities with the texts of Berkeley and Jaspers, which differed from them only in their grounding principles:

	PERSPECTIVE	REALITY	METHOD	PRINCIPLE
Zen masters, etc.	*diaphanic*	*existential*	*agonistic*	*elemental*
Berkeley, Jaspers	*diaphanic*	*existential*	*agonistic*	*creative*

A difference of one variable creates radical divergences in these theories.

Berkeley bases his existential sense of reality on the paradoxical relation between divine and human perceptions. Our perceptions both express God's thoughts and reveal him to us. Berkeley's principle of the efficacity of spirits is a version of the Christian creationist doctrine, as he is at pains to point out. Apart from this semantic factor, Berkeley's "new theory of vision" has an old ring to it—it shares with Buddhism its refutation of enduring essences and material substrates alike.[23]

The existential Buddhist text also invites comparison with the text of the Hellenistic Skeptics. The two differ only in perspective, as we see in summary form:

	PERSPECTIVE	REALITY	METHOD	PRINCIPLE
Buddhists	*diaphanic*	*existential*	*agonistic*	*elemental*
Skeptics	*objective*	*existential*	*agonistic*	*elemental*

Zen Buddhists produced a theory of salvation out of their agonistic discourse, whereas the skeptics did not.[24]

It is appropriate that the existential focus of the standard Buddhist text be expressed in negative form. *Sunyata* is the emptiness of emptiness. Accordingly, the Buddha-nature is not a self, not a substance. It is not some transcendent essence in the noumenal sense; nor again is it some immanent essence in the phenomenological sense. It is to be identified neither with a substratum of material dharmas nor with a putative energy field of physical substances and their mutations.

What the absolute Buddha-nature "is" is precisely the passing moment of actualization, which both "is and is not." The individual act (or dharma) of lived experience is the very "place" of nirvanic experience. Each dharma moment is a concrete location of absolute reality. The Mahayana phrases, "Becoming the Buddha in this very body" and "Becoming the Buddha in this very mind," are only two of virtually innumerable variations on this existential paradox. The body and the mind are here dharma-positions of the evanescent moment, which is the absolute presence manifesting itself even as it vanishes.

The Yogacara Mind-only mysticism of Hua-yen and the dynamic practice of Dōgen's Zen share the same archic profile. They both adopt the brain-shattering "Ho!" of Lin-chi.[25] The "Ho!" is the instant of the self-realization of the absolute reality; it is also "the place of nothingness," in Nishida's phrase.[26]

The joining of an elemental principle with two Sophistic elements in Buddhist theory produces a "divination text." The philosophy of Nishida Kitarō becomes intelligible in the light of this paradigm. All of Nishida's complicated philosophical analyses revolve around the "acts of consciousness," each of which represents a unique point in the infinite matrix of absolute reality. This "place of nothingness" is simultaneously locative of all acts and located by all acts. Each "historically formative act" is thus a self-determination of the concrete reality in the form of an absolutely contradictory identity. Thus Nishida cites the ancient Buddhist phrase: "Having no place wherein it abides, this mind arises." This saying sums up perfectly Nishida's archic profile.[27]

The special character of Nishida's modern reinterpretation of the Buddhist text lies in its agonistic assimilation of Christianity and of the major Western philosophical trends. Thus Nishida developed his "logic of the East" in contrast to the logics of Aristotle, Leibniz, Kant, and Hegel. He later became interested in distinguishing his existential "place of nothingness" from the noumenal realities of Leibniz and Kant, as well. But in so doing Nishida wrote from the transcendental perspective of his own Buddhist text. Nishida's disciple, Nishitani Keiji, performed a similarly agonistic appropriation of Western texts for the sake of Buddhist polemics.[28]

Nevertheless, modern spokesmen of the Buddhist tradition such as Nishida and Nishitani have shown that Buddhism is closely related to the apophatic, mystical stream of Christian Neoplatonism in Erigena, Eckhart, Boehme, and Cusanus through their integrating principles and authorizing perspectives. The One of Plotinus, *die Gottheit* of Meister

Eckhart, and *Dharmakaya,* or *sunyata,* in its many forms derive from similar sources, as do the texts of Taoism, Hinduism, Sufism, or Schelling. However, these non-Buddhist texts—with the exception of Taoism, which has a substrative ontological focus—are all dialectical expressions of a noumenal reality. The Buddhist texts, which are predominantly existential in ontological focus, speak in the paradoxical terms of the nonduality of samsara and nirvana.[29]

Old and New Testament Religions

In theory and in practice, the Old and New Testaments form a pair of intertwined religious texts. With the Koran, they comprise a trinary system. Allowing for irregularities within these traditions, their archic profiles are as follows:

	PERSPECTIVE	REALITY	METHOD	PRINCIPLE
Old Testament	*diaphanic*	*essential*	*dialectical*	*creative*
New Testament	*diaphanic*	*noumenal*	*dialectical*	*creative*
Koran	*diaphanic*	*noumenal*	*agonistic*	*creative*

The Koran's agonistic method accounts for the concept of holy war, which is a conspicuous feature of Islamic teaching.

The Old Testament chronicles the history of the Jews as it reveals divine justification. It is a morality play, or story, enacted in the generations of Abraham and the later prophets.

In the New Testament, by contrast, Christ says that his kingdom is not of this world. He is exalted in his resurrection, as are his followers. In all the forms of evangelical Christianity the drama of salvation bespeaks a noumenal reality: the heavenly father has sent his son to redeem mankind from the historical process itself. The Christian redemption is consummated in an eternal life to come. The New Testament dovetails with Plato's (and Plotinus's) text in this respect.

Through the Christian Neoplatonic texts the noumenal sense of a higher reality of God and destiny of the soul was transmitted to the Rhineland mystics. This noumenal focus reappears in the texts of Spinoza, Leibniz, Kant, Fichte, Schelling, and Kierkegaard.

Despite their differences, the methodological form of both the Old and New Testaments is dialectical. From a single source in a single chosen people or in the Gospels salvation spreads outward to embrace all human beings. God and man collaborate in the unfolding of the redemptive experience. The very meaning of the Old Testament's concept of covenant is governed by this semantic factor. In the New Testament the covenant centers on the figure of Christ, the God-man. In theory and in liturgical practice, all souls participate in the greater drama of salvation, whose form is essentialist in Judaism and noumenal in Christianity.

All forms of trinitarian and Christian theology involve the dialectical method, as do all the cosmical (in Kant's sense) religious traditions based on a spiritual union of heaven, earth, and man. By contrast, the orthodox text of Islam differs from all the above in its agonistic method.

The Book of Genesis clearly reveals a creative principle. The *creatio ex nihilo* proceeds from the sheer power of God. The prophets, such as Abraham, perpetuate the creative act, fathering countless generations of believers. The creative principle controls the dialectical form of the immanent moral drama in Judaism and the transcendent drama of Christian salvation. It functions as the generative and integrating factor in the agonistic salvation drama of Islam. Every orthodox adherent of the Jewish, Christian, and Muslim faiths assumes this creative principle in the "continued miracle" (in Hume's phrase) that takes place in their believing hearts.[30]

However, a whole set of Christian Neoplatonic mystical writers depart from the creative principle of the Old and the New Testaments by adopting the elemental principle of Plotinus's text. The text of Saint Thomas Aquinas contains a version of Aristotle's reflexive principle in its definition of *esse* as pure act.[31] Aquinas's text therefore diverges from both the orthodox (Augustinian) creationist text and the unorthodox (pseudo-Dionysian) Neoplatonic text of the Middle Ages.

Another striking example of this shift in governing principle is found in the text of Leibniz, which prominently displays its doctrine of creation. Indeed, Leibniz's *Discourse on Metaphysics* begins by stating that God must have created the best of all possible worlds in the perfect outpouring of his wisdom and love.[32] This text clearly has a Christian ring to it; in fact Leibniz liked to incorporate New Testament teachings into his philosophical writings. Yet, in Leibniz's text, God must be an infinitely perfect moral creator. God creates not merely out of metaphysical necessity (as in Spinoza), but out of moral necessity. The principle of the whole, which organizes all its members in a perfect hierarchy, takes precedence in Leibniz's text over the creative principle. In this respect Leibniz, the theological metaphysician *par excellence*, departed from the orthodox Christian theology of such authors as Augustine, Anselm, and Bonaventure, each of whom upholds the creative principle in his writings.

Leibniz's contemporaries, Newton and Locke, also cite the Bible in support of their doctrines. They were actually more orthodox than Leibniz in their reliance on creative principles. Berkeley also used the Bible to support his doctrine of the sole creativity of spirits, human and divine.

Thus it was Leibniz who deviated from the norm in subordinating the creative principles of the texts of Newton, Locke, and Berkeley to his own version of a comprehensive principle.

Leibniz's text provides us with an important hermeneutical lesson. He "makes sense of" the creative principle of the Biblical tradition on his own terms. Some commentaries on a religious text or group of such texts and commentaries remain semantically faithful to their material. Others take different directions in their interpretations. Yet each "makes sense of" the world, self, and God within the parameters of its own text.

Whitehead, for example, captures the sense of the Old Testament's ontological focus in his own "cosmological story." He writes in *Modes of Thought:* "The effective aspect of this source (of ideals) is Deity as immanent in the present experience. The sense of historic importance is the intuition of the universe as everlasting process, unfading in its deistic unity of ideals."[33]

Whitehead's text, through its dialectical method of discourse, proceeds to assimilate the New Testament's noumenal focus into its own essential sense of reality. The final chapter of his *Process and Reality,* entitled "God and the World," exemplifies this process of interpretive assimilation. In his doctrine of Christ, the companion and fellow sufferer who understands, and of a kingdom of heaven that is with us today, Whitehead revives the Old Testament version of the "cosmological story."[34]

Whitehead explicitly drew attention to his essentialist sense of reality in *Process and Reality,* but it appears throughout his writings.[35] His text therefore differs in the most significant variable from the standard Christian text. Kierkegaard's text, on the other hand, displays a noumenal ontological focus. However unorthodox it is in rejecting the mediating forms of ecclesiastical community, it is consistently Christian in teaching that Christ's kingdom is not of this world. Religious existentialists such as James or Jaspers play down the supernatural ontology of orthodox Christianity. Their texts thus represent irregularities within the mainstream religious traditions.

To attend the conventions of theologians and philosophers today is frequently to witness reenactments of these various appropriations of the multiple possibilities of the Old and New Testament "texts." For our comparative hermeneutic, it is first a matter of intuiting what the regular paradigms are in their own right. We shall then be in a better position to appreciate their irregular conjugations.

Heidegger's text, which has inspired a generation of Christian theological interpretations, is identical in its principal features to the Old Testament. The archic profile of Heidegger's text is diaphanic, essentialist, dialectical, and creative. Whitehead and Heidegger differ only in perspective.

Heidegger speaks like an Old Testament prophet; in his later works he becomes a shepherd of being. He goes figuratively to the top of the mountain, where being discloses itself in poetically metaphysical tablets. Heidegger's nothingness (*das Nichts*) is another form of this diaphanically essentialist view. For Heidegger, history begins with Being. The poets, philosophers, and other spirit creatures bear testimony to this radical "historicization" of Being—to the event of Appropriation. In Heidegger, there is only the Sovereign, with his appropriation and property, mirrored on the canvas of creation. Heidegger's diaphanic cultural essentialism also accounts for his support of the Nazi movement.

Comparing Leibniz, Whitehead, and Heidegger, Leibniz's text departs from the archic profile of Christianity in its integrating principle and in discursive method, but retains the crucial variable, its noumenal focus. In various remarks on Christianity in his second *Critique* and other works Kant also adopted this Platonic variable. The texts of Whitehead and Heidegger, with their versions of the creative principle and dialectical method, resemble the evangelical and orthodox text of Christianity, but diverge from its noumenal reality. This is why the texts of Leibniz and Kant appear to be irregular forms of the New Testament paradigm, whereas Whitehead's appears to be an irregular form of the Old Testament paradigm. Heidegger's archic profile exactly matches the Old Testament's.

All of these observations illustrate paradigm shifts, based on changes in the interpretation of a text's meaning. They exhibit a wide range of theoretical forms associated with Old and New Testament religions. These examples show the resilience and adaptability of the great religious texts.

I have not included all the world's religions in this brief overview. I have simply tried to show how fruitful a more detailed exploration of this field might be. Each of the world religions makes a profound contribution to civilization. An architectonic theory, which would consider each one on its own terms, provides the proper framework for such an investigation.

10

The Architecture of Theories

Architectonic Theory in Kant and Peirce

In the preface to the first edition to his *Critique of Pure Reason* Kant clearly states his grounding principle. Pure reason, he says, functions so perfectly as a unity that if it were insufficient for the solution of even a single one of all the questions to which it itself gives birth, "we should have no alternative but to reject the principle, since we should then no longer be able to place implicit trust upon it in dealing with any of the other questions."[1] With that sentence Kant established the essential link between his principle of the self-sufficiency of mind and those of Anaxagoras, Aristotle, Aquinas, Bacon, Descartes, and Spinoza.

In the preface to the second edition of the same work Kant added this explanation of the synoptic method, whose roots go back to Hippocrates, Aristotle, and Aquinas:

> Reason, holding in one hand its principles, according to which alone concordant appearances can be admitted as equivalent to laws, and in the other hand the experiment which it has devised in conformity with these principles, must approach nature in order to be taught by it. It must not, however, do so in the character of a pupil who listens to everything the teacher chooses to say, but of an appointed judge who compels the witnesses to answer questions which he has himself formulated.[2]

It is the judicial function of human reason to order the matter and form of its own inquiries. Combining this principle and method with a disciplinary perspective, Kant produced one of the greatest architectonic texts in the history of philosophy.

Kant addresses explicitly the architectonic function in his first *Critique,* in the section entitled "The Architectonic of Pure Reason": "By architectonic I understand the art of constructing systems. As systematic unity is that which raises common knowledge to the dignity of science, that is, changes a mere aggregate of knowledge into a system, it is easy to see that architectonic is the doctrine of what is really scientific in our knowledge, and forms therefore a necessary part of the doctrine of method."[3] Kant's three *Critiques* exemplify his architectonic ideal by establishing the complete schema of a transcendental philosophy.

Kant also included a brief passage entitled "The History of Pure Reason" in the *Critique of Pure Reason.* But there, we note, Kant does not attempt to distinguish the historical periods in which the principles of philosophy underwent their changes; nor does he endeavor to establish any essential connections with his predecessors. He describes only certain differences in ideas, which he considers to have caused the principal revolutions. Kant does not go into detail, confining himself to a few brief remarks about the objects of knowledge, the origin of the pure concepts of reason, and method.[4]

The title, "The History of Pure Reason," Kant tells us, "stands here only in order to indicate the place in the system which remains empty for the present and has to be filled hereafter. I content myself with casting a cursory glance, from a purely transcendental point of view, . . . on the labours of former philosophers, which presents to my eyes many structures, but in ruins only."[5]

What is remarkable about this passage is that it indicates that Kant saw in the history of philosophy the mere shadow of an architectonic system. He seems to squint at the great texts of philosophy, unable to discern their interrelationships. Through a comparative analysis of Kant's text we can explain this blind spot in Kant's vision. While it is Aristotelian in perspective, method, and principle, Kant's text is noumenal in its sense of reality. True to the ontological form of his own text, Kant did not envision the possibility of a phenomenology of the major philosophical texts.

In this respect Kant's text reveals a flaw in its own theory-formation. Kant, a noumenal Aristotelian, concentrated his efforts on transcendental analysis, thereby opening himself to criticism for the merely formal character of his architectonics of meaning. With this point in mind, let us turn now to Peirce, who teaches us a different lesson in architectonic theory-formation, as well as in the limitation of a particular theory.

Among post-Kantians, Peirce alone developed a systematic "architecture of theories." Although some scholars have been confused by the disparate nature of Peirce's essays, it is no exaggeration to claim that his whole corpus was devoted to that end.[6]

In an essay of 1891 entitled "The Architecture of Theories," Peirce begins by noting that "fifty or a hundred systems of philosophy . . . have been advanced at different times of the world's history." He dismisses those that appear to be arbitrary—that is, those that fill in available niches in a mental landscape by a process of accidental variation.

Such arbitrary theories illustrate what Peirce calls firstness. They may be thought of as useful experiments in theorizing, just as papier-mâché models might offer valuable insights to builders but would prove worthless as real houses. Certain "one-idea'd philosophies," Peirce concludes, "are exceedingly interesting and instructive, and yet are quite unsound."[7]

Peirce spent his life surveying the methods of the sciences and philosophies. In effect, he translated Kant's sense of transcendental architecture into his own systematic approach to what he sometimes calls a universal phenomenology or semiology.[8] Peirce's solution to the problems of philosophy and science took the form of the doctrine of the three categories—concepts whose archic assumptions are essentialist, synoptic, and reflexive. This doctrine elaborates degrees of truth and reality, based on the progressive teleology of the three categories themselves. His text identifies and orders general modalities of human experience and of the universe at large according to this pattern.

Peirce drew on Kant to support his sense of architectonic theory, as the following passage shows:

> The universally and justly laudable parallel which Kant draws between a philosophical doctrine and a piece of architecture has excellencies which the beginner in philosophy might easily overlook; and not the least of these is its recognition of the cosmic character of philosophy. I use the word "cosmic" because *cosmicus* is Kant's own choice; but I must say I think *secular* or *public* would have approached nearer to the expression of his meaning. Works of sculpture and painting can be executed for a single patron and must be by a single artist. . . . But a great building, such as alone can call out the depths of the architect's soul, is meant for the whole people, and is erected by the exertions of an army representative of the whole people. It is the message with which an age is charged, and which it delivers to posterity. . . . If anybody can doubt whether this be equally true of philosophy, I can but recommend to him the splendid third chapter of the Methodology, in the *Critic of the Pure Reason*.[9]

Peirce takes his perspective from the objective procedures and forms of the logical, mathematical, and physical sciences, as his essays on how to make our ideas clear, on the scientific attitude and fallibilism, on some consequences of four incapacities, and on abduction and induction demonstrate. His perspective is central to the thrust of his pragmaticism, theory of signs, and cosmogonic philosophy. Peirce therefore oriented his pragmaticism to the world's future. He elaborated a social theory of reality that transcends every private idiosyncrasy and is destined to appear "in the long run" from that perspective. He conceived of theory-formation in the same vein.

But we note that Peirce's own philosophical theory—great building that it is—legislates this concept of "the long run," while claiming to have a completely developed system. (Every major world-text is such a completely developed system.) Peirce's metaphor requires that a great building, public and secular in character, be complete in essential form. That is the only way it can become the message with which an age is entrusted and which it passes down to posterity.

Returning to Kant's concept of the "cosmical" character of philosophy, we see that Peirce has subordinated Kant's meaning to his own. While Peirce's main intention in his commentary on Kant's text is to replace personalistic perspectives with his own objective perspective, he ends up dislodging Kant's disciplinary perspective as well.

Kant used the concept of the "cosmical," however, precisely to distinguish the function of philosophy from the work of "the mathematician, the student of nature, and the logician," whom Kant considered to be "merely artists of reason." The philosopher, on the other hand, "stands before us, not as an artist, but as the lawgiver of human reason"[10] and is therefore "an ideal teacher, who controls them all, and uses them as instruments for the advancement of the essential aims of human reason." "This ideal teacher," Kant continues, "exists nowhere, while the idea of his legislation exists everywhere in the reason of every human being."[11] Kant exhorts us to uphold that idea.

Peirce, by contrast, did not uphold Kant's idea of "cosmical concept." He altered it to give precedence to the epistemic fallibilism and the open-ended projects of "the mathematician, the student of nature, and the logician." In this way Peirce remained true to his own education and training. I contend, however, that Kant's is the better perspective from which to interpret the essential character of philosophical texts, Peirce's included. Peirce's theory defines the rules of human reason but is vulnerable to the obsolescence of scientific theories that represent mere stages in the technologies of mind.

Departing in this way from Kant's "cosmical" concept of philosophy, Peirce commits himself to a vaguer doctrine of the ongoing signification of signs. It is no accident that certain contemporary deconstructionists are using Peirce's semiotics to reinforce their doctrine of the indefinite proliferation of signifiers.

This book constitutes a counterargument either to Peirce's doctrine of the open-ended meaning of the real signified or to the deconstructionist doctrine of the indefinite supplemention of signifiers. It is clear that great texts of the world civilizations are semantically complete. They represent enduring forms of mental culture. The texts of Plato, Confucius, Lao Tzu, Aristotle, Spinoza, Kant, or Peirce are comparable to the violin or clarinet, two musical instruments perfected at a certain point of history and apparently incapable of any further technical improvement.

Our comparative hermeneutic emphasizes precisely this sense of essential realization, or completion, in which a work of art or philosophy can be considered to have reached its highest form and yet continues to yield new meanings for succeeding generations. Moreover, we judge the great works of civilization, including the immortal works of the philosophers. All these considerations reinforce Kant's Aristotelian perspective on the universal, or world-forming, character of philosophy itself. The texts of the philosophers, with their essential formulations of the principles of mind, form the basis for mankind's judgments.

Watson's Architectonics of Meaning

Walter Watson's *The Architectonics of Meaning: Foundations of the New Pluralism* escapes the limitations of Kant's noumenal ontology, on the one hand, and Peirce's extrapolation from the mathematical, logical, and physical sciences, on the other. Watson accomplishes this by treating Aristotle's four causes as a set of hermeneutic variables that can be deployed to form an "archic matrix" combining the properties of utmost generality and precision in its definition of essential terms. This matrix is grounded in the history of philosophy, unlike Kant's transcendental program, and forms a complete set, unlike Peirce's fallibilistic model.

Watson's work therefore introduces a level of systematic generalization and essential complexification unavailable to the earlier thinkers. If we compare, for example, Peirce's three categories, themselves a variation on Kant's three critiques, with Watson's four control concepts, we see at once the great advance he has accomplished in the study of theory-formation.

Watson postulates that Aristotle's efficient cause represents the semantic factor of the theoretical agency in theory-formation itself.[12] He further explores the possibility of employing the four causes as control concepts for the four types of perspective—namely, the personal, objective, disciplinary, and diaphanic. Using the same principles of analysis, he defines the four types of primary realities, methods, and intentional principles I have employed in the comparative analyses of this book. Watson's four-by-four archic matrix generates 256 possibilities of textual formations. It accounts for Kant's, Peirce's, and its own text into the bargain.[13]

Watson's work achieves a distinct variation on Aristotle's metaphysical project in architectonic theory, while remaining true to the pluralistic functionalism of Aristotle's text. Since each of the 256 possibilities of theory-formation represents a configuration of first principles, we now have at our disposal an unprecedented overview of the possible variety of first principles.[14]

Watson's work yields this veritable windfall of first principles. Given the abundance of philosophical texts that contemporary ideologues and scholars are generating today, his insight is a timely one. We find ourselves in a unique position to match the variety of worldviews to their formal principles of signification.

At the same time, I find that Watson's modernization of Aristotle's text illustrates the truth—to which both philosophers subscribe—that the great works of civilization are inexhaustibly rich yet perfectly definite. I will attempt to show here how this is so, by establishing a connection between his architectonics of meaning and what I call the architecture of theories, East and West.

Our architecture of theories will involve allocating the position of the mixed archic modes in relation to the four pure modes. I thus work with a concept of semantic transference, or conversion, among the archic modes, further specified as to symmetrical and asymmetrical types.

On the surface the highest degree of symmetrical "displacement," and therefore of "transferability," must occur among the four pure archic modes, while there will be various types of asymmetrical convertibility in the relationships of the pure to the mixed modes, and again among the mixed modes with respect to one another. But on further reflection, it becomes impossible to accept without reservations Watson's concept of the "parity" of the four pure modes,[15] because the Aristotelian mode provides the parameters of theory-formation in terms of which the other archic modes are rendered intelligible in the first place. Therefore, as the controlling theory of theories, the Aristotelian mode is asymmetrically related to the other pure modes.

In Aristotle's own words, "The faculty of knowing is never moved but remains at rest."[16] He also states, "But if there is anything that has no contrary, then it knows itself and is actual and possesses independent existence."[17] Throughout his writings we learn that intellectual activity—and ultimately the eternal activity of mind—is to be distinguished from mere change or motion. Change and motion involve contraries, whereas intellectual activity does not.

This theory of the activity of mind underlies Aristotle's insistence that knowledge is not sensation and is not altered by its objects. It also informs his view that, in the individual, potential knowledge is prior to actual knowledge, but in the universe at large actual knowledge precedes potential knowledge.[18] Things are things known, and are known determinately in the first instances as beings or substances. The philosophical mind itself is actively universal and knows worlds in the light of its substantial, historical universality. All these things being true, perfect philosophical knowledge is inherent in all of these worlds, as when a philosopher grasps the first, generic principles embodied in actual or possible worldviews.

Watson shows how philosophical texts displace each other's meanings, becoming in effect contraries to each other. He therefore writes that it "may be questioned whether the pure modes are in some way superior to the mixed modes. The pure modes have a coherence, simplicity, and elegance that distinguish them from the mixed modes and give them an archetypal role, but, on the other hand, they can easily degenerate into thinness and triviality. The synthesis of heterogeneous elements in the mixed modes presents difficulties at the sutures, but, on the other hand, the unity of discordant elements can give a philosophy unusual interest and power."[19] He also asserts: "The archic variables are formally independent, and there is no formal reason to prefer the pure to the mixed modes, or indeed any modes to any other. . . . There is, we may say, a formal parity of all archic modes, whether pure or mixed."[20]

For our purposes, however, the archetypal nature of the pure modes is expressed in their generality and their particular dimensions of theory-formation. Moreover, the pure modes already shine forth in the texts of the Sophists, Democritus/Santayana, Plato, and Aristotle, and may be exemplified by future texts. Formally and materially considered, the unnatural sutures in the mixed modes produce contractions in the generality and lucidity of the pure modes.

If we insist that it is the acknowledged masterworks of philosophy that are substantively significant, then we must recognize that they do not express the same truth about the world. They envision different dimensions and degrees of truth, as measured by the pure modes and ultimately by the Aristotelian mode. The emphasis shifts to evaluating the archic profiles of individual texts within a generically normative theory.

The conclusion of our comparative hermeneutic is that the Aristotelian mode, being generically normative for theory-formation, has no contrary and is immovable and incapable of reconstruction or deconstruction by any logic of semantic transpositions. It represents philosophical activity at its best. It therefore becomes the measure of the degrees of truth and reality attainable in theories.

The Architecture of Theories

At the end of his first *Critique* Kant considered writing a "history of pure reason." He did not accomplish this phenomenological goal in his own text, which displays a noumenal reality. Of Kant's successors, it was Hegel who undertook this project, modified to his purpose. In his *Phenomenology of Mind* Hegel produced a blueprint for a monumental architecture of theories. He worked out the details of this phenomenology in many other writings, each of which has its place in an overall encyclopedia of the philosophical sciences encompassing the mind and life of *Geist*, the divine spirit. Even though Hegel developed a diaphanic form of architectonic theory, he must be credited with having contributed to the advance of Kant's idea.

At the heart of Hegel's concept of history and phenomenology lies a sense of gradated realizations, of the evolution of ideas. Like Aristotle's, Hegel's essential sense of reality made him see the concrete expressions of nature and history as embodied types of reason.

But unlike Aristotle or Kant, Hegel wrote from a diaphanic perspective—from the self-consciousness of "absolute knowledge"—and used a well-known dialectical method of articulation. Hegel's version of an essentialist ontology exhibits the peculiar trait of conceiving of the full realization of essence only at the completion of the system. The forms of logic, nature, and human spirit are of course essential forms, transcending the merely accidental determinations of appearance. But they are "less concrete" forms than the fully realized divine spirit, which is the concrete universal itself.

Both Peirce and Watson draw attention to Hegel's essentialist ontology. They do not subscribe to his dialectical and diaphanic interpretation of the history of philosophy. They assert, however, that the history of philosophy is of primary importance for philosophers. Each uses a version of Kant's synoptic method, governed by reflexive principles, to explore the history of ideas for the raw materials of his own architectonic project.

Most practicing philosophers are serious students of the history of philosophy, and with good reason. Philosophers deal in ultimate perceptions, utterances, or judgments of the world and are therefore drawn to fellow philosophers. Even when they neglect it, the history of ideas provides them with their raison d'être.

In Hegel's, Peirce's, and Watson's treatments of this idea, we become aware of the range of great texts that address fundamental questions. And we sense that the major worldviews represent so many degrees and dimensions of philosophical mind. But we have no justification for thinking that history defers to the future the full realization of philosophical essences.

To expand on Aristotle here, however much all things may be "so and not so"—that is, different—"still there is a more or less in the nature of things." All men make unqualified judgments, if not about all things, still about what is better and worse.[21] Reflexively employed here, this rule must also apply to the variety of theory-formations: the great texts must represent more or less adequate theories of the world.

Our task then is to assess the worldviews as degrees and dimensions of mind, and thus as exemplifying, in their various symmetrical and asymmetrical relationships, so many primary forms of human utterance. When this is done, they will have been assigned their just and rightful places within an encompassing world-theory.

This consideration has far-reaching implications for architectonic theory, as well as for pedagogical practice. Peculiarly relevant becomes a reconsideration of the power of magnitude of Watson's archic matrix, introduced in chapter 1 and employed systematically in the various interpretive readings of this book.

If the ordinary and, for want of a better word, dogmatical texts of the history of philosophy each have an archic profile whose values specify the general set of archic variables (namely, perspective, reality, method, and principle), then Watson's archic matrix itself must be measured in terms of the square of four (or sixteen). It produces this comparative degree of generality with respect to the dogmatical texts. Surely this represents substantial progress in philosophical awareness.[22]

Of particular importance is Watson's analysis of the four pure modes:

	PERSPECTIVE	REALITY	METHOD	PRINCIPLE
Sophistic	*personal*	*existential*	*agonistic*	*creative*
Democritean	*objective*	*substrative*	*logistic*	*elemental*
Platonic	*diaphanic*	*noumenal*	*dialectical*	*comprehensive*
Aristotelian	*disciplinary*	*essentialist*	*synoptic*	*reflexive*

In this system, it is impossible to move to higher levels of generality. The pure modes represent the four semantically perfect kinds of texts, in the sense that they express the highest degree of affinity among the archic variables in each configuration and the greatest possible differences from one another. All other texts are based on the 252 mixed configurations of their possible values.

Imagine for a moment that the four perfect modes represent the top of a pyramid composed of these 256 possible kinds of archic profiles, or texts. The bottom of this pyramid must consist of a set of the 24 most mixed modes, representing complete dis-affinity, or heterogeneity, in archic values, as opposed to the natural affinity of the four pure modes.

The most mixed modes' complete dis-affinities in archic values represent the highest degrees of mental unnaturalness, so to speak. They produce the worldviews that are hardest to maintain without alterations in the transmission of their original semantic intentions. They are always liable to break down into more naturally enduring forms. The text of Mencius, for example, has four heterogeneous elements; it survived historically as a companion to the texts of the *Analects* and the *Hsün Tzu*, and was later incorporated by those of Chu Hsi and Wang Yang-ming.

In this hypothesis, then, generality of outlook is a function of the natural affinity among archic values. But we are also working with a concept of semantic transferability among the archic values, further specified as to symmetrical and asymmetrical types of intertextual relations. The highest degree of generic parity (and thus of mutual appropriation or displacement) takes place among the four pure modes, while there are various orders of asymmetrical convertibility in the intertextual relationships obtaining among the pure and mixed modes.

To explore this hypothesis further, let us now assign each of the archic factors—perspective, reality, method, and principle—a value of 1, and compute the degree of affinity in archic values by a simple notation. We can symbolize the degree of homogeneity, or affinity, in the pure modes by the notation of 4 : 0, and the degree of heterogeneity in the 24 most mixed modes by the notation of 1 : 1 : 1 : 1. Between the most pure and impure archic modes lie the various mixed texts, which can have three possible distributions—3 : 1, 2 : 2, and 2 : 1 : 1.[23]

Closest to the pure modes would be the texts having only one heterogenous element, expressed by the notation of 3 : 1. There are many such texts in the history of philosophy.

Illustrating this 3 : 1 ratio, the text of Anaxagoras reveals three Democritean values but an Aristotelian principle. Bacon's archic text revived this Anaxagorean paradigm at a crucial stage of early modern Western philosophy. Pythagoras has three Platonic variables but a Democritean sense of reality. (Kepler reinterpreted this Pythagorean configuration, as did the Chinese philosopher Shao Yung.)

The Bhagavad Gita, Plotinus, the Neoplatonic and Sufi mystics, and Schelling depart from the Platonic paradigm only in their elemental principles. Augustine, Anselm, and Bonaventure depart from the Neoplatonic paradigm in their creative principles, and thus reaffirm the archic assumptions of the New Testament. Dante has the same archic text as Thomas Aquinas. Aquinas departed from the Aristotelian paradigm only in his noumenal sense of reality.

Tung Chung-shu, Chou Tun-i, Chang Tsai, the Ch'eng brothers, Chu Hsi, and generations of Neo-Confucians in the Ch'eng-Chu line of orthodox transmission in China, Korea, and Japan were Platonists, but with essential realities. They all drew upon the Book of Changes, which has a similar distribution of archic values.

Leibniz was a logistic Platonist.

Newton, Locke, Adam Smith, and Darwin were modern Democriteans with creative principles. Their archic profiles were anticipated by Thales, Epicurus, and Lucretius.

Hume (Russell et al.) was an existential Democritean.

Erasmus's text was that of an elemental Sophist; so was Voltaire's. Berkeley's text was diaphanically Sophistic. Kierkegaard's was noumenally Sophistic. James's was Sophistic, but with a synoptic method. Sartre's and Merleau-Ponty's texts were Sophistic, but with dialectical methods. Unamuno's text displays three Sophistic variables with a Democritean reality. Foucault's text is Sophistic, but from an objective perspective. Jaspers's text echoes Berkeley's in its own fashion.

Hippocrates anticipated the Aristotelian text, but with a substrative reality. Aquinas and Kant were noumenal Aristotelians; Montesquieu, an agonistic Aristotelian; Peirce, an objective Aristotelian; Husserl, a logistic Aristotelian; and Dewey, a creative Aristotelian.

Freud's text is related to those of Empedocles and Democritus; he views life as an objective Empedoclean or as an agonistic Democritean. Freud also revived the archic paradigm of Wang Ch'ung, which had already appeared in the Carvaka teaching of ancient India. It is also found in certain kinds of naturalistic literary and artistic texts of Japan and the West, both ancient and modern.

Texts having only one heterogenous variable occupy the next rank in philosophical generality, internal dimensionality, clarity of worldview, and strategic importance, and generate semantic continuities on their own.[24] In fact, the texts of Plotinus and the Christian Neoplatonists, as well as those of the Augustinian and Thomistic strains, became dominant forces during centuries of Western spiritual life. Similarly, the Hindu and Neo-Confucian traditions defined the central value systems of India and East Asian cultures, respectively, for significant periods of time. It is worth dwelling on the comparative stability of these great texts, all of which are 3 : 1-valued theories.

Many of the outstanding philosophical texts of the seventeenth and eighteenth centuries have only one heterogenous archic value, including those of Bacon, Leibniz, Newton, Locke, Berkeley, Hume, Adam Smith, Montesquieu, and Kant.

In the classical American tradition, the texts of Peirce, William James, and Dewey have 3 : 1 archic ratios. Each generates its own possibilities in the various human sciences and technologies, grounded further in the generality of the purely Sophistic, Democritean, Platonic, and Aristotelian modes.

The mixed modes show us that the unnatural splicing of disparate archic variables produces crimps, or contractions, in the generality, dimensionality, and lucidity achievable by the pure modes. This contraction is already noticeable in the transformation of 4 : 0 into 3 : 1 texts, and may be expected to have consequences in the passage to 2 : 2 and 2 : 1 : 1 texts. This process provides further justification for our recommendation that the great texts of philosophy not be deconstructed by lesser texts of the present, but be allowed to shine forth in their original clarity. The reverse side of this coin is worth noting: The lesser texts should be reconstructed by the greater ones—that is, those with greater generality, dimensionality, and clarity of outlook.

The return from a 3 : 1 to a 4 : 0 text signals a liberation of the general possibilities of thought. Such a change took place most notably in the Renaissance with the rediscovery of the original theories of Plato, Aristotle, Democritus, and the ancient grammarians after centuries of medieval theology and pedagogy. The Renaissance's reinterpretation of classical thought gave impetus to many new worldviews, beginning with those of Bacon and Descartes.

Bacon effectively inaugurated the modern period of Western natural philosophy with a rare form of a 3 : 1 archic text. Descartes followed with an unprecedented form of a 2 : 1 : 1 text. Spinoza introduced another excellent but rare 2 : 1 : 1 text. At almost the same time, Hobbes wrote a 2 : 2 text. Leibniz, Newton, Locke, Berkeley, Hume, and Kant reworked the same ideas into 3 : 1 texts.

It is possible not only to enter intuitively into these transmissions of thought at critical historical junctures, but also to experience them in the changes in one's own intellectual life. One feels a similar liberation of intellectual possibilities when returning from the mixed Aristotelian texts of Peirce, Husserl, or Dewey to that of Aristotle himself. One finds a new Renaissance of the Democritean paradigm in the writings of Santayana, which range beyond those of Peirce or Dewey in generality of outlook.

At the next lower level of this hierarchy of theories are the archic profiles of texts whose heterogenous elements form two pairs. These texts will have the ratio of 2 : 2. For example, we saw that Parmenides' text had two Democritean and two Platonic values. His text, it may be argued, is harder to understand and preserve than 4 : 0 and 3 : 1 texts. This is because it compresses logistic and elemental values into combination with diaphanic and noumenal values, when the whole force of the intertextual relation between Democritus and Plato is to keep them apart.

The texts of Fichte and Hegel consist of two Platonic and two Aristotelian values, although in different pairs. These two form theoretical contractions, joining what the original Platonic and Aristotelian texts had established as naturally discordant. Fichte and Hegel overcome this discordance through dialectical methods, a topic we shall return to shortly.

Nietzsche and Derrida are half-Democritean and half-Sophistic, although in different elements. If Fichte and Hegel produce overly idealistic texts, Nietzsche, Derrida, and other deconstructionists go to the opposite extreme, subverting all idealistic projects. They have the right tools for doing so, but combine archic values that were separated in the texts of Democritus and the Sophists.

Hobbes's text is also half-Sophistic and half-Democritean, as are those of the Chinese Legalists, although in a different distribution of archic values.

The Tao Te Ching rests on two Democritean and two Platonic assumptions. The Koran is based on two Platonic and two Sophistic assumptions.

Wittgenstein's text, like that of Giles Deleuze, reaffirms the archic profile of the Hellenistic Skeptics. It grants precedence to two Democritean and two Sophistic elements, but not the same ones as Nietzsche's or Hobbes's. Justus Buchler's version of American naturalism has two Aristotelian and two Sophistic values.

Such 2 : 2 texts can produce highly charged theoretical formations. The balance of discordant elements, as Watson has observed, can give texts unusual interest and power. As we might also expect, such texts are predominantly two-voiced in their discursive organizations. Fichte and Hegel combine Platonic and Aristotelian values with dialectical methods. Lao Tzu harmonizes two Platonic and Democritean values. The Chinese Legalists, exponents of Islam, as well as Nietzsche, Wittgenstein, Derrida, and Deleuze produce discordant utilities through agonistic methods.

Among major philosophers, Hobbes appears to be the exception to the rule that the 2 : 2 texts are either dialectically or agonistically formed. Hobbes's well-known doctrine of man's conflict with his fellow man is grounded in a concept of the state of nature that is personal in perspective, substrative in reality, logistic in method, and creative in principle—a combination that informs his "Body Politick."

Justus Buchler's text has two Aristotelian variables: it is disciplinary in perspective (the attitude of generically normative theories) and synoptic in method (the method of defining complex natural orders). It has two Sophistic elements as well: his existential sense of the ontological parity of natural complexes and his creative principle of query. Buchler's creative principle drives his method into endless factorability of natural complexes, an openness that permits no absolute beginning, middle, or end and thus undermines any claim to a simple, or absolute, completion of analysis.[25]

This distribution of archic values in Buchler's text predisposes him to espouse James's doctrine of the indefinite factorability of existential complexes, as opposed to the essentialist doctrines of Peirce and Dewey. But by a natural semantic transference, Buchler's 2 : 2 text is liable to change into a 3 : 1 Sophistic form. That is, Buchlerians are prone to turning it into an agonistic instrument of deconstructive query, since the principle of ontological parity is inherently inimical to any systems that produce logical, epistemic, or ontological priorities of any sort.

As in the case of Hobbes's "Body Politick," what the 2 : 2 texts gain in specialization, they lose in generalization and pluralistic potential. Consider, for example, the multiple dimensions of the 4 : 0 philosophical texts of Plato, Aristotle, or Santayana, or of the musical text of Mozart. Measure these against the more contracted forms of 2 : 2 texts. I do not refer to volumes of printed pages, but to the semantic properties of these theories. With the 4 : 0 text one is introduced to far more extensive, yet variegated worldviews, whether in the cognitive, political and ethical, or aesthetic aspects of life.

It follows from this consideration that the narrower theories tend to underestimate (and misinterpret) the broader ones. The 2 : 2 texts are always forcing the 4 : 0 and 3 : 1 texts into their narrower frameworks. To work a long time on the intertextual relations between Fichte or Hegel and of Plato or Aristotle, for example, is eventually to feel the constraints Fichte or Hegel put on Plato or Aristotle, or again on the 3 : 1 text of Kant. Derrida's critique of Plato produces a tedious play. For all its rhetorical brilliance and hyperbole, Nietzsche's worldview is far less dazzling than Shakespeare's. (Nietzsche as a young man favored the music of the "purely Germanic" Richard Wagner and disparaged the more cosmopolitan Mozart.) Buchler's naturalism reduces Santayana's materialism to Buchler's ordinal definitions, whereas Santayana's penetrating gaze gives us one of the most colorful and subtly shaded descriptions of the human condition in the history of philosophy.

At the next level on our scale of "mixedness" we can place those texts comprising one homogenous pair of archic values and two heterogenous ones. These will have a notation of 2 : 1 : 1. Such would be, in differing respects, the texts of Anaximander, Heraclitus, Empedocles, Confucius, Mo Tzu, Hsün Tzu, Chuang Tzu, Wang Yang-ming, Nagarjuna and most of the Buddhists up to the time of Nishida, the Old Testament, the Stoics, Descartes, Spinoza, Rousseau, Marx, Schopenhauer, F. H. Bradley, Bergson, Whitehead, Scheler, and Heidegger. Such texts can be considered to be more specialized in range and reference.

Here again we might expect the 2 : 1 : 1 texts to be predominantly two-voiced in their discursive organization. The texts of the Old Testament, Wang Yang-ming, Rousseau, Marx, Bergson, F. H. Bradley, Whitehead, and Heidegger are in fact dialectical in method, while those of Anaximander, Heraclitus, Empedocles, Confucius, Hsün Tzu, Chuang Tzu, Nagarjuna, and most other Buddhists down to the Kyoto School writers are agonistic. Schopenhauer's synoptic method does not fit this pattern; nor do the logistic methods of Mo Tzu, Descartes, and Spinoza.

We may be able to account for these deviations from the general rule on the basis of the looser bonding of archic values in the 2 : 1 : 1 form.

Nonetheless, the predominance of dialectical and agonistic methods in the 2 : 2 and 2 : 1 : 1 texts provides food for further thought. Agonistic texts—as in Homer, Heraclitus, the Buddhists, Chuang Tzu, Nietzsche, Scheler, and Derrida—call attention to their powers of expression. Although they tend to be more concerned with hard categories, texts that are dialectical in method and creative in principle—as in Sartre, Marx, Bergson, Whitehead, and Heidegger—also tend to be rhetorically vivid. According to the synoptic logic of this hypothesis, one could say that the rhetorical brilliance of such texts compensates for their loss of formal generality and precision, compared to the 4 : 0 and 3 : 1 texts.

Buddhist texts, for example, are often rhetorically brilliant, even as they reduce the many dimensions of life to a flux of evanescent moments. The texts of Wittgenstein and Derrida run on memorable examples and tropes. Wittgenstein makes remarks about shewing the fly out of the philosophical bottle, houses of cards, and language going on holiday. Derrida encourages language games and writing games in which the great works of philosophy are considerably reduced in substance. Elusively Sophistic, these philosophers achieve what may be called zero metaphysical profiles. When their followers, as theoretically handcuffed as they are, try to interpret their ideas in an ethical and even religious direction, they sometimes adopt a Buddhist attitude.

Every teacher and student of philosophy has encountered texts of lesser generality. We adjust our mental registers upward or downward when reading, for example, Democritus or Newton on atoms and the void, Plato or Berkeley on perception, Plato or Derrida on writing, or Aristotle or Confucius on ethics and politics.

According to this classification of theories, the 4 : 0, 3 : 1, 2 : 2, and 2 : 1 : 1 texts will exhibit various degrees of asymmetry. Compare the ethics of Aristotle with those of the Stoics; the Stoics certainly take a more extravagant approach to the good life. We will have to make greater efforts to understand the other 2 : 1 : 1 texts as well. The 1 : 1 : 1 : 1 texts will require even greater feats of interpretation, although they are still possible forms of thought.

It will take a highly differentiated analysis to plot all the implications of this reading of the philosophical texts. Suffice it to say that the texts related by continuities of archic values are the most accessible for our comparative hermeneutic.

The ethics of Aristotle, the Stoics, Kant, Hegel, and Peirce, for example, are all governed by reflexive principles, although they differ in other respects. The ethics of Democritus, Mencius, Wang Yang-ming, Hume, Rousseau, Voltaire, Schopenhauer, and Nietzsche are all based on elemental principles, but diverge in their other archic values. Comparing the Stoics with Voltaire or Nietzsche, or Kant with Mencius or Hume, we eventually have to trace each form of ethical discourse to its source (in the Aristotelian and Democritean modes, respectively). Otherwise, we end up merely contrasting them—for they are ultimately incompatible—and this will tend to abort the interpretive enterprise at an early stage. (Some modern hermeneuts do just that.)

This brief discussion of the degrees, dimensions, and limits of theories is only intended to suggest the possibilities of comparative research, which might lead to a far more sophisticated understanding of the architecture of theories than has hitherto been envisioned. Let us remember Peirce's opinion that it takes as much preliminary planning and preparation of materials to construct a good theory as it does to build a good house. Such detail falls outside the scope of the present work, which addresses itself to the foundations of such an architectural project. The foundations, I repeat, are the four pure modes.

In musical terms, the pure modes are the solo players in a classical string quartet. The scoring formula for the string quartet defines the chief technical program for this ensemble of instruments. Historically, as in Haydn, this entailed the technique of "*thematische Arbeit,*" or, in Beethoven's later phrase, "obbligato accompaniment," performed by each of the four instruments. Such obligatory writing for the four soloists emancipated the cello from the continuo and all-bass doublings, and allowed the viola and cello to function as equals with the violin. The independence and potential equality of the four parts led to the exploration of distinct musical possibilities through a complex process of transformations and exchanges.

Inspired by Haydn's String Quartets Opus 33, Mozart composed a set of six string quartets of his own, which were to release a new flow of creative writing on Haydn's part. The great masters of composition, in another version of obbligato accompaniment, began to express the form of the classical string quartet in their exchanges.

We can say that the perfection of the classical string quartet—like that of the instruments for which Haydn and Mozart wrote—represents a pure form. Similarly, the texts of the Sophists, Plato, Democritus, and Aristotle may be assigned the role of the four soloists in the philosophical obbligato accompaniment of their time, or that of the great masters of composition.

Nietzsche remarked that all subsequent ages have raged with envy at the Greeks—and have done everything possible to undermine their monumental achievements.[26] This observation must include Nietzsche's own pronouncements on the Platonic and Aristotelian modes of thought. For our comparative hermeneutic, Nietzsche's text provides a prime example of a somewhat malicious interpretation of Plato and

Aristotle based on a combination of Democritean and Sophistic variables.

We need not resent the achievements of any of the Greek philosophers, and certainly not the greatest of all (no more than we should the musical masterpieces of Haydn and Mozart). We should strive to reclaim them in their pristine forms, knowing that their texts provide the foundation for numerous other philosophical theories.

Seeing the gross distortions of Plato, Aristotle, and other major figures, which are obsessively repeated in postmodern and Pragmatist circles, one wishes for a little more of Jaspers's good sense in "seeking the company of the great philosophers." Meanwhile, as they rage on, we are entitled to entertain the suspicion that less mature minds are attacking more mature ones.

We must remember, however, that even these Greek philosophers have not exhausted the paradigms bearing their names. The now fragmentary text of Democritus was preceded by that of Anaximenes; both these texts yield to the more fully developed "pure materialism" of Santayana. With his consummate style, his cosmopolitan philosophical outlook and literary culture, and the range of his published works, which include books, essays, poetry, and even a novel (*The Last Puritan*), Santayana produced a contemporary worldview of rare genius. His writings have the generality and cogency of a pure archic mode.

Santayana also possessed the philosophical and literary erudition needed to enter into intertextual relations with a whole range of the world's philosophers. Santayana's interpretations of his fellow philosophers provide us with a contemporary example of the imbalance between a pure and various mixed worldviews.

We identified Mozart as another "pure materialist" whose musical text has the qualities of very rare genius. The masterworks of Mozart are often praised as penetratingly objective, profoundly moving even in their most joyous or comic moods, absolutely economical, and quintessentially elegant and complete. To this might be added their sheer variety. We cannot pursue the comparison between the Mozart and Santayana here. Suffice it to say that the "ethics of cheerfulness" of the pure materialist text runs through the fragments of Democritus, the life and music of Mozart, and the life and philosophy of Santayana.[27]

I offer these interpretations of the gradations in generality of the great texts as suggestions for further thought and research. It may be more helpful to see the four pure modes as the bases of this architecture of theories. In their sheer generality and precision of insight, they prepare the way for the various lesser philosophical texts. Each of these lesser texts intuits the world according to its fundamental insights and displaces the others. At the same time, each theory establishes its place within a set of possible theories—that is, within the realm of philosophical awareness.

The Aristotelian mode, as we saw, moderates all other theories. Aristotle placed his philosophy between the extremes of the Platonic and Democritean paradigms. He also avoids the disadvantages of the Sophistic text, which stresses idiocentric, existential, and contentious points of view.

If all texts, as theory-formations, represent generalities of mind, the Aristotelian mode is best suited to explain the process of theory-formation. It accounts for the variety of human sciences and arts as general possibilities of mind. It interprets the world's great philosophical texts as rich sources of first principles, which it organizes synoptically into pedagogical models. It accomplishes these goals by according each actual or potential philosophical text full semantic self-sufficiency.

The Aristotelian text, however, must simultaneously manifest its own meaning. It must lay the foundations of theoretical intertextuality in its own apprehension of the essential forms of thought. Comparing and therefore judging the first principles of thought, it must establish the standard for all possible theory-formations.

Only such a text can rescue the history of philosophy from Kant's "ruins." The purpose and strength of philosophical reason lies in realizing its essential forms, both as historical phenomena and as enduring resources for all times.

Appendix: The Archic Matrix

Archic Variables

Perspective: the text's voice, as self-validating epistemic warrant
Reality: the text's reference to what is ultimately real, not just apparent
Method: the text's logical or conceptual form
Principle: the text's motivating and integrating intention

Specific Archic Values

Perspectives
- Personal: subjective, idiocentric
- Objective: impersonal, normal, unexceptional
- Diaphanic: religious, revelatory of higher view
- Disciplinary: schooled, expert, competent, universally referent

Realities
- Existential: immediately lived, contingently experiential
- Substrative: material, underlying, recondite, cryptic, suppressed
- Noumenal: supersensibly general and ideal
- Essential: historically general and ideal

Methods
- Agonistic: paradoxical
- Logistic: computational
- Dialectical: sublational
- Synoptic: problematic

Principles
- Creative: volitional, making a difference
- Elemental: simple, self-same, repetitious, recycling

Comprehensive: totalistic, hierarchically encompassing
Reflexive: autonomously active and self-completing

The following graph representing the archic matrix of the pure modes, is itself a text, whose archic modality is disciplinary, essential, synoptic, and reflexive.

	PERSPECTIVE	REALITY	METHOD	PRINCIPLE
Sophistic	*personal*	*existential*	*agonistic*	*creative*
Democritean	*objective*	*material*	*logistic*	*elemental*
Platonic	*diaphanic*	*noumenal*	*dialectical*	*comprehensive*
Aristotelian	*disciplinary*	*essential*	*synoptic*	*reflexive*

Notes

1. Resources for an Intellectual Renaissance Today

1. See Wolfgang Hildesheimer, *Mozart,* trans. Marion Faber (New York: Vintage Books, 1983), pp. 55, 284, 366, and H. C. Robbins Landon, *1791: Mozart's Last Year* (New York: Schirmer Books, 1988), p. 10.

2. During the Renaissance, Francis Bacon and the humanists claimed to be *moderni,* a term later taken over by some of the Enlightenment *philosophes* of the eighteenth century. But such thinkers as Machiavelli, Vico, Rousseau, and Hume devised strategies to look back positively to ancient ways, as did Nietzsche and Santayana, two conspicuous critics of modernism in more modern times. Today, postmoderns, trading in the currency of Heidegger and the Parisian Heideggerians, claim to be making a new break with the traditions. Other concepts of modernization have exercised generations of social scientists and have served as heuristic tools for Asian specialists, as well. More important for our comparative hermeneutic, the classical worldviews recur in the various modern forms; moreover, in any epoch, they coexist in their variety. Their continuities and synchronicities require a more sophisticated account than is engendered by the diachronic models, some of which give precedence to such concepts as "crises," "breakthroughs," "historical obsolescence," and the like.

3. Immanuel Kant, *Critique of Pure Reason,* A:835–38, B:863–66, trans. F. Max Müller (Garden City: Doubleday and Co., 1966), pp. 533–34.

4. Ibid., A:850, B:878, p. 541.

5. For a revelant critique of some of the political assumptions that inform the prevailing styles of the academy today, see Allan Bloom, *The Closing of the American Mind* (New York: Simon and Schuster, 1987).

6. See Allan Bloom, *The Closing of the American Mind,* pp. 336–82. Bloom argues that liberal education must and can be "both synoptic and precise" (p. 343), and deplores the fact that today "there is no synopsis" (p. 347). He then astutely describes the agonistic relationships that comprise the disciplines of the university today (pp. 356ff.). What Bloom does not do is provide a positive architec-

tonic—either of the Great Books on a world scale or of the disciplines of the modern university.

7. This technical nomenclature is adapted from Walter Watson, *The Architectonics of Meaning: Foundations of the New Pluralism* (Albany: SUNY Press, 1985), pp. 151–54 and passim.

8. As only one example of this baneful practice, see the deconstructive strategy of cutting off a classical author's meaning in mid-paragraph. In his *Dissemination* (trans. Barbara Johnson [Chicago: University of Chicago Press, 1981]), Jacques Derrida does this to Plato's *Phaedrus* at the critical juncture when Plato's mythical King Thamus is about to censure Theuth, who turns out to function for Derrida as a symbol of deconstructive writing (p. 75). King Thamus has to wait for twenty-seven pages of Derrida's text before he can finish his judgment.

9. René Descartes, *Second Replies to Objections*, cited in *Philosophers Speak for Themselves: From Descartes to Locke*, ed. T. V. Smith and Marjorie Grene (Chicago: University of Chicago Press, 1940), p. 117. See *The Philosophical Works of Descartes*, vol. 2, trans. Elizabeth S. Haldane and G. R. T. Ross (Cambridge: Cambridge University Press, 1911), pp. 47–51.

10. Immanuel Kant, *Prolegomena to Any Future Metaphysics*, 263–64, trans. Lewis White Beck (Indianapolis: Bobbs-Merrill Co., 1950), p. 11. See also Immanuel Kant, *Critique of Practical Reason*, trans. L. W. Beck (Indianapolis: Bobbs-Merrill Co., 1956), p. 10.

11. That the order of inquiry does not coincide with the order revealed by inquiry is well illustrated in the Kant's *Prolegomena to Any Future Metaphysics* and again in his *Grounding for the Metaphysics of Morals*, trans. James W. Ellington (Indianapolis: Hackett Publishing Co., 1981). In either case, Kant proceeds from the givens of ordinary human consciousness to the formal principle of their possibility. In the *Critiques* of pure and practical reason Kant proceeds to deduce the formal structures of our cognitive and moral faculties from their first principles, the cognitive and volitional applications of reason, respectively. What is revealed by these analytical inquiries is definitive for Kant: pure reason defines the transcendental forms of its own cognitive and moral faculties.

12. On Kant's concept of metaphysics as science, see Lewis White Beck's "Translator's Introduction" to *Critique of Practical Reason*, pp. ixff.

13. Ibid., A:110, pp. 106–7.

14. On this notion of unifying act see Kant, *Critique of Pure Reason*, trans. F. Max Müller, A:68, p. 54; see pp. 60, 77–79, 84–85, 94–96, 104, 145, and passim.

15. Immanuel Kant, *Critique of Judgment*, trans. J. H. Bernard (New York: Hafner Press, 1951), p. 21: "There is in nature a subordination of genera and species comprehensible by us. Each one approximates to some other according to a common principle, so that a transition from one to another, and so on to a higher genus, may be possible. Though it seems at the outset unavoidable for our understanding to assume different kinds of causality for the specific differences of natural operations, yet these different kinds may stand under a small number of principles, with the investigation of which we have to busy our-

selves." Kant calls this "the law of the specification of nature in respect of its empirical laws" (p. 22).

16. Kant goes on to amplify this concept of natural purpose, or internal purposiveness in organized beings, in the section entitled "Analytic of the Teleological Judgment," (ibid., pp. 208–31).

17. Aristotle *On the Soul* 3.4.429b5–9, trans. J. A. Smith in *Basic Works of Aristotle*, ed. Richard McKeon (New York: Random House, 1941). See *The Complete Works of Aristotle*, rev. Oxford ed., 2 vols., ed. Jonathan Barnes, (Princeton: Princeton University Press, Bollingen Series, 2d ed., 1985).

18. Aristotle *On the Soul* 1.1.402b16–25: "It seems not only useful for the discovery of causes of the derived properties of substances to be acquainted with the essential nature of those substances . . . but also conversely, for the knowledge of the essential nature of a substance is largely promoted by an acquaintance with its properties: for, when we are able to give an account conformable to experience of all or most of the properties of a substance, we shall be in the most favorable position to say something worth saying about the essential nature of that subject." In all scientific demonstration, Aristotle goes on to say, a working definition of the subject matter is required as a starting point of inquiry. But definitions that do not enable us to discover its real properties must obviously be merely dialectical and futile.

19. Ibid., 2.1.412a20, 412b5–6.

20. Aristotle *Nicomachean Ethics* 1.1.1094a1–18, trans. W. D. Ross, in *Basic Works of Aristotle*, ed. Richard McKeon (New York: Random House, 1941).

21. Ibid., 1.2.1094a28–1094, 1094b1–12.

22. Aristotle *Posterior Analytics* 2.19.100a9–13, trans. G. R. G. Mure, in *Basic Works of Aristotle*, ed. Richard McKeon: "We conclude that these states of knowledge are neither innate in a determinate form, nor developed from other higher states of knowledge, but from sense-perception. It is like a rout in battle stopped by first one man making a stand and then another, until the original formation has been restored. The soul is so constituted as to be capable of this process."

23. Aristotle *Metaphysics* 1.2.928a5–26, in *Basic Works of Aristotle*, ed. Richard McKeon.

24. Aristotle *Metaphysics* 1.3.985a15–16.

2. Prolegomena to Any Future Hermeneutic

1. These categories are adapted from the writings of Justus Buchler. See his *Toward a General Theory of Human Judgment*, 2d ed. (New York: Dover Publications, 1979); *Nature and Judgment* (New York: Columbia University Press, 1955), pp. 20–49 and passim; *The Concept of Method* (New York: Columbia University Press, 1961); and *The Main of Light: On the Concept of Poetry* (New York: Oxford University Press, 1974), pp. 97–116. In these three concepts, I seek to reinvest meanings suggested by the texts of Aristotle, Kant, and Peirce. In my under-

standing, these categories are essential features of the synoptic concept of "text." Thus they are general properties of texts. They correspond to Aristotle's three types of "theoretical," or intellectual, activity—namely, the cognitive, practical, and productive—and reappear in a related form in Kant. In his theory of phanerons, or phenomenology, Peirce related his own doctrine of the three categories to the subjects of Kant's three *Critiques* (firstness to the domain of aesthetic feeling, secondness to that of volition, and thirdness to thought).

2. Compare John Locke, *An Essay Concerning Human Understanding,* bk. 4, chap. 21, "Of the Division of the Sciences," pars. 1–5.

3. As I employ them, the three categories of judgment are preeminently characteristics of philosophical texts. These properties in turn are functions of the ontological reference of such worldviews. I stress this point to anticipate special claims for the priority of the propositional over the active or performative kinds of utterances, or vice versa, which can be found in many sorts of interpretive texts. A world-theory, I hold, is always simultaneously propositional, practical, and expressive in modality. Indeed, this is always so in theories that assert and/or enact an absolute priority of some sort. Consider, for example, either Pragmatist or Marxist theories of the "primacy of action," or "praxis." Consider also certain religious discourses—that of Zen Buddhism, for example—and also deconstructionist writings, which tend to deliberately confuse these modalities of judgment for special effects.

4. See, for example, Jacques Derrida, *Dissemination,* trans. Barbara Johnson (Chicago: University of Chicago Press, 1981), where deconstructive "writing" (the *pharmakon*) is asserted to have "no ideal identity; it is aneidetic. . . ." (p. 126).

5. See Robert Magliola, *Derrida on the Mend* (West Lafayette: Purdue University Press, 1984), p. 191.

6. See, for example, John Dewey, *Reconstruction in Philosophy,* enl. ed. (Boston: Beacon Press, 1948), pp. v–vi.

7. Among the theories that pass themselves off as nontheories, one finds strains of philosophical definition that eschew "foundational thinking." For a representative example and discussion of a wider literature, see Joseph Margolis, *Pragmatism Without Foundations: Reconciling Realism and Relativism* (Oxford: Basil Blackwell, 1986). But in our comparative hermeneutic, all philosophical discourses are foundational. Kant is right on this point: the distinguishing feature of philosophical texts is that they are nomothetic. This is equally true of allegedly nonfoundational theories as well.

8. See, for example, Plato *Republic* 511b, trans. R. Hackforth, cited in *The Collected Dialogues of Plato,* ed. Edith Hamilton and Huntington Cairns, Bollingen Series (New York: Pantheon Books, 1961).

9. Ibid., 533d.

10. Walter Watson's *The Architectonics of Meaning: Foundations of the New Pluralism* (Albany: SUNY Press, 1985), although prefigured in the work of Richard McKeon, will be recognized as the historically pivotal statement of such a global

hermeneutic. I have deliberately drawn upon Watson's terminology, regarding it as a function of the disciplinary perspective of this collegial project that I can do so. The emphasis in this chapter on the three modes of world-texts is my own, although essentially compatible with Watson's.

3. The Principles of Athenian and Hellenistic Philosophy

1. From Diogenes Laertius 9.30, cited in *Fifth-Century Atomists,* selected and translated by Walter Watson, with the assistance of K. Freeman and W. K. C. Guthrie, from the text of H. Diels and W. Kranz, eds., *Die Fragmente der Vorsokratiker,* 7th ed. (Berlin: Weidmannsche Verlagsbuchhandlung, 1954), unpublished MS, 1, p. 1.

2. Diels-Kranz 2, p. 1.

3. Diels-Kranz 66, p. 2, from Aetius 1.26.2: "Necessity for Democritus is the resistance, motion, and impact of matter."

4. Diels-Kranz 30, p. 1, from Aetius 4.8.5.

5. Diels-Kranz 9, p. 4, from Sextus Empiricus 7.135.

6. *Fifth-Century Atomists,* trans. W. Watson, Diels-Kranz 159, p. 7.

7. See Walter Watson, "Democritus on the Gods" (unpublished paper), pp. 1–27.

8. Aristotle *Generation of Animals* 2.742b17, in *Fifth-Century Atomists,* trans. Walter Watson, Diels-Kranz 65a, p. 2.

9. Aristotle *Metaphysics* 1.6.987b1–12, trans. W. D. Ross, in *Basic Works of Aristotle.*

10. Watson, *Architectonics of Meaning,* p. 61.

11. Aristotle *Metaphysics* 1.6.987a31–34, trans. W. D. Ross, in *Basic Works of Aristotle.*

12. Ibid., 4.5.1009b37.

13. See Watson, *The Architectonics of Meaning,* p. 151.

14. See Watson, *The Architectonics of Meaning,* pp. 151–54.

15. Diogenes Laertius on Pyrrho and the Skeptics, trans. J. Hicks (Loeb Classical Library series), cited in *Philosophers Speak for Themselves: From Aristotle to Plotinus,* ed. T. V. Smith (Chicago: University of Chicago Press, 1934), p. 172.

16. Ibid., p. 173. See *The Hellenistic Philosophers,* vol. 1, translations of the principal sources, with philosophical commentary, by A. A. Long and S. N. Sedley (Cambridge: Cambridge University Press, 1987), pp. 13–24, 468–88. Also consult *Sextus Empiricus: Selections from the Major Writings on Scepticism, Man, and God,* ed. Philip P. Hallie, trans. Sanford G. Etheridge, new rev. ed. (Indianapolis: Hackett Publishing Co., 1985).

17. The Skeptics' teaching of "laying down nothing, not even the laying down of nothing"—and their final recourse to silence—is reminiscent of a recurrent theme of Buddhist literature. The Skeptics' argument by silence is also reminiscent of the famous ending of Wittgenstein's *Tractatus Logico-Philosophicus.* In our

comparative analysis the Buddhists transform the perspective of the Skeptics' paradigm into a diaphanic one, while the Skeptics' and Wittgenstein's texts presuppose objective perspectives. Hume's "moderate scepticism" departs from the precedent of the Hellenistic Skeptics and from the text of Wittgenstein in its logistic method. Wittgenstein had only one career-text, the one that he formulated in the *Philosophical Investigations;* he begins to readopt the skeptical paradigm in the closing pages of his *Tractatus Logico-Philosophicus.*

18. Lucretius *De Rerum Natura* 2.251–62, 289–93, cited in *The Philosophy of Epicurus: Letters, Doctrines, and Parallel Passages from Lucretius,* trans., with commentary and an introductory essay on ancient materialism, by George K. Strodach (Evanston, Ill.: Northwestern University Press, 1963).

19. Epicurus *Sententiae Vaticanae,* trans. Cyril Bailey, cited in Norman Wentworth DeWitt, *Epicurus and His Philosophy* (Westport, Conn.: Greenwood Press, 1973), p. 177. See *The Hellenistic Philosophers,* vol. 1, pp. 25–157.

20. See DeWitt, *Epicurus and His Philosophy,* pp. 171–96, 328–58.

21. Lucretius *The Nature of the Universe* 1.1–49, trans. R. E. Latham (Baltimore: Penguin Classics, 1951).

22. Ibid., 5.925–1457.

23. See *The Hellenistic Philosophers,* vol. 1, pp. 158–437, and *Philosophers Speak For Themselves: From Aristotle to Plotinus,* ed. T. V. Smith, pp. 154–170, 203–245. The Stoics' reflexive principle of reason, in the form of the eternal decrees of God and of the lawmaking tendency of man's rational nature, recurs most notably in the philosophies of Spinoza and Vico. In the *The Third New Science: Principles of a New Science Concerning the Common Nature of Nations,* Vico writes: "This axiom proves that the divine providence exists and that it is a divine legislative mind which, from passions of men concerned only with their own personal advantage, in pursuit of which they would live as wild beasts in solitude, has created the civil orders through which they may live in a human society" (*Vico: Selected Writings,* ed. and trans. by Leon Pompa [Cambridge: Cambridge University Press, 1982], p. 162). Vico's text has a mixed archic profile, composed of two Aristotelian and two Democritean elements.

24. Plotinus *Enneads* 6.9.9., trans. Thomas Taylor, cited in *Philosophers Speak for Themselves: From Aristotle to Plotinus,* ed. T. V. Smith.

4. Archic Configurations in Pre-Socratic Philosophy

1. For this cardinal doctrine, see Aristotle *De Anima* 3.5.430a14–25, 7.431a1–9, trans. J. A. Smith, in *Basic Works of Aristotle.*

2. From the *Nature of Man,* in *The Extant Writings of Hippocrates,* trans. W. H. S. Jones (Loeb Classical Library series) cited in *The Presocratics,* ed. Philip Wheelwright (Indianapolis: Bobbs-Merrill, The Odyssey Press, 1960), 3, p. 268.

3. From *The Sacred Malady,* in *The Presocratics,* ed. P. Wheelwright, 2, p. 265; from *On Ancient Medicine,* cited in the same work, 1, pp. 269–70.

4. From *On Ancient Medicine*, in *The Presocratics*, 2, p. 270.

5. From *Precepts and Maxims*, in *The Presocratics*, 4, p. 273.

6. See Aristotle *Posterior Analytics* 2.19.100a1–100b17, trans. G. R. G. Mure, in *Basic Works of Aristotle.* Another Hippocratic text has it: "In the healing art, as in wisdom generally, use is not something that can be taught. Nature was at work before any teaching began, and it is the part of wisdom to make adjustments to the situation that nature has provided" (*Precepts and Maxims*, in *The Presocratics*, ed. P. Wheelwright, 6, p. 274).

7. *Precepts and Maxims*, in *The Presocratics*, 5, pp. 273–74.

8. *Precepts and Maxims*, in *The Presocratics*, 7, p. 274.

9. From *The Sacred Malady*, in *The Presocratics*, 21, p. 266.

10. From *The Sacred Malady*, in *The Presocratics*, 21, pp. 263, 267, 272. Illness, which begins with an excess of some physiological function over the rest, is overcome by assisting the physical body in generating its own self-healing process (*pepsis*). The physician's art therefore consists in watching for the "opportune moment" (*kairos*) to intervene, thus contributing in a salutary manner at the "turning point" (*krisis*). *Pepsis* therefore expresses a telic principle, which in turn governs the methodological procedures embedded in the concepts of *kairos* and *krisis*.

11. From *The Nature of Man*, in *The Presocratics*, 2, p. 268.

12. From *The Nature of Man*, in *The Presocratics*, 5, p. 269.

13. Plato *Phaedo* 86b, trans. H. Tredennick, in *The Collected Dialogues of Plato*, p. 68; Aristotle *Metaphysics* 1.5.985b22, 987a13; 13.6.1080b16; 14.3.1090a20.

14. *The Presocratics*, ed. P. Wheelwright, T 30, p. 223.

15. Ibid., 1, p. 54.

16. Aristotle *Physics* 3.4.203b6, cited in *The Presocratics*, p. 55.

17. From Diogenes Laertius 1.1–2, cited in *The Presocratics*, T 5, pp. 55–56.

18. From Pseudo-Plutarch *Stromata*, cited in *The Presocratics*, T 10, p. 57.

19. Ibid., 1, 2, p. 69.

20. Ibid., 24, p. 71.

21. Ibid., 120, p. 79.

22. Ibid., 123, 122, p. 79.

23. Copernicus, *De Revolutionibus Orbium Coelestium*, bk. I, chap. 10, cited in John Herman Randall, *The Career of Philosophy: From the Middle Ages to the Renaissance* (New York: Columbia University Press, 1962), p. 312.

24. *The Presocratics*, ed. P. Wheelwright, 1, 2, 10, 16, pp. 231–234.

25. See Albert Einstein, *The World As I See It*, trans. Alan Harris (New York: The Wisdom Library, n.d.), p. 29.

26. It is tempting to develop this analogy further in view of the seemingly Pythagorean language with which Einstein expresses what he calls cosmic religious feeling. In a passage reminiscent of the Pythagorean metaphor of the soul imprisoned in the body, Einstein writes: "The individual feels the nothingness of human desires and aims and the sublimity and marvelous order which reveal themselves both in nature and in the world of thought. He looks upon indi-

vidual existence as a sort of prison and wants to experience the universe as a single significant whole" (ibid., p. 26). An archic analysis reveals, however, that Einstein's method of articulation is agonistic and his perspective objective, which aligns his text in principle, method, and perspective with that of Anaximander. It differs from the latter, and Pythagoras and Plato as well, in its existential sense of reality.

27. Aristotle *Metaphysics* 1.3.984a5, cited in *The Presocratics*, ed. P. Wheelwright.

28. *The Presocratics*, p. 60.

29. Ibid., T 5, p. 62.

30. Ibid., T 6, p. 62.

31. Ibid., T 7, p. 62.

32. Ibid., T 9, p. 62.

33. Ibid., T 13, p. 63.

34. Ibid., T 14, p. 63.

35. Ibid., 6, 8, 11, p. 127.

36. Ibid., 6, p. 97.

37. Ibid., 1, 3, p. 96.

38. Ibid., 7 (A), p. 97.

39. Ibid., 7 (C), (D), p. 98. The power of Parmenides' elemental principle is further exhibited in such teachings as the following: "Thinking and the object of thought are the same. For you will not find thought apart from being, nor either of them apart from utterance. Indeed, there is not anything at all apart from being, because Fate has bound it together so as to be whole and immovable" (ibid., 1, 7 (E), p. 96); and "Since there has to be limit, Being is complete on every side, like the mass of a well-rounded sphere, equally balanced in every direction from the center. . . . The All is inviolable. Since it is equal to itself in all directions, it must be homogeneous within the limits" (ibid., p. 97).

40. *The Presocratics*, 1, p. 258. See W. K. C. Guthrie, *The Sophists* (Cambridge: Cambridge University Press, 1971). Aristotle, in the *Metaphysics*, 4.2.1004b22–26, trans. W. D. Ross, has his own version of this: "For sophistic and dialectic turn on the same class of things as philosophy, but this differs from dialectic in the nature of the faculty required and from sophistic in respect of the purpose of the philosophic life. Dialectic is merely critical where philosophy claims to know, and sophistic is what appears to be philosophy but is not."

41. Plato *Protagoras* 328b, trans. W. K. C. Guthrie: "I have adopted the following method of assessing my payment. Anyone who comes to learn from me may either pay the fee I ask for or, if he prefers, go to a temple, state on oath what he believes to be the worth of my instruction, and deposit that amount."

42. Aristotle *Metaphysics* 4.4.1007b20, trans. W. D. Ross.

43. Aristotle *Metaphysics* 1.5.986b21, cited in *The Presocratics*, ed. P. Wheelwright; W. D. Ross, in *Basic Works of Aristotle*, translates it as follows: "Xenophanes, the first of these partisans of the One (for Parmenides is said to have been his pupil) gave no clear statement. . . ." (p. 699).

44. *The Presocratics*, ed. P. Wheelwright, T 4, p. 37; see Wheelwright's arrangement of extant fragments, 1–4, p. 32. On Xenophanes' reflexive principle, see Watson, *The Architectonics of Meaning*, pp. 136–37.

45. *The Presocratics*, ed. P. Wheelwright, T 8, p. 38. This passage demonstrates not only Xenophanes' reflexive principle, but also his personal perspective; for the latter, see also Fragments, 5–10, 12, 20, 22, 24, pp. 33–36, and Watson, *The Architectonics of Meaning*, pp. 16–17. Xenophanes' essentialism is made clear in his distinction between God and men, his praise of ritual and intelligence, and his sense of the gradations in human excellence; see Wheelwright's Fragments 21–22, pp. 34–35. The archic profile of Xenophanes' text reappears in a modern form in Allan Bloom's *The Closing of the American Mind*. Bloom writes from a personal perspective in an agonistic form, while his emphasis on the resources of the "great books"—with their doctrines of the dignity of the soul, the teleology of human nature, and autonomy of mind—reveals an essential reality and reflexive principle. Given its configuration of archic elements, Bloom's text satirizes the current state of affairs in the university and in modern society at large, but does not provide any positive solution to the problems it describes.

46. *The Presocratics*, T 9, 38.

47. Aristotle *De Anima* 1.2.405a20; 1.5.411a.7, trans. J. A. Smith.

48. Aristotle *Metaphysics* 1.3.983b20–27, trans. W. D. Ross. Thales put his creative principle to work as a military engineer, as reported by Herodotus (*The Persian Wars* 1.170), and demonstrated his practical acumen in cornering an olive market (from Aristotle *Politics* 1.11.1259a5–22; cf. *The Presocratics*, ed. P. Wheelwright, p. 44.

5. The Principles of Confucian Philosophy

1. *Mo Tzu: Basic Writings*, trans. Burton Watson (New York: Columbia University Press, 1963), pp. 15, 21, 63ff.

2. Ibid., p. 86.

3. Ibid., pp. 40, 83–84, 88.

4. *A Source Book in Chinese Philosophy*, trans. and comp. Wing-tsit Chan (Princeton: Princeton University Press, 1963), p. 212.

5. *Mo Tzu: Basic Writings*, trans. Burton Watson, pp. 6, 50ff.

6. Ibid., pp. 131ff.

7. Ibid., pp. 18, 22, 29.

8. Ibid., pp. 83–84, 91–92.

9. See *A Source Book in Chinese Philosophy*, trans. and comp. Wing-tsit Chan, pp. 14–18; *Sources of Chinese Tradition*, ed. Wm. T. de Bary, 2 vols. (New York: Columbia University Press, 1964), vol. 1, pp. 15–20. See also Arthur Waley, *The Analects of Confucius* (London: Allen and Unwin, 1939); Fung Yu-lan, *A History of Chinese Philosophy*, 2 vols., trans. Derk Bodde (Princeton: Princeton University

Press, 1952–53); and *A Short History of Chinese Philosophy* (New York: Macmillan, 1948).

10. *Analects,* bk. 2, chap. 3; bk. 3, chap. 15; bk. 19, chap. 23; bk. 5, chap. 15; bk. 6, chaps. 23, 25; bk. 8, chap. 2; bk. 12, chaps. 11, 15–17, 19, 32, in *Confucius: Confucian Analects, The Great Learning, and the Doctrine of the Mean,* translated with exegetical notes by James Legge (New York: Dover Publications, 1971). See Julia Ching, *Confucianism and Christianity: A Comparative Study* (Tokyo: Kodansha International, 1977), and Herbert Fingarette, *Confucius: The Secular as Sacred* (New York: Harper Torchbook, 1972).

11. *Analects,* bk. 1, chap. 2; bk. 8, chaps. 19–20.

12. Ibid., bk. 6, chap. 25.

13. Ibid., bk. 14, chap. 13: "Tze-lu asked what constituted a complete man. The Master said, Suppose a man with the knowledge of Tsang Wu-chung, the freedom from covetousness of Kung-ch'o, the bravery of Chwang of Pien, and the varied talents of Tsan Ch'iu; add to these the accomplishments of the rules of propriety and music:—such an one might be reckoned a complete man."

14. See the thematic analysis of the *Analects* provided by Wing-tsit Chan in *A Source Book in Chinese Philosophy,* p. 18.

15. *Analects,* bk. 4, chap. 15; bk. 15, chap. 2.

16. *The Great Learning,* Text, 3, in *Confucius,* trans. J. Legge, p. 357.

17. Ibid.

18. Ibid., Commentary, 5, pp. 365–66.

19. *The Doctrine of the Mean,* in *Confucius,* trans. J. Legge, bk. 1, chap. 1, p. 383.

20. Passages such as the following can be traced through centuries of Confucian philosophy in East Asia:

> How great is the Way of the Sages!
> Like overflowing water, it sends forth and nourishes all things, and rises up to the height of Heaven.
> All-complete is its greatness! It embraces the three
> hundred rules of ceremony, and the three thousand rules of demeanor.
> It waits for the proper man, and then it is trodden.
> Hence it is said, 'Only by perfect virtue can the perfect path, in all its courses, be made a fact.'
>
> Therefore, the superior man honors his virtuous nature, and mantains constant inquiry and study, seeking to carry it out to its breadth and greatness, so as to omit none of the more exquisite and minute points which it embraces, and to raise it to its greatest height and brilliancy, so as to pursue the course of the Mean. He cherishes his old knowledge, and is continually acquiring new. He exerts an honest, generous earnestness, in the esteem and practice of all propriety. (*The Doctrine of the Mean,* bk. 27, in *Confucius,* trans. J. Legge)

21. Ibid., bk. 1, chap. 4, pp. 384–85.

22. Ibid., bk. 14, chap. 1, p. 395.

23. *Mencius*, bk. 1, pt. 1, chap. 3, sec. 3, in *The Works of Mencius*, translated, with critical and exegetical notes, by James Legge (New York: Dover, 1970). See *Mencius*, trans. and arranged W. A. C. H. Dobson (Toronto: University of Toronto Press, 1963).

24. *Mencius*, bk. 1, pt. 1, chap. 7, sec. 5, in *The Works of Mencius*, trans. J. Legge.

25. Ibid., bk. 1, pt. 1, chap. 7, sec. 9.

26. Ibid., bk. 1, pt. 2, chap. 1, sec. 8; chap. 3, secs. 2–3; chap. 5, secs. 4–5.

27. Ibid., bk. 4, pt. 1, chap. 1, secs. 1–3.

28. Ibid., bk. 2, pt. 1, chap. 2, sec. 7.

29. Ibid., bk. 4, pt. 2, chap. 12.

30. Ibid., bk. 2, pt. 1, chap. 7, sec. 2.

31. Ibid., bk. 4, pt. 1, chap. 28.

32. Ibid., bk. 4, pt. 1, chap. 9, sec. 2.

33. Ibid., bk. 6, pt. 1, chap. 1, secs. 1–3.

34. Ibid., bk. 2, pt. 1, chap. 2, secs. 11–16.

35. Ibid., bk. 2, pt. 1, chap. 6, secs. 1–7; bk. 6, pt. 1, chap. 6, sec. 4; bk. 2, pt. 2, chap. 7, secs. 2–4.

36. *Hsün Tzu: Basic Writings*, trans. Burton Watson (New York: Columbia University Press, 1963), pp. 15–16, 18, 30.

37. *Hsün Tzu: Basic Writings*, trans. Burton Watson, sec. 9, pp. 44, 46–47.

38. Ibid., sec. 7, p. 86; see sec. 9, pp. 43, 48.

39. Ibid., sec. 23, p. 158: "Mencius states that man is capable of learning because his nature is good, but I say that this is wrong. It indicates that he has not really understood man's nature nor distinguished properly between the basic nature and conscious activity. The nature is that which is given by Heaven; you cannot learn it, you cannot acquire it by effort. Ritual principles, on the other hand, are created by sages; you can learn them, you can work to bring them to completion."

40. *Mo Tzu: Basic Writings*, trans. Burton Watson, sec. 29, pp. 130–36.

41. *Analects*, bk. 2, chap. 10; bk. 5, chap. 27; bk. 6, chap. 2; bk. 11, chap. 16; bk. 19, chap. 17.

42. Ibid., bk. 2, chap. 23; bk. 3, chap. 24.

43. Ibid., bk. 7, chaps. 1–3.

44. Ibid., bk. 16, chap. 8.

45. Ibid., bk. 14, chap. 27; bk. 7, chap. 22.

46. Ibid., bk. 20, chap. 3.

47. *Mencius*, bk. 1, pt. 2, chap. 3, secs. 2–3; chap. 4, sec. 3; chap. 15, sec. 3; bk. 4, pt. 1, chap. 4, sec. 3; bk. 2, pt. 1, chap. 7, sec. 12.

48. Ibid., bk. 4, pt. 1, chaps. 1ff.; chap. 2, secs. 1–2.

49. Ibid., bk. 7, pt. 1, chap. 1, secs. 1–3; chap. 2.

50. Ibid., bk. 4, pt. 1, chap. 12, secs. 2–3.

51. *The Great Learning*, Commentary, sec. 1, subsecs. 1–2.

52. Ibid., sec. 6, subsec. 1.

53. *The Doctrine of the Mean*, bks. 21, 23, 24.

54. Ibid., bk. 20, chap. 18.

55. Ibid., bk. 14, chap. 4; bk. 17, chap. 4.

56. Ibid., bk. 1, chap. 1.

57. *Hsün Tzu: Basic Writings*, trans. Burton Watson, pp. 21–38.

58. Ibid., p. 125.

59. Ibid., pp. 141–43, 147, 149.

60. Ibid., pp. 79–81.

61. Ibid., p. 85.

62. *Mencius*, bk. 1, pt. 1, chap. 1, sec. 3.

63. Ibid., bk. 4, pt. 2, chap. 19, secs. 1–2.

64. Ibid., bk. 3, pt. 1, chap. 4, secs. 17–18; bk. 7, pt. 1, chaps. 46–47; pt. 2, chap. 17.

65. Ibid., bk. 1, pt. 1, chap. 5, sec. 2.

66. Ibid., bk. 6, pt. 1, chaps. 15 and 19.

67. *Hsün Tzu: Basic Writings*, trans. Burton Watson, p. 18.

68. Ibid., p. 87.

69. Ibid., p. 87.

70. Ibid., p. 94.

71. *The Doctrine of the Mean*, bk. 22.

72. See *Analects*, bk. 7, chaps. 1, 3; bk. 4, chap. 5; bk. 10, chap. 12; bk. 6, chap. 20; bk. 11, chap. 11, and passim.

73. *A Source Book in Chinese Philosophy*, trans. and comp. Wing-tsit Chan, pp. 18 and ref.; de Bary, *Sources of Chinese Tradition*, vol. 1, pp. 30–32.

74. See *The I Ching or Book of Changes*, trans. Richard Wilhelm and Cary F. Baynes, 3d ed. (Princeton: Princeton University Press, 1967); Richard Wilhelm, *Lectures on the I Ching: Constancy and Change*, trans. Irene Eber (Princeton: Princeton University Press, 1979); Hellmut Wilhelm, *Change: Eight Lectures on the I Ching*, trans. Cary F. Baynes (Princeton: Princeton University Press, 1973).

75. *A Source Book in Chinese Philosophy*, trans. and comp. Wing-tsit Chan, p. 244.

76. Ibid., p. 262–63.

77. Ibid., p. 244.

78. Ibid., p. 247.

79. Ibid.

80. Ibid., pp. 249–50.

81. Ibid., pp. 248–49.

82. Ibid., pp. 271–72.

83. Ibid., pp. 279–88.

6. Chinese Philosophies in World Perspective

1. *Tao Te Ching*, 1, in *The Way of Life according to Lao Tzu*, trans. Witter Bynner (New York: Capricorn Books, 1944), p. 25. Cf. *The Way and Its Power*, trans.

Arthur Waley (London: Allen and Unwin, 1935); Wing-tsit Chan, *The Way of Lao Tzu, A Translation and Study of the Tao-Te Ching* (New York: Bobbs-Merrill, 1963); *Tao Teh Ching,* trans. John C. H. Wu (New York: St. John's University Press, 1961); *Tao Te Ching,* trans. Gia-fu Feng and Jane English (New York: Vintage Books, 1972); *A Source Book in Chinese Philosophy,* trans. and comp. Wing-tsit Chan, pp. 136–176.

2. Witter Bynner also captures the point that Lao Tzu's Tao is an elemental life-force in such passages as the following:

> Bountiful life, letting anyone attend,
> Making no distinction between left and right,
> Feeding everyone, refusing no one,
> Has not provided this bounty to show how much it owns,
> Has not fed and clad its guests with any thought of claim. (34)
>
> Who will prefer the jingle of jade pendants if
> He once has heard stone growing in a cliff! (39)
>
> There is no difference between the quick and the dead,
> They are one channel of vitality. (60)

Tao Te Ching, trans. Witter Bynner, pp. 46–47, 51, 63

3. Ibid., 43, trans. Witter Bynner, p. 53.

4. Ibid., 59, trans. Witter Bynner, p. 63.

5. Ibid., 35, trans. Witter Bynner, p. 47.

6. Ibid., 80, trans. Witter Bynner, pp. 75–76.

7. *Chuang Tzu: Basic Writings,* trans. Burton Watson (New York: Columbia University Press, 1964), pp. 6–7. See *The Complete Works of Chuang Tzu,* trans. Burton Watson (New York: Columbia University Press, 1968); *Chuang Tzu: Mystic, Moralist, and Social Reformer,* trans. Herbert A. Giles (London: Allen and Unwin, 1961); *A Source Book in Chinese Philosophy,* trans. and comp. Wing-tsit Chan, pp. 177–210.

8. *Chuang Tzu: Basic Writings,* trans. Burton Watson, p. 27.

9. Ibid., pp. 41–42.

10. Ibid., pp. 50, 53.

11. Ibid., p. 35.

12. Ibid., p. 77.

13. Ibid., p. 82.

14. Ibid., pp. 83, 90–91.

15. Ibid., p. 108.

16. Ibid., pp. 48–80.

17. Ibid., pp. 95, 102.

18. Ibid., p. 140.

19. Ibid., p. 23.

20. Ibid., p. 26.

21. Ibid., p. 31.

22. Ibid., p. 33.
23. Ibid., pp. 34, 37.
24. Ibid., p. 113.
25. Ibid., pp. 114–15.
26. Ibid., pp. 24–25, 31, 33.
27. Ibid., p. 54.
28. *Han Fei Tzu: Basic Writings*, trans. Burton Watson (New York: Columbia University Press, 1963), pp. 84–85, 101.
29. Ibid., pp. 5, 11, 34, 40, 85.
30. Ibid., pp. 16–19, 34, 37–39.
31. Ibid., p. 30. The comparison of the Legalist doctrine with that of Machiavelli's *The Prince* inevitably suggests itself. There are two archic differences. Machiavelli's text is disciplinary in perspective and elemental in principle. This elemental principle manifests itself in his constant refrain that a prince must study the lessons of the past. He writes: "I bring forward very exalted instances, for men walk almost always in the path trodden by others, proceeding in their actions by imitation." His agonistic method is typically evidenced in the following: "A prince should therefore have no other aim or thought, nor take up any other thing for his study, but war and its organisation and discipline. . . . The chief cause of the loss of states, is the contempt of this art, and the way to acquire them is to be well versed in the same." Machiavelli consistently focuses on a substrative reality of human passions. See Niccoló Machiavelli, *The Prince*, trans. Luigi Ricci (New York: New American Library, 1952), pp. 48, 81, 92, and passim. See also *Machiavelli, The Prince and The Discourses* (New York: Modern Library, 1940).
32. See *A Source Book in Chinese Philosophy*, trans. and comp. Wing-tsit Chan, p. 232.
33. Ibid., pp. 235–42.
34. Kung-sun Lung, "On Names and Actuality," chap. 6 in *A Source Book in Chinese Philosophy*, p. 243.
35. Ibid., p. 232.
36. *Chuang Tzu*, chaps. 24 and 33, excerpted in *A Source Book in Chinese Philosophy*.
37. Ibid., pp. 233–34.
38. Wang Ch'ung, *Lun Heng*, 2 vols., pt. 1: Philosophical Essays of Wang Ch'ung, and pt. 2: Miscellaneous Essays of Wang Ch'ung, trans. Alfred Forke (London: Luzac, 1907–11). Forke's introductory essay is still good. It discusses the life, works, and philosophy of Wang Ch'ung, and summarizes the table of contents of the *Lun Heng*. Written in the first century A.D., this is surely one of the classics of Chinese and world philosophy.
39. See *A Source Book in Chinese Philosophy*, trans. and comp. Wing-tsit Chan, pp. 292–93.
40. Wang Ch'ung, *Lun Heng*, sec. 56, in *A Source Book in Chinese Philosophy*, p. 304.

41. *Lun Heng*, sec. 13, in *A Source Book in Chinese Philosophy*, pp. 293–96, 298.

42. "Yang Chu Chapter," in *A Source Book in Chinese Philosophy*, p. 310.

43. *A Source Book in Chinese Philosophy*, p. 311.

44. Ibid., pp. 310–11.

45. Ibid., p. 589.

46. Ibid. See *Reflections on Things at Hand: The Neo-Confucian Anthology, Compiled by Chu Hsi and Lu Tsu-ch'ien*, trans. Wing-tsit Chan (New York: Columbia University Press, 1967); *Neo-Confucian Terms Explained (The Pei-hsi tzu-i), by Ch'en Ch'un, 1159–1223*, trans. and ed. with intro. by Wing-tsit Chan (New York: Columbia University Press, 1986).

47. On Lo Ch'in-shun's position, see Irene Bloom, "On the 'Abstraction' of Ming Thought: Some Concrete Evidence from the Philosophy of Lo Ch'in-shun," in *Principle and Practicality: Essays in Neo-Confucianism and Practical Learning*, ed. Wm. T. de Bary and Irene Bloom, (New York: Columbia University Press, 1979), pp. 69–126; *Knowledge Painfully Acquired: The K'un-chih chi by Lo Ch'in-shun*, ed. and trans. Irene Bloom (New York: Columbia University Press, 1987).

48. See the series of Neo-Confucian Studies published by Columbia University Press: *Self and Society in Ming Thought*, by Wm. T. de Bary and the Conference on Ming Thought (1970); *The Unfolding of Neo-Confucianism*, by Wm. T. de Bary and the Conference on Seventeenth-Century Chinese Thought (1975); *Principle and Practicality: Essays in Neo-Confucianism and Practical Learning*, ed. Wm. T. de Bary and Irene Bloom (1979); Wm. T. de Bary, *Neo-Confucian Orthodoxy and the Learning of the Mind-and-Heart* (1981); *Yuan Thought: Chinese Thought and Religion Under the Mongols*, ed. Hok-lam Chan and Wm. T. de Bary (1983); Wm T. de Bary, *The Liberal Tradition in China* (1983); *The Rise of Neo-Confucianism in Korea*, ed. Wm. T. de Bary and JaHyun Kim Haboush (1985).

49. In an important work of intellectual history, *The Message of the Mind in Neo-Confucian Thought, 1200–1850* (New York: Columbia University Press, 1988), Wm. T. de Bary traces the "succession of the Way" (*tao-t'ung*) of the Ch'eng-Chu school from the Sung through the Ch'ing dynasties. He demonstrates that the Lu-Wang school is primarily a brain-child of Wang Yang-ming himself, and describes the line of "orthodox" and "neo-orthodox" adherents to Chu Hsi thought up into the mid-nineteenth century. De Bary provides detailed analyses of the Ming thinkers Ts'ao Tuan (1376–1434), Hsüeh Hsüan (1389–1464), Hu Chü-jen (1434–84), Chou Ch'i (n.d.), Wu Yü-pi (1392–1461), Ch'en Chien (1497–1567), T'ang Po-yüan (*chin shih* degree, 1574), Teng Yüan-shi (1529–93), and Chang Huang (1527–1608), the last two affiliated with a more conservative Wang Yang-ming school; and of the Ch'ing thinkers Sun Ch'i-feng (1585–1675), T'ang Pin (1627–87), Lü Liu-liang (1629–83), Chang Lü-hsiang (1611–74), Lu Shih-i (1611–72), Li Yung (1627–1705), Lu Lung-ch'i (1630–93), Li Kuang-ti (1642–1718), Chang Po-hsing (1652–1725), Chu Shih (1665–1736), and Fang Tung-shu (1772–1851).

50. Chou Tun-i, *Explanation of the Diagram of the Great Ultimate and Penetrating*

the Book of Changes, chaps. 1–4, trans. Wing-tsit Chan, in *A Source Book in Chinese Philosophy*, pp. 463–67.

51. See Shao Yung, *Supreme Principles Governing the World*, chaps. 27, 29, 30; Chang Tsai, *The Western Inscription*, and *Correcting Youthful Ignorance*, chaps. 3, 20, 22, 24, 30, and passim; in *A Source Book in Chinese Philosophy*, trans. and comp. Wing-tsit Chan, pp. 493–94, 497–98, 507–8, and passim.

52. Ibid., p. 483. Shao Yung, *Supreme Principles Governing the World*, chaps. 7, 9, 12, 17, 23, and passim, in *A Source Book in Chinese Philosophy*, pp. 487–91.

53. See the systematization of Chu Hsi's sayings in Wing-tsit Chan, *A Source Book in Chinese Philosophy*, p. 593, Principle (*li*) and Material Force (*ch'i*), secs. 100–13, pp. 634–38; and *Sources of Chinese Tradition*, vol. 1, ed. Wm. T. de Bary, pp. 481ff.

54. Ch'eng Hao, Selected Sayings, 12, trans. Wing-tsit Chan, in *A Source Book in Chinese Philosophy*, p. 531.

55. See Wang Yang-ming, *Instructions for Practical Living and Other Neo-Confucian Writings*, trans. Wing-tsit Chan (New York: Columbia University Press, 1963); Julia Ching, *To Acquire Wisdom: The Way of Wang Yang-ming* (New York: Columbia University Press, 1976); *A Source Book in Chinese Philosophy*, trans. and comp. Wing-tsit Chan, pp. 654–91; *Sources of Chinese Tradition*, vol. 1, ed. Wm. T. de Bary, pp. 514–29.

56. As one example of this archic shift, Chu Hsi, with his comprehensive principle and dialectical method, had included the heteroarchic Mencius in the Neo-Confucian canon of the Four Books (while excluding Hsün Tzu). Wang Yang-ming, however, called upon Mencius's own principle of original mind to displace the basis of Chu Hsi's thought. He did so from the strength of his own elemental principle, an exemplary version of which we see in the following citation:

> The Teacher said, The innate knowledge of man is the same as that of plants and trees, tiles and stones. Without the innate knowledge inherent in man, there cannot be plants and trees, tiles and stones. This is not true of them only. Even Heaven and Earth cannot exist without the innate knowledge that is inherent in man. For at bottom Heaven, Earth, the myriad things, and man form one body. The point at which this unity manifests its most refined and excellent form is the clear intelligence of the human mind. Wind, rain, dew, thunder, sun and moon, stars, animals and plants, mountains and rivers, earth and stones are essentially of one body with man. (Wang Yang-ming, *Instructions for Practical Living*, sec. 274, trans. Wing-tsit Chan, p. 685)

For Wang Yang-ming and his followers, everything follows from this elemental identity of man and the universe.

57. For the Wang Yang-ming school in the Ming dynasty, see especially the monumental work, *The Records of Ming Scholars, by Huang Tsung-shi*, a selected translation, ed. by Julia Ching, with the collaboration of Chao-ying Fang (Hono-

lulu: University of Hawaii Press, 1987). Huang Tsung-shi (1610–95), a Ming loyalist, is credited with writing over one hundred books. His *Ming-ju hsüeh-an* has been especially appreciated as a classic of intellectual history in its own genre. A work in sixty-two *chüan,* it gathers and preserves approximately 200 individual lines of Ming thought. Twenty-seven of those *chüan,* almost two-fifths of the book, are devoted to the central figure of Wang Yang-ming (1472–1529), and to the regional variations of the Wang Yang-ming schools of the Ming dynasty. This English edition provides a selective translation of sixteen schools, plus a group of miscellaneous thinkers, amounting to some forty representative Ming philosophers. Julia Ching complements her own extensive introduction and epilogue with various useful appendices. These include a chart of the schools of the Ming, a sixteen-page glossary of technical terms, selected bibliographies, and a glossary of transliterations.

58. For basic sources and an overview, see *Sources of Japanese Tradition,* ed. R. Tsunoda, Wm. T. de Bary, and D. Keene (New York: Columbia University Press, 1958), vol. 1, chaps. 16, 17, 18, and 21. For formulations of the pluralistic nature of Tokugawa Neo-Confucianism, which gradually attained its full potential in keeping with Chinese traditions, see Wm. T. de Bary, "Sagehood as a Secular and Spiritual Ideal in Tokugawa Neo-Confucianism," and David A. Dilworth, "Jitsugaku as an Ontological Conception: Continuities and Discontinuities in Early and Mid-Tokugawa Thought," in *Principle and Practicality: Essays in Neo-Confucianism and Practical Learning,* ed. Wm. T. de Bary and Irene Bloom, pp. 127–188 and pp. 471–514, respectively. These views stand in contrast to those of Maruyama Masao, *Studies in the Intellectual History of Tokugawa Japan* (Princeton: Princeton University Press, 1974), who emphasized the "dissolution" of seventeenth-century "orthodoxy" by the school of Ogyū Sorai. More recently, Herman Ooms, *Tokugawa Ideology: Early Constructs, 1570–1680* (Princeton: Princeton University Press, 1985), has provided a radically "political," that is, "ideological," portrait of early Tokugawa intellectual history. Challenging the interpretations of de Bary, Maruyama, and others, Ooms changes philosophical ideas as civilizational resources into localized "constructs" of contingent power. This is a reductionistic function of the Sophistic elements of his own hermeneutical act. Ooms in fact aligns himself with a variety of like-minded interpreters, such as Polanyi, Habermas, Foucault, Barthes, Derrida, and others. See Ooms, *Tokugawa Ideology,* chap. 1, "Introduction: Beginnings," pp. 3–17, and passim.

59. I am especially indebted to Mary Evelyn Tucker for many discussions of these materials of Tokugawa intellectual history. See her *Moral and Spiritual Cultivation in Japanese Neo-Confucianism: The Life and Thought of Kaibara Ekken (1630–1714)* (Ph.D. dissertation, Columbia University, 1986), chap. 1, "Neo-Confucianism in the Tokugawa Period," pp. 2–43 and references. In archic profile, the texts of the *kogaku* scholars Yamaga Sokō, Itō Jinsai, and Itō Tōgai all derive from that of Confucius (which is diaphanic, essential, agonistic, and comprehensive); Ogyū Sorai differed from this group, as well as from the Neo-

Confucian schools, by returning to the creative principle of Hsün Tzu and the Legalists (his archic profile is diaphanic, essential, agonistic, and creative). See *Sources of Japanese Tradition*, ed. Tsunoda, de Bary, and Keene, vol. 1, chap. 18, "The Rediscovery of Confucianism," pp. 384–423; and *Ogyū Sorai's Distinguishing the Way*, trans. Olof G. Lidin (Tokyo: Sophia University Press, 1970).

7. Early Modern Western Philosophy

1. Francis Bacon, *Novum Organum*, bk. 2, sec. 52, in *The English Philosophers: From Bacon to Mill*, ed. Edwin A. Burtt (New York: Random House, 1939), p. 123.

2. Francis Bacon, *The Great Instauration*, Prooemium, in *The English Philosophers*, p. 5.

3. Bacon, *The Great Instauration*, Preface, in *The English Philosophers*, p. 6.

4. Ibid., p. 12.

5. Ibid., p. 16.

6. See David Hume, *A Treatise of Human Nature*, ed. L. A. Selby-Bigge and P. H. Nidditch, 2d ed. (Oxford: Oxford University Press, 1978), Introduction, p. xvii.

7. Ibid., p. 23.

8. Bacon, *Novum Organum*, Preface, in *The English Philosophers*, p. 24.

9. Bacon, *The Great Instauration*, in *The English Philosophers*, p. 17. Bacon goes on to say: "And thus I conceive that I perform the office of a true priest of sense (from which all knowledge in nature must be sought, unless men mean to go mad) and a not unskillful interpreter of its oracles; and that while others only profess to uphold and cultivate the sense, I do so in fact" (pp. 17–18).

10. Ibid., p. 18.

11. Bacon, *Novum Organum*, Aphorisms, bk. 1, secs. 38–62, in *The English Philosophers*.

12. Ibid., sec. 63.

13. Ibid., sec. 72: "But the elder of the Greek philosophers, Empedocles, Anaxagoras, Leucippus, Democritus, Parmenides, Heraclitus, Xenophanes, Philolaus, and the rest (I omit Pythagoras as a mystic), did not, so far as we know, open schools: but more silently and severely and simply,—that is, with less affectation and parade,—betook themselves to the inquisition of truth. And therefore they were in my judgment more successful. . . ."

14. Ibid., sec. 70.

15. Ibid., bk. 2, sec. 7. In a later passage Bacon repeats this point, saying "We must make therefore a complete solution and separation of nature, not indeed by fire, but by the mind, which is a kind of divine fire" (sec. 16).

16. Ibid.

17. Ibid., sec. 17.

18. As a subordinate version of the latter he produces a lexicon of prerogative

instances, supports of induction, rectification to induction, and so on. Under prerogative instances alone he details twenty-seven kinds (ibid., secs. 11, 12, 13, and 15).

19. A century later Hume was to reformulate Bacon's logistic method, now transmuted by an existential ontology, in his theory of the association of ideas; he applied the same method in his theory of morals. See *An Enquiry Concerning the Principles of Morals,* sec. 5, pt. 2, no. 178, in David Hume, *Enquiries Concerning Human Understanding and Concerning the Principles of Morals,* ed. L. A. Selby-Bigge and P. H. Nidditch, 3d ed. (Oxford: Oxford University Press, 1975), p. 219.

20. Bacon changes the Democritean paradigm by a reflexive principle. Thus he disagrees with Democritus's elemental principle of the self-sameness of the material particles, but articulates his own version of the latter's logistic method, combined with an objective perspective and substrative reality. See *Novum Organum,* bk. 2, sec. 8.

21. Aristotle characterizes Anaxagoras's text as substrative in reality and logistic in method in *Metaphysics* 1.3.984a12–16: "Anaxagoras of Clazomenae . . . says the principles are infinite in number; for he says almost all the things that are made of parts like themselves, in the manner of water or fire, are generated and destroyed in this way, only by aggregation and segregation, and are not in any sense generated or destroyed, but remain eternally." He identified Anaxagoras's reflexive principle in *Metaphysics* 1.3.984b15–20: "When one man said, then, that reason was present—as in animals, so throughout nature—as the cause of order and of all arrangement, he seemed like a sober man in contrast with the random talk of his predecessors. We know that Anaxagoras certainly adopted these views, but Herotimus of Clazomenae is credited with expressing them earlier. Those who thought thus stated that there is a principle of things which is at the same time the cause of beauty, and that sort of cause from which things acquire movement." Aristotle then criticizes Anaxagoras in *Metaphysics* 1.4.955a19–21: "For Anaxagoras uses reason as a *deus ex machina* for the making of the world, and when he is at a loss to tell from what cause something necessarily is, he then drags reason in, but in all other cases ascribes events to anything rather than to reason" (Trans. W. D. Ross, in *Introduction to Aristotle,* ed. Richard McKeon [New York: Modern Library, 1947]).

22. Bacon's Anaxagorean joining of a reflexive principle with an objective perspective, substrative reality, and logistic method is illustrated by the following: "For a true and perfect axiom of knowledge then the direction and precept will be, that another nature be discovered which is convertible with the given nature, and yet is a limitation of a more general nature, as of a true and real genus. Now these two directions, the one active and the other contemplative, are one and the same thing; and what in operation is most useful, that in knowledge is most true" (*Novum Organum,* bk. 2, sec. 5).

23. See Descartes, *Second Replies to Objections,* Axioms or Common Notions, 6: "There are diverse degrees of reality, that is, of being: for substance has more

reality than accident or mode, and infinite substance than finite. Hence also there is more objective reality in the idea of substance than in that of accident, and in the idea of infinite than in the idea of finite substance" (*Secundae Responsiones,* Adam and Tannery ed., [Paris, 1904], 155ff., as cited in *Philosophers Speak for Themselves: From Descartes to Locke,* ed. T. V. Smith and Marjorie Grene [Chicago: University of Chicago Press, 1940], p. 121.) See Descartes, *Meditations on First Philosophy:* "For, without doubt, those that represent substances are something more, and contain in themselves, so to speak, more objective reality (that is, participate by representation in higher degrees of being or perfection), than those that represent only modes or accidents. . . ." (trans. John Veitch, in *Philosophers Speak for Themselves,* p. 74).

24. Descartes, *Discourse on Method,* pt. 1, trans. John Veitch, in *The Rationalists* (Garden City, N.Y.: Doubleday and Co., 1960), p. 40. For exemplary formulations of the logistic rule see Descartes, *Rules for the Direction of the Understanding,* esp. Rules 4–8, in *Philosophers Speak for Themselves: From Descartes to Locke,* ed. T. V. Smith and Marjorie Grene, pp. 16–49.

25. Descartes, *Discourse on Method,* pt. 1, trans. John Veitch, in *The Rationalists,* p. 40.

26. See Descartes, *Meditations on First Philosophy,* Preface to the Reader, trans. John Veitch, cited in *Philosophers Speak for Themselves,* p. 51. See also his *Second Replies to Objections,* in *Philosophers Speak for Themselves,* p. 116.

27. For the combination of the two Cartesian elements, one Aristotelian and one Democritean, in Spinoza's thought, see Benedict de Spinoza, Letter 42 (37), in *On the Improvement of the Understanding, The Ethics, Correspondence,* trans. R. H. M. Elwes (New York: Dover, 1955), pp. 360–61.

28. Spinoza, *Ethics,* bk. 1, Appendix, trans. R. H. M. Elwes, in *The Rationalists.*

29. Ibid.

30. Ibid., bk. 1, definition 1.

31. Ibid., bk. 1, prop. 10. In *Ethics,* bk. 1, prop. 10, Spinoza teaches that "each particular attribute of one substance must be conceived though itself." This is a logistic conception. In the sequel, prop. 11, he says: "God, or substance, consisting of infinite attributes, of which each expresses eternal and infinite essentiality, necessarily exists." This entails both logistic and noumenal presuppositions. Although the human mind is limited to knowing the two attributes of thought and extension, God is "absolutely infinite or perfect" and therefore has an infinite number of attributes.

32. Ibid., bk. 5, prop. 36. It will be seen that Leibniz set out consciously to displace Spinoza's perspective and principle. But he understood Spinoza. Indeed, Leibniz may have been one of the few major philosophers to understand Spinoza. Such thinkers as Hume, Voltaire, Kant, Fichte, Schelling, Hegel, Goethe, Nietzsche, Scheler, Nishida, Einstein, and Santayana interpret Spinoza in ways that are ultimately more revealing of their own views than of Spinoza's. The nineteenth-century philosophers especially tended to misunderstand "the God-drunk Spinoza" as a materialist and an atheist. Running through such

commentaries is a consistent failure to perceive Spinoza's noumenal sense of reality and reflexive principle.

33. Ibid., bk. 5, prop. 22.

34. Ibid., bk. 5, prop. 23.

35. Ibid., bk. 5, prop. 33.

36. Ibid., bk. 5, prop. 36.

37. Ibid., bk. 5, prop. 35.

38. Ibid., bk. 5, prop. 36, Corollary.

39. Ibid., bk. 5, prop. 37.

40. Ibid., bk. 1, Appendix.

41. Leibniz, *Discourse on Metaphysics*, sec. 2b, trans. George Montgomery, in *The Rationalists*, p. 439.

42. Ibid., sec. 28, p. 441.

43. Ibid.

44. "Wise and virtuous persons work in behalf of everything which seems conformable to presumptive or antecedent will of God, and are, nevertheless, content with what God actually brings to pass through his secret, consequent and determining will, recognizing that if we were able to understand sufficiently well the order of the universe, we should find that it surpasses all the desires of the wisest of us, and that it is impossible to render it better than it is, not only for all in general, but also for each one of us in particular, provided that we have the proper attachment for the author of all, not only as the Architect and efficient cause of our being, but also as our Lord and the Final Cause, who ought to be the whole goal of our will, and who alone can make us happy" (Leibniz, *The Monadology*, 89, trans. George Montgomery, in *The Rationalists*, pp. 470–71).

45. See Thomas Hobbes, *De Corpore* and *Of Human Nature*, in *Philosophers Speak for Themselves: From Descartes to Locke*, ed. T. V. Smith and Marjorie Grene, pp. 128–57.

46. Thomas Hobbes, *Leviathan*, ed. Francis B. Randall (New York: Washington Square Press, 1964), Introduction, p. xxvii.

47. Ibid.

48. Hobbes, *Leviathan*, in *English Works of Thomas Hobbes*, ed. Sir Wm. Molesworth (1839–45), vol. 3, p. 113, cited in John Herman Randall, *The Career of Philosophy*, vol. 1, p. 556.

49. Ibid., p. 557.

50. We can map the relationships between the texts of the Chinese Legalists, Machiavelli, and Hobbes in the following set:

	PERSPECTIVE	REALITY	METHOD	PRINCIPLE
Han Fei Tzu	*objective*	*substrative*	*agonistic*	*creative*
Machiavelli	*disciplinary*	*substrative*	*agonistic*	*elemental*
Hobbes	*personal*	*substrative*	*logistic*	*creative*

51. Isaac Newton, *Principia Mathematica Philosophiae Naturalis,* Preface to the First Edition, in *Newton's Philosophy of Nature: Selections From His Writings,* ed. H. S. Thayer (New York: Hafner, 1953), p. 10.

52. Ibid., pp. 41–67, 176.

53. For Newton's substrative reality and creative principle, see also *Newton's Principia: The Mathematical Principles of Natural Philosophy by Sir Isaac Newton,* trans. Andrew Motte (New York: 1846), cited in *Philosophers Speak for Themselves: From Descartes to Locke,* ed. T. V. Smith and Marjorie Grene (Chicago: University of Chicago Press, 1940), p. 337.

54. John Locke, *An Essay Concerning Human Understanding,* bk. 1, chap. 9, par. 27, ed. A. C. Fraser (1894), cited in John Herman Randall, *The Career of Philosophy* (New York: Columbia University Press, 1965), vol. 1.

55. Ibid., bk. 1, chap. 156.

56. Ibid., bk. 2, chap. 184. See also Locke, *An Essay Concerning Human Understanding,* bk. 2, chap. 23, par. 2, "Our Ideas of Sustance in General," cited in *Philosophers Speak for Themselves: From Descartes to Locke,* ed. T. V. Smith and Marjorie Grene. This is the well-known passage that says the world is supported by a great elephant, which rests on a tortoise, and so on indefinitely.

57. See Locke, *An Essay Concerning Human Understanding,* bk. 2, chap. 61, cited in J. H. Randall, *The Career of Philosophy,* vol. 1.

58. See H. R. Fox Bourne, *The Life of John Locke,* 1876, vol. 1, pp. 403–4, as cited in John Locke, *Second Treatise of Government,* ed. with an introduction by C. B. Macpherson (Indianapolis: Hackett Publishing Co., 1980), pp. xi–xii.

59. Locke, *Second Treatise of Government,* par. 96.

60. Ibid., par. 6.

61. Ibid., par. 26.

62. Ibid., par. 27.

63. Ibid., par. 30.

64. Ibid., par. 32.

65. See *The Enlightenment: A Comprehensive Anthology,* ed. Peter Gay (New York: Simon and Schuster, 1973), pp. 571–617.

66. Max Lerner, in Adam Smith, *Inquiry into the Nature and Causes of the Wealth of Nations,* ed. with an intro. by Edwin Cannan, with intro. by Max Lerner (New York: Modern Library, 1937), p. vi.

67. Adam Smith, ibid., p. 423.

68. Ibid., pp. 3–12; *The Enlightenment,* ed. Peter Gay, pp. 577ff. For the sources of Adam Smith's logistic method and creative principle, see Locke, *Second Treatise of Government,* pars. 40 and 42.

69. See Charles Darwin, *Origin of Species and The Descent of Man* (New York: Modern Library, n. d.). Darwin's sense of biological nature is materialistic in its ultimate presupposition. His central metaphors of competition and the survival of the fittest are functions of the real substrate, just as they were for Adam Smith. His text is that of a patient, logistic observer of an ecosystem. Darwin's text reveals a creative principle in its cardinal doctrine of the origin of new species in

biological evolution. (In all archic respects, therefore, Darwin produced another version of Epicurus's swerving atoms.) See Watson, *The Architectonics of Meaning*, Index, Darwin, p. 197 and references.

70. David Hume, *Enquiry Concerning Human Understanding*, sec. 4, pt. 2, in *Enquiries*, ed. Selby-Bigge and Nidditch.

71. See Hume, *A Treatise of Human Nature*, 2nd ed., ed. Selby-Bigge and Nidditch, Introduction, p. xvi.

72. Edward Gibbon, *The Decline and Fall of the Roman Empire*, 3 vols. (New York: The Modern Library, n. d.).

73. For Hume's existential sense of reality, see *A Treatise of Human Nature*, ed. Selby-Bigge and Nidditch, bk. 1, pt. 1, sec. 7.

74. Ibid., Appendix, pp. 661–62.

75. See George Berkeley, *Three Dialogues between Hylas and Philonous*, in *Philosophers Speak for Themselves: Berkeley, Hume, Kant*, ed. T. V. Smith and Marjorie Grene (Chicago: University of Chicago Press, 1940), pp. 1–95.

76. *Karl Jaspers: Basic Philosophical Writings, Selections*, ed. Leonard H. Ehrlich, Edith Ehrlich, and George B. Pepper (Athens: Ohio University Press, 1986), p. 21.

77. Ibid., p. 174.

78. Hume, *Enquiry Concerning Human Understanding*, sec. 12, pt. 2, p. 155; sec. 12, pt. 3.

79. Ibid., sec. 2, par. 13.

80. Ibid., sec. 7, pt. 1.

81. Hume, *A Treatise of Human Nature*, bk. 1, pt. 4, sec. 6.

82. Hume, *Enquiry Concerning Human Understanding*, sec. 5, pt. 1, pp. 43–44; sec. 5, pt. 2, pp. 54–55, and passim.

83. This is another place naturally to distinguish the types of skepticism found in the works of the Hellenistic skeptics, the Han critic Wang Ch'ung, and Hume. Hume calls himself a "moderate sceptic," and the reason for this lies in his archic profile. In intertextual analysis:

	PERSPECTIVE	REALITY	METHOD	PRINCIPLE
Skeptics	*objective*	*existential*	*agonistic*	*elemental*
Wang Ch'ung	*objective*	*substrative*	*agonistic*	*elemental*
Hume	*objective*	*existential*	*logistic*	*elemental*

84. Hume, *Enquiry Concerning the Principles of Morals*, sec. 1.

85. Ibid., sec. 5, pt. 2, pp. 219–20. See Hume, *A Treatise of Human Nature*, bk. 3, pt. 1, sec. 1, pp. 455–70; sec. 2, pp. 471–76.

86. Ibid., sec. 9, pt. 1. See also David Hume, *Dialogues Concerning Natural Religion*, ed. with intro. by Norman Kemp Smith (Indianapolis: Bobbs-Merrill Co., 1947).

87. David Hume, "My Own Life," in *Dialogues Concerning Natural Religion*, pp. 233–40.

88. Both Vico and Rousseau may be mentioned again in this historical context. Vico's men are driven out of the primeval forests by their reason, which is implanted and governed by a divine legislative act; they progress to civilized society in sequential phases. In "The Idea of a Jurisprudence of Mankind," Vico writes: "The cause of the just is not variable utility but eternal reason which, in immutable geometric and mathematical proportions, distributes the variable utilities upon the occasion of different human needs" (*The First New Science*, bk. 1, sec. 12, in *Vico, Selected Writings*, ed. and trans. by Leon Pompa [Cambridge: Cambridge University Press, 1982], p. 100). This "ideal eternal history" is reflected in three main stages of mankind: the poetic, heroic, and rational. He faults Descartes, and the tradition of political philosophy from Hobbes to Grotius, for taking its point of departure from the rational stage, instead of the true beginning in poetic mankind.

Rousseau's archic profile differs from Vico's as follows:

	PERSPECTIVE	REALITY	METHOD	PRINCIPLE
Vico	*disciplinary*	*substrative*	*logistic*	*reflexive*
Rousseau	*personal*	*substrative*	*dialectical*	*elemental*

In Rousseau's ideal state, the social compact is guided by the general will. The general will is the dialectical force of all individual wills providing that everyone is free to exercise his own will. "Each of us places his person and all his power in common under the supreme direction of the general will; and as one we receive each member as an indivisible part of the whole" (Jean-Jacques Rousseau, *On the Social Contract and Discourses*, ed. and trans. by Donald A. Cress, [Indianapolis: Hackett Publishing Company, 1983], p. 24.)

89. The archic profile of Montaigne (1533–92) is personal in perspective, substrative in reality, agonistic in method, and reflexive in principle; see Michel de Montaigne, *Essays*, trans. with intro. by J. M. Cohen (New York: Viking Penguin Classics, 1958). For Voltaire (1694–1778), see the selections in *The Portable Voltaire*, ed. by Ben Ray Redman (New York: Viking Press, 1949). An exception to this rule is Montesquieu, Charles Louis de Secondat (1689–1755), whose *Persian Letters* (1721), *De l'Esprit des Lois* (1748), and other writings are disciplinary in perspective, essential in sense of reality, agonistic in method, and reflexive in principle.

90. See Immanuel Kant, *Prolegomena to Any Future Metaphysics*, Preface, 260, trans. Paul Carus, revised by James W. Ellington (Indianapolis: Hackett Publishing Co., 1977), p. 5.

91. Kant, *Critique of Pure Reason*, A:805, B:833, p. 515.

8. The Changes of the Books in Nineteenth- and Twentieth-Century Thought

1. "But pure reason is a sphere so separate and self-contained that we cannot touch a part without affecting all the rest. We can therefore do nothing without first determining the position of each part and its relation to the rest. For inasmuch as our judgment cannot be corrected by anything outside of pure reason, so the validity and use of every part depends upon the relation in which it stands to all the rest within the domain of reason, just as in the structure of an organized body the end of each member can only be deduced from the full conception of the whole. It may, then, be said of such a critique that it is never trustworthy except it be perfectly complete, down to the smallest elements of pure reason. In the sphere of this faculty you can determine either everything or nothing" (Kant, *Prolegomena to Any Future Metaphysics*, 263–64, trans. L. W. Beck, p. 11). Kant clearly reasserts his synoptic method in the opening pages of his *Critique of Practical Reason*, trans. L. W. Beck (Indianapolis: Bobbs-Merrill Co., 1956), p. 10.

2. See J. G. Fichte, *The Science of Knowledge* (1794), "First Introduction," ed. and trans. Peter Heath and John Lachs (Cambridge: Cambridge University Press, 1970), pp. 3–28.

3. The word *agon* appears on the opening page of Nietzsche's first work, *The Birth of Tragedy from the Spirit of Music* (1872), which echoes Schopenhauer's *The World as Will and as Representation* (1818; final version, 1859). Nietzsche analogizes the dreamlike, or Apollonian, and the intoxicated, or Dionysian, aspects of experience after Schopenhauer's two foundational concepts—representation and will, respectively. Nietzsche interpreted the formations of classical Greek culture in the terms of a struggle between Apollonian and Dionysian forces. In later works, the *agon* between Apollonian and Dionysian forces is generally transmuted into an unresolvable tension between two physiologically based systems of morals—of good and bad, and of good and evil.

4. For Schopenhauer's repudiation of the Sophistic paradigm of rhetoric, see *The World as Will and as Representation*, 2 vols., trans. E. F. J. Payne (New York: Dover Publications, 1969), vol. 1, bk. 1, par. 9.

5. Reminiscing on the formative influences on his education, Peirce wrote around 1897: "I devoted two hours a day to the study of Kant's *Critic of the Pure Reason* for more than three years, until I almost knew the whole book by heart, and had critically examined every section of it" (*Collected Papers*, 1.3–14, cited from *Philosophical Writings of Peirce*, selected and ed. by Justus Buchler [New York: Dover, 1955], p. 2). Peirce adapted Kant's synoptic method of transcendental analysis to his own purposes of studying the holistic forms of theory formation, especially as illustrated in the history of the logical, mathematical, and physical sciences. This will be seen to be one of the net effects illustrated by Peirce's papers collected under the titles of "Philosophy and the Sciences: A

Classification," and "The Principles of Phenomenology," in *Philosophical Writings of Peirce*, pp. 42–97.

6. See Edmund Husserl, *Cartesian Meditations*, trans. Dorion Cairns (The Hague: Martinus Nijhoff, 1973).

7. For Husserl's archic profile, see Walter Watson, *The Architectonics of Meaning*, pp. 20, 65–66, 72.

8. C. S. Peirce, *Collected Papers*, 1.286, in *Philosophical Writings of Peirce*, ed. Justus Buchler (New York: Dover Publications, 1955), p. 75.

9. See Bertrand Russell, "Introduction," pp. 7–23, in Ludwig Wittgenstein, *Tractatus Logico-Philosophicus*, trans. C. K. Ogden (London: Routledge and Kegan Paul, 1922).

10. See Herman Saatkamp, Jr., "Santayana's Autobiography and the Development of His Philosophy," *Overheard in Seville: Bulletin of the Santayana Society*, no. 4 (Fall 1986): 21–27; and Angus Kerr-Lawson, "Spirit's Primary Nature is to be Secondary," *Overheard in Seville: Bulletin of the Santayana Society*, no. 2 (Fall 1984): 12.

11. See Angus Kerr-Lawson, "Six Aspects of Santayana's Philosophy," *Overheard in Seville: Bulletin of the Santayana Society*, no. 4 (Fall 1986): 32.

12. George Santayana, *Dialogues in Limbo* (New York: Charles Scribner's Sons, 1948).

13. J. G. Fichte, *The Science of Knowledge*, ed. and trans. Peter Heath and John Lachs, Translators' Preface, pp. vii–xviii.

14. Fichte plays out his dialectical method in *The Vocation of Man*, trans. Roderick M. Chisolm (Indianapolis: Bobbs-Merrill Co., 1956), where the realm of faith—that is, of the a priori domain of the idealistic, practical will—accomplishes a synthesis of the opposition between object and subject. See also J. G. Fichte, *The Science of Knowledge*, Translators' Preface, pp. xi–xiv, and Fichte's text, *passim*.

15. See Francis Herbert Bradley, *Appearance and Reality* (Oxford: Clarendon Press, 1893), bk. 2, chap. 24, "Degrees of Truth and Reality," pp. 318–54; he concludes chapter 27, "Ultimate Doubts," by asserting, "The presence of Reality in all appearances, but to different degrees, is the last word of philosophy" (pp. 488–89). Bradley's Platonic principle is also clearly evidenced in the introductory (pp. 1–4) and concluding (pp. 470–73) remarks of his *Essays on Truth and Reality* (Oxford: Clarendon Press, 1914).

16. For cited texts and a discussion of Einstein's archic profile, see chapter 3 above (Archic Prefigurations in the Presocratics), nn. 25 and 26; and Walter Watson, *The Architectonics of Meaning*, pp. 47, 75, 134, 152.

17. See George Santayana, *Egotism in German Philosophy* (New York: Charles Scribner's Sons, 1915).

18. Advocating moral will, Fichte writes: "To the idealist, the only positive thing is freedom; existence, for him, is a mere negation of the latter. On this condition alone does idealism have a firm foundation, and remains consistent with itself" (*The Science of Knowledge*, trans. Peter Heath and John Lachs, p. 69).

To Hegel, on the other hand, spiritual freedom must be historically embodied: "The truth is the whole. The whole, however, is merely the essential truth reaching its completeness through the process of its own development. Of the absolute it must be said that it is essentially a result, that only at the end is it what it is in very truth; and just in that consists its nature, which is to be actual, subject, or self-becoming, self-development" (*The Phenomenology of Mind*, Preface, trans. J. B. Baillie [New York: Harper and Row, 1967], pp. 81–82). See also G. W. F. Hegel, *The Philosophy of History*, trans. J. Sibree, with a new introduction by C. J. Friedrich (New York: Dover Publications, 1956).

19. Schelling's archic profile reappears below in chapter 9, "The World Religions," with a discussion of the texts of Hinduism, Sufism, and Neoplatonism. A lengthy discussion of a concept of the natural constellations of archic elements appears in chapter 10, "The Architecture of Theories."

20. See "Marx on the History of his Opinions" (preface to *A Contribution to the Critique of Political Economy*), pp. 3–6, "Discovering Hegel," pp. 7–8, and subsequent entries in *The Marx-Engels Reader*, 2nd. ed., ed. Robert C. Tucker (New York: W. W. Norton, 1978). Worth noting here is that Marx's archic text diverges from that of Locke only in its dialectical method (Locke's is logistic). The difference is decisive for the former's repudiation of Locke's concept of private property and, with that, the entire legal structure of "civil society." In another comparative profile, Marx's text resembles the archic text of Rousseau both in dialectical method and substrative sense of reality; but it diverges from the latter's personal perspective and elemental principle.

21. Soren Kierkegaard, *Concluding Unscientific Postcript*, trans. David F. Swenson and Walter Lowrie (Princeton: Princeton University Press, 1941), pp. 140–219. In *Fear and Trembling*, Kierkegaard's paradoxical logic and concept of incommensurable subjectivity are personified in the biblical Abraham. See *Kierkegaard's Writings*, vol. 6, ed. and trans. Howard V. Hong and Edna H. Hong (Princeton: Princeton University Press, 1983).

22. See Friedrich Nietzsche, *The Gay Science*, trans. Walter Kaufmann (New York: Vintage Press, 1974), p. 273 and *passim;* and *The Will to Power*, trans. Walter Kaufmann and R. J. Hollingdale (New York: Vintage Books, 1968), pp. 544–50.

23. See Nietzsche, *The Will to Power*, trans. Kaufmann and Hollingdale, p. 550. On Nietzsche's subjective perspectivism, see also *The Gay Science*, trans. Walter Kaufmann, p. 215, and *passim*. Schopenhauer's diaphanic perspective appears in *The World as Will and Representation*, vol. 1, bk. 4, "The World as Will: Second Aspect," and Appendix, "Criticism of the Kantian Philosophy."

24. Sigmund Freud, *Civilization and Its Discontents*, trans. James Strachey (New York: W. W. Norton and Co., 1961), p. 90, and *passim*. See James Strachey, ed., *The Standard Edition of the Complete Psychological Works of Sigmund Freud*, 24 vols. (London: Hogarth Press, 1953–74).

25. Freud, *An Autobiographical Study*, trans. James Strachey (New York: Norton and Co., 1952), pp. 109–10.

26. See Jacques Derrida, *Dissemination*, trans. Barbara Johnson (Chicago: University of Chicago Press, 1981), and other writings.

27. Ibid., p. 93, 133. Numerous texts can be cited to show the consistency of Derrida's form of articulation—that is, its own logocentrism. See, for example, Jacques Derrida, *Positions*, I, 36, cited in *Of Grammatology*, trans. Gayatri Chakravorty Spivak (Baltimore: Johns Hopkins University Press, 1976), Translator's Preface, p. lxxii; and Robert Magliola, *Derrida on the Mend* (West Lafayette: Purdue University Press, 1984), p. 191.

28. Ludwig Wittgenstein, *Philosophical Investigations*, 3d ed., trans. G. E. M. Anscombe, pt. 1, 19: "And to imagine a language means to imagine a form of life" (p. 8); pt. 1, 23: "But new types of language, new language-games, as we may say, come into existence, and others become obsolete and get forgotten" (p. 11); pt. 1, 24: "If you do not keep the multiplicity of language-games in view you will perhaps be inclined to ask questions like: 'What is a question?'" (p. 12); pt. 1, 38: "For philosophical problems arise when language goes on a holiday" (p. 19); pt. 1, 47: "But what are the simple constituent parts of which reality is composed?" (p. 21); pt. 1, 65: "Instead of producing something common to all that we call language, I am saying that these phenomena have no one thing in common which makes us use the same word for all,—but that they are related to one another in many different ways" (p. 31); pt. 1, 66: "Consider for example the proceedings that we call 'games.' . . .—but look and see whether there is anything common to all. . . . To repeat: don't think, but look!" (p. 31).

29. Wittgenstein's remark in the *Investigations* that "philosophical problems arise when language goes on holiday" (pt. 1, 38, p. 19) is essentially linked to his often-quoted "What is your aim in philosophy?—To shew the fly the way out of the fly-bottle" (pt. 1, 309, p. 103), and other such pronouncements that reenact the elemental principle of the Hellenistic Skeptics (the purpose of which is to achieve "tranquillity" or "insensibility" of mind by freeing one up from the dogmatism of views). Wittgenstein's advocacy of "silence," and the "senselessness" of his own propositions, in his *Tractatus*, are other instances of the skeptical principle that "determines nothing, not even the determining of nothing." The Buddhists, we saw, maintain the same theory, transformed however by a diaphanic perspective. Characteristically skeptical (in the archic sense we have established) are the following propositions in Ludwig Wittgenstein, *Tractatus Logico-Philosophicus*, trans. by C. K. Ogden (London: Routledge and Kegan Paul, Ltd., 1922), pp. 183–89: "All propositions are of equal value" (6.4.); "For all happening and being-so is accidental" (6.41); "It is clear that ethics cannot be expressed" (6.421); "How the world is, is completely indifferent for what is higher" (6.432); "The solution of the problem of life is seen in the vanishing of this problem" (6.521); "The right method of philosophy would be this. To say nothing except what can be said, i.e. the propositions of natural science, i.e. something that has nothing to do with philosophy" (6.53); "He must surmount these propositions; then he sees the world rightly" (6.54); "Whereof one cannot speak, thereof one must be silent" (7).

30. Jaspers's *Existenz*-philosophy shatters every man-centered interpretation of existence by a reorientation of philosophical thinking to the revelatory language of Being which takes place in our own existential world-being. Thus he writes that reading "the cipher-script" of his own self-transcending existence, his objects "become transparent language in such a way that they aim at me out of the Encompassing" and—conversely, by simultaneously being constituted by himself—"cast beams of light into the Encompassing" (Karl Jaspers, *Basic Philosophical Writings, Selections,* ed. Leonard H. Ehrlich, Edith Ehrlich, and George B. Pepper [Athens, Ohio: Ohio University Press, 1986], p. 174). See also pp. 159, 177, 192.

31. In the chapter below on the world religions.

32. See note 15 above. Bradley's existential focus is seen in his insistence that "Sentient experience, in short, is reality, and what is not this is not real" (*Appearance and Reality,* bk. 2, 14, "The General Nature of Reality," p. 127, and *passim*). Whitehead says that he was greatly influenced by Bradley's essay, "On Our Knowledge of Immediate Experience" (*Essays on Truth and Reality,* chap. 5, with Appendix, "Consciousness and Experience," and Supplementary Note, chaps. 6 and 7). Whitehead, however, transmuted Bradley's existential sense into an essentialist one, as exemplified by his doctrine of the ingression of eternal objects into the concrescent realities of actual occasions.

33. Alfred North Whitehead, *Process and Reality,* corrected ed., ed. David Ray Griffin and Donald W. Sherburne (New York: Free Press, 1978), pp. xii–xiii.

34. See Bradley, *Essays on Truth and Reality,* chap. 4, "On Truth and Practice"; chap. 5, "On Truth and Copying"; chap. 5, Appendix 1, "On the Ambiguity of Pragmatism"; chap. 5, Appendix 2, "On Professor James' 'Meaning of Truth' "; chap. 5, Appendix 3, "On Professor James' 'Radical Empiricism' "; pp. 65–158.

35. See *Collected Papers of Charles Sanders Peirce,* vols. 1–6, ed. by Charles Hartshorne and Paul Weiss, and vols. 7–8, ed. by Arthur W. Burks (Cambridge: The Belknap Press of Harvard University Press, 1931–58): "Chance is First, Law is Second, the tendency to take habits is Third; Mind is First, Matter is Second, Evolution is Third" (6.32). Looking at life phaneroscopically, Peirce everywhere discovers monadic, dyadic, and triadic experiences (1.351, 7.528); possibilities, events, and thoughts (1.431, 537); the immediate present, actual past, and generality of the future (1.343); originality, obsistence, and transuasion (2.89); presentness, struggle, and law (5.41, 45, 59); variety, uniformity, and passage from the first to the second (6.97); tychasm, anancasm, and agapasm (6.302); chance, logic, and love (1.409). These three "Kainopythagorean categories," as he calls them (7.528ff.), form the inner latticing of Peirce's thought, subtending its various special articulations. See also *Philosophical Writings of Peirce,* ed. Justus Buchler, chap. 6, "The Principles of Phenomenology," pp. 74–97. Peirce's text is essentialist in so marking generalities and teleological gradations of natural life and mind, and synoptic in defining their formal networking.

36. When Peirce came to name his philosophy, he said that tychism, or firstness, is subsidiary to continuity, or thirdness, and thus he called it synechism

(6.202). The governing assumption of Peirce's synechism is what he called "the principle of Habit," or "the self-development of Reason," or again, "thought as an active force in the world" (1.337, 340, 348). Peirce's entire text functions according to this noetic principle of progressive ordination, through which thought or reason develops in the universe (1.615). The principle of habit as the mind's—and the universe's—generalizing tendency, undergirds his various formulations of the spread, plasticity, and insistency of ideas, which are manifestations of evolution in the widest sense (1.390, 409, 621, 140; 6.204, 289). This law of the growth of mind functions in turn as the *lumen naturale,* the guiding light of active intellection in Kepler's instinctive judgments in science (1.80, 6.10). Evolution in this sense accounts for the very possibility of abduction, hypothesis-making, or retroductive reasoning rooted in the connaturality of mind and universe (1.81, 5.172, 7.46).

37. Nietzsche, *Beyond Good and Evil,* trans. Walter Kaufmann (New York: Vintage Books, 1966), par. 20, p. 27.

38. *Collected Papers of Charles Sanders Peirce,* 6.25; see also 1.362, 615.

39. See Martin Heidegger, *The End of Philosophy,* trans. Joan Stambaugh (New York: Harper and Row, 1973), pp. 32–33; "The Origin of the Work of Art," *Poetry, Language, and Thought,* trans. Albert Hofstadter (New York: Harper and Row, 1975), pp. 26ff.; "The Age of the World Picture," *The Question Concerning Technology and Other Essays,* trans. William Lovitt (New York: Garland Publishing, 1977), pp. 131 ff. See also Jacques Derrida, "The Ends of Man," trans. E. Morot-Sir, W. C. Piersol, H. L. Dreyfus, and B. Reid, *Philosophy and Phenomenological Research,* vol. 30, no. 1 (Sept. 1969): 31–57.

40. See Martin Heidegger, *Identity and Difference,* trans. Joan Stambaugh (New York: Harper and Row, 1969), pp. 36–41. Cf. Derrida, *Dissemination,* trans. Barbara Johnson, where Thoth (Derrida's symbol of deconstructive "writing") works precisely at "the subversive dislocation of identity in general, starting with that of theological regality" (p. 86). Derrida typically writes: "All the metaphysical determinations of truth, and even the one beyond metaphysical onto-theology that Heidegger reminds us of, are more or less immediately inseparable from the instance of *logos,* or of a reason thought within the lineage of *logos,* in whatever sense it is understood: in the pre-Socratic or the philosophical sense, or in the anthropological sense, in the pre-Hegelian and the post-Hegelian sense. Within this *logos,* the original and essential link to the *phoné* has never been broken" (*Of Grammatology,* trans. Gayarti Chakravorty Spivak, pp. 10–11).

41. Jaspers invests a new meaning in Kant's doctrine of Reason (*Vernunft*), and invokes it methodologically to accomplish a shipwrecking or foundering (*Schiffbruch*) of the human scientific understanding (*Verstand*). This finally entails *Existenz*'s opportunity to recover thought itself from the Kantian restrictions of its determinacy, "as a releasement to Being in its encompassing openness" (Karl Jaspers, *Basic Philosophical Writings,* ed. Leonard H. Ehrlich, Edith Ehrlich, and

George B. Pepper, p. 331). The same function of periontological *Vernunft* informs Jaspers's concept of the Axial Age, which he thematizes over against the objectifying modalities of modern scientific understanding (pp. 381ff.).

42. Edward Said's *Orientalism* (New York: Vintage Books, 1979) may be cited here. Although taking issue with Foucault's objective perspective (the French writer's notion of the "absent subject"), Said's "hybrid perpective" is broadly "anthropological," as he says, and engenders a species of deconstructive intellectual history (see Introduction, pp. 1–28, and esp. p. 23). Allan Bloom's *The Closing of the American Mind* (New York: Simon and Schuster, 1987) includes a critique of these various deconstructive efforts. Bloom remarks on "the American reconstruction of Heidegger" (pp. 226, 310), and portrays the field of comparative literature in America as "now fallen largely into the hands of a group of professors who are influenced by the post-Sartrean generation of Parisian Heideggerians, in paricular Derrida, Foucault, and Barthes" (p. 379).

43. *Collected Papers of Charles Sanders Peirce*, 5.121.

44. Ibid., 5.64.

45. See George Santayana, *Scepticism and Animal Faith* (New York: Dover Publications, 1955): "My system, finally, though, of course, formed under the fire of contemporary discussions, is no phase of any current movement. . . . It is not unwillingness to be a disciple that prompts me to look beyond the modern scramble of philosophies: I should gladly learn of them all, if they had learned more of one another. Even as it is, I endeavor to retain the positive insight of each, reducing it to the scale of nature and keeping it in its place; thus I am a Platonist in logic and morals, and a transcendentalist in romantic soliloquy, when I choose to indulge in it. Nor is it necessary, in being teachable by any master, to become eclectic. All these vistas give glimples of the same wood, and a fair and true map of it must be drawn to a single scale, by one method of projection, and in one style of calligraphy" (p. viii). Santayana presents the image of himself as a "soliloquist" and "wandering scholar" in his various writings.

46. James's personal perspective determines the sphere of relevance of his various writings. In *Pragmatism: A New Name for Some Old Ways of Thinking* (1907; New York: Meridian Books, 1955), it determines his portrayal of two types of mental make-up, the tender and tough minded (p. 22). Echoing a conspicuous tenet of his earlier *Principles of Psychology* (1890), James begins "The Types of Thinking," the first lecture of *A Pluralistic Universe* (1909), on the same note: "Different men find their minds more at home in very different fragments of the world" (p. 11). James's subjectively lived "each form," as distinguished from the "all form" of monistic theory, appears in the same work, pp. 34, 325, and *passim*. In *The Varieties of Religious Experience* (1902; New York: Collier Books, 1961) he says that he will take his point of departure not from anthropological and other institutional data, but from personal documents (pp. 22ff.); and he goes on to celebrate the subjective varieties of religious experience. Reminiscent

of Emerson and Walt Whitman, James typically writes that a personalistic theory that "makes the man seem as if he were individually helping to create the actuality of the truth whose metaphysical reality he is willing to assume, will be sure to be responded to in large numbers" (from "The Sentiment of Rationality," in John J. McDermott, ed., *The Writings of William James* [Chicago: Chicago University Press, 1977], p. 334).

47. The ontological focus of James's text is "radically empiricist," or existential. Thus to James, "pure experience" is always "the instant field of the present" (William James, *Essays in Radical Empiricism and a Pluralistic Universe* [New York: Longmans, Green and Co., 1955], p. 23). It is only a collective name for "all these sensible natures" (ibid., p. 27) of the empiricist universe that float and dangle like those dried human heads with which the Dyaks of Borneo deck their lodges (ibid., p. 46). They do not float and dangle in any essential order. Pure experience is rather "the stream of concretes, or the sensational stream," indefinitely multivariate in character, in which the conjunctive and the disjunctive parts are perfectly confluent (ibid., p. 95). It can figure "twice, thrice, or four times, or any number of times, by running into as many different mental contexts, just as the same point, lying at their intersection, can be continued into many different lines" (ibid., p. 80). Simultaneously, James's text presupposes a volitional principle, and in that respect asserts its relationship to the traditions of American biblical theology. In James's vision, the world is still pursuing its adventures and novelties are forever leaking in; the creation is still going on, and thus we are actively collaborating with God in the making of fact. We experience this "front edge" of pure experience in the lived immediacy of our own individual, energetic lives (ibid., pp. 181–82). He argues that such an existential philosophy harmonizes best with a radical pluralism, with novelty and indeterminism, moralism, theism, and humanism (ibid., p. 90).

48. For Santayana's discussion of Dewey's position, see especially George Santayana, *Obiter Scripta,* ed. Justus Buchler and Benjamin Schwartz (New York: Charles Scribner's Sons, 1936), "Dewey's Naturalistic Metaphysics," pp. 213–40. Santayana critiques Dewey's position as amounting to a "half-hearted and short-winded" naturalism, committed to "the dominance of the foreground" and other illusions of the mere surface of natural existence.

49. See the series of letters to James in Peirce's *Collected Papers,* vol. 8, chap. 6, pp. 186–213, which offer first-hand information of how one philosopher disagrees with the archic assumptions of another.

50. Santayana's opinion of his former teacher, William James, is revealed in his letters. See references to William James in the index to *The Letters of George Santayana,* ed. Daniel Cory (New York: Charles Schribner's Sons, 1955), p. 448; and especially see Letters, pp. 30, 61, 67, 76, 78, 81, 372. Santayana's chapter, "William James," in *Character and Opinion in the United States* (Garden City, N.Y.: Doubleday Anchor Books, n.d., pp. 39–59), first appeared in 1920. It is a critique of James's "agnostic" individualism and existentialism of the psychological flux. Earlier, in his *Three Philosophical Poets* (Cambridge: Harvard University Press,

1910, 5th impression, 1935), Santayana obliquely referred to James as he repudiated Goethe's Faust's turn to a life of "pure experience" (see pp. 198–99, 203). See also George Santayana, *Persons and Places*, critical edition, ed. William C. Holzberger and Herman J. Saatkamp, Jr. (Cambridge: MIT Press, 1987), p. 401.

51. George Santayana, *Dominations and Powers: Reflections on Liberty, Society, and Government* (New York: Charles Scribner's Sons, 1951), p. 27.

52. Hegel's chief contribution, Peirce opined, consists in his concept of generality or continuity, "the very idea the mathematicians and physicists have been chiefly engaged in following out for three centuries" (*Collected Papers*, 1.41–42). But Peirce rejected Hegel's dialectical method of sublation (5.90–91). Of his own category of thirdness Peirce wrote: "The third stage is very close indeed to Thirdness, which is substantially Hegel's *Begriff*. Hegel, of course, blundered monstrously, as we shall all be seen to do; but to my mind one fatal disease of his philosophy is that, seeing that the *Begriff* in a sense implies Secondness and Firstness, he failed to see that nevertheless they are elements of the phenomenon not to be *aufgehoben*, but as real and able to stand their ground as the *Begriff* itself" (8.268). Elsewhere Peirce characterizes Hegel's philosophy as follows: "The Hegelian philosophy is such an anancasticism. With its revelatory religion, with its synechism (however imperfectly set forth), with its 'reflection,' the whole idea of the theory is superb, almost sublime. Yet, after all, living freedom is practically omitted from its method. The whole movement is that of a vast engine, impelled by a *vis a tergo*, with a blind and mysterious fate of arriving at a lofty goal" (6.305). Hegel's archic profile—diaphanic in perspective, essentialist in ontological focus, dialectical in method, and reflexive in principle—recurs in Royce's text; see *The Philosophy of Josiah Royce*, ed. John K. Roth (Indianapolis: Hackett Publishing Co., 1982).

53. Ontologically speaking, an essence is inexhaustible—a resource for "indefinite" representation, amplification, ramification, or, in Peirce's own word, generalization in the intertextual process. But a distinguishing feature of a disciplinary perspective is the concomitant assumption that an essence can be seen as "finally" realized in true, good, and sufficient forms of cognition, action, or expression—and also retain its character as such a good form or function in natural and/or historical processes. (The "texts" of Aristotle, Rembrandt, Mozart, or Peirce, for example, are such historical accomplishments, whose generic traits continue to function as intertextual resources. But this point can be illustrated by any of the significant accomplishments in the sciences, arts, and crafts, from the invention of the wheel on down to the most sophisticated "texts" of contemporary life.) Here we are in agreement with F. H. Bradley and Dewey, among others, whose disciplinary perspectives motivate them to critique Peirce's semiotic of the indefinite "long run." For Dewey's critique, based on his definition of qualitative realization in consummatory experiences, see Ralph W. Sleeper, *The Necessity of Pragmatism* (New Haven: Yale University Press, 1987), p. 140.

54. Santayana, *Dominations and Powers*, pp. vi–vii.

9. The World Religions

1. Sigmund Freud, *Civilization and Its Discontents,* trans. James Strachey (New York: W. W. Norton and Co., 1961), pp. 47ff.

2. Plato *Phaedrus* 242c, trans. R. Hackforth, in *The Collected Dialogues of Plato.*

3. Hegel, *The Phenomenology of Mind,* trans. J. Baillie (New York: Harper and Row, 1967), pp. 789–908.

4. Martin Heidegger, *Identity and Difference,* trans. with intro. Joan Stambaugh (New York: Harper and Row, 1969), pp. 14, 36–41. Joan Stambaugh points out (p. 14) that the etymology of *Ereignis,* event, derives from *er-eignen,* with the senses of *eigen* (to own, and thus to come into one's own, to come to where one belongs), and *er-äugnen* (*Auge,* eye, thus to catch sight of, to see with the mind's eye, to see face-to-face). In "Heidegger and the Limits of Representation" (paper delivered at the Society for Phenomenological and Existential Philosophy conference, Chicago, October 1985), Dorothea Olkowski clarifies this point by citing Craig Owen's characterization of the classical system of representation as presupposing the presence in absence of an absolutely sovereign person. Human sovereignty is only an abrogation of this higher Sovereignty that reveals itself through the *Ereignis* to which Heidegger's text bears witness.

5. *Karl Jaspers: Basic Philosophical Writings, Selections,* ed. Leonard H. Ehrlich, Edith Ehrlich, and George B. Pepper (Athens, Ohio: Ohio University Press, 1986), pp. 24, 204, 212, 330–35.

6. Ibid., p. 206.

7. See Mark Musa, "An Introduction to Dante and His Works," in *Dante: The Divine Comedy,* vol. 1: *Inferno* (New York: Penguin Classics, 1984), pp. 15–56. For Dante's authorial perspective, see the cast of persons, beginning with Dante himself, in the *Divina Commedia.* The entire work illustrates the poet's personal loves, hates, hopes, and politics. But Dante's archic profile, as seen in his other poetical and political writings, is disciplinary, noumenal, synoptic, and reflexive. His career-text, a system of justice for this life and the next, is isomorphic with those of Aquinas and Kant.

8. See Albert Einstein, *The World as I See It,* pp. 26–29; John Dewey, *A Common Faith* (New Haven: Yale University Press, 1934), pp. 1–28, 59–87.

9. *The Bhagavad Gita,* trans. Franklin Edgerton (Cambridge: Harvard University Press, 1944), chap. 8, v. 18, and *A Sourcebook in Indian Philosophy,* ed. Sarvepalli Radhakrishnan and Charles A. Moore (Princeton: Princeton University Press, 1957), p. 130. In traditional classification systems the Carvaka, Jaina, and Buddhist systems were defined as heterodox for not accepting the authority of the Vedas and Upanishads. All three appear to be agonistically heterodox, both in opposition to Hinduism and in their internal discursive forms. The Carvaka school considers wealth and sensual pleasure the only ends of life. It mounts a strong attack against logistic inference; this deconstructive function is carried over into the Jain and Buddhist schools, which emphasize logics of perspectival and semantic differences. The Carvaka-vada is objective in perspective, sub-

strative in reality, and elemental in principle. The Jainist and Buddhist schools appear to have diaphanic perspectives and elemental principles; the Jainist texts appear to have noumenal realities; while the Buddhist texts are generally existential in ontological reference (some Hinayana and Pure Land Schools appear to be noumenal). See *A Sourcebook in Indian Philosophy*, ed. Radhakrishnan and Moore, pp. 227–346.

10. Hegel, *The Phenomenology of Mind*, trans. J. B. Baillie, p. 79.

11. Schelling, *Philosophical Inquiries into the Nature of Human Freedom*, trans. James Gutman, p. 34. On the relation between Schelling and Hegel, see F. W. J. Schelling, *Bruno, or On the Natural and the Divine Principle of Things*, ed. and trans. with an introduction by Michael J. Vater, pp. 81–97.

12. For the Sufi tradition, see Fakhruddin 'Iraqi, *Divine Flashes*, trans. and intro. by William C. Chittick and Peter Lamborn Wilson (New York: Paulist Press, 1982).

13. Ibid., pp. 63–64.

14. See Schelling, *Bruno, or On the Natural and the Divine Principle of Things*, pp. 3–112.

15. Plotinus *Enneads* 5.2.11.1, in *The Essential Plotinus*, trans. Elmer O'Brien (Indianapolis: Hackett Publishing Co., 1964). In effect, Plotinus assimilates the principles of Plato, Aristotle, and the Stoics by returning to the One of Parmenides, while otherwise retaining Plato's diaphanic perspective, noumenal reality, and dialectical method. *Enneads* 1.3.20 is devoted in its entirety to the dialectical powers of the soul. Plotinus' Parmenidean (that is, Democritean) principle is illustrated in *Enneads* 1.6.1.7, 1.6.1.9, 6.9.9.2, 6.9.9.3, and 6.9.9.5.

16. See Plotinus *Enneads* 6.9.9.9 and 6.9.9.11.

17. See Nishida Kitarō, *Last Writings: Nothingness and the Religious Worldview*, trans. with an introduction by David A. Dilworth (Honolulu: University of Hawaii Press, 1987), Index, Kierkegaard, p. 153 and references.

18. See Keiji Nishitani, *Religion and Nothingness*, trans. Jan Van Bragt (Los Angeles: University of California Press, 1982). In addition to Nishitani's text, see also the entries in Van Bragt's glossary under "*sive*" (*soku*) and "*sive/non*" (*soku hi*), and further references in chap. 5, n. 19, p. 291. Other works of the Kyoto School include Tanabe Hajime, *Philosophy as Metanoetics*, trans. Takeuchi Yoshinori, with Valdo Viglielmo and James W. Heisig (Berkeley and Los Angeles: University of California Press, 1986); Takeuchi Yoshinori, *The Heart of Buddhism*, ed. and trans. James W. Heisig, (New York: Crossroad Publishing Co., 1983); Masao Abe, *Zen and Western Thought*, ed. William LaFleur (London: Macmillan Press Ltd., 1985).

19. We can compare these with a genre of Buddhist literature which centers on "questions which tend not to edification." In a typical early Buddhist text: "These theories which The Blessed One has left unelucidated, has set aside and rejected—that the world is eternal, that the world is not eternal, that the world is finite, that the world is infinite, that the soul and the body are identical, that the soul is one thing and the body another, that the saint exists after death, that the

saint does not exist after death, that the saint both exists and does not exist after death,—these The Blessed One does not elucidate to me" (Sutta 63, *Majjhima-Nikaya,* in *Buddhism in Translation,* trans. Henry Clarke Warren [New York: Atheneum Press, 1976]). Still, these are the teachings of The Blessed One, whose enlightenment is shared by all expositors of the truth of Buddhism. The *Prajnaparamita Sutra* literature, its philosophical exposition by Nagarjuna, and all the later writers in this tradition down to Nishida and the Kyoto School followed suit in producing versions of this diaphanic Skepticism. The archic difference is that the Skeptics and Wittgenstein have objective perspectives, while all Buddhist texts have diaphanic ones.

20. Saint Shinran, founder of the Japanese True Pure Land school (*Jōdo shinshū*), is portrayed in Nishida and the other Kyoto School writers as having propounded an existential form of Pure Land teaching. Existential Zen masters—Dōgen and Hakuin, for example—are generally to be found denouncing the not-of-this-world soteriology of the Pure Land teachings.

21. Richard Robinson, *The Buddhist Religion: A Historical Introduction* (Belmont, Calif.: Dickenson Publishing Co., 1970), pp. 51–52.

22. See Gadjin Nagao, "On the Theory of the Buddha-body (*Buddha-kaya*)," trans. Umeyo Hirano, *The Eastern Buddhist,* n.s. 6, no. 1 (May 1973): 45–53. In Zen, the Bliss-body (*sambhogakaya*) is interpreted existentially, while in Pure Land it has a noumenal signification.

23. In a previous chapter we noted that Jaspers's archic profile is isomorphic with Berkeley's, differing only in its post-Kantian formulation of the phenomenality of being. In this context it is relevant to note that Jaspers, while acknowledging a general similarity with the text of Buddhism, sharply attacked its "principle of indifference." In archic terms, he displaced Buddhism's elemental principle with his own creative principle. See *Karl Jaspers: Basic Philosophical Writings, Selections,* ed. Leonard H. Ehrlich, Edith Ehrlich, and George B. Pepper, pp. 419, 427, 431, 432–33.

24. In chapter 3 above, we noted that the Skeptics transmuted the pure Sophistic paradigm by introducing an elemental principle. The standard Buddhist text further contracts the Sophistic paradigm. These intertextual relations can be summarized as follows:

	PERSPECTIVE	REALITY	METHOD	PRINCIPLE
Sophists	*personal*	*existential*	*agonistic*	*creative*
Skeptics	*objective*	*existential*	*agonistic*	*elemental*
Buddhists	*diaphanic*	*existential*	*agonistic*	*elemental*

In these terms the Buddhists are diaphanic Skeptics, and thus the true religious Pyrrhonians in the history of philosophy. See also n. 19 above.

25. See *The Zen Teaching of Rinzai,* trans. Irmgard Schloegl (Berkeley: Sham-

bhala, 1976); Chang Chung-yuan, *The Original Teachings of Ch'an Buddhism* (New York: Pantheon, 1969).

26. See Nishida Kitarō, "The Logic of the Place of Nothingness and the Religious Worldview," sec. 2, trans. David A. Dilworth, in *Last Writings: Nothingness and the Religious Worldview*, pp. 68–70, and passim.

27. Ibid., pp. 24, 82, 89.

28. Ibid., pp. 125–26. See n. 18 above.

29. See William R. LaFleur, *The Karma of Words: Buddhism and the Literary Arts in Medieval Japan* (Berkeley and Los Angeles: University of California Press, 1983). Our comparative hermeneutic allows us to open this topic up to a wider analysis. Limiting the discussion to the ontologies found in the Nara, Heian, Kamakura, Muromachi, and Tokugawa eras, we find four forms coexisting in each of these periods: (1) an existential worldview, taking a religious form in Tendai, Shingon, and Zen materials, and a secularized form in such works as Murasaki Shikibu's *The Tale of Genji* and Sei Shōnagon's *The Pillow Book;* (2) noumenal religious orientation, as in some of the Japanese Pure Land schools; (3) a worldly, moral essentialism exemplified by the Confucian and Neo-Confucian traditions in Japan; and (4) a naturalistic, substrative strain. This last ontological focus typically appears in the various Shinto religions. As the force of human instinct and passion, this substrative sense of reality is prominent in the secular literary arts of Japan. Thus various forms of erotic, nostalgic, karmically retributive, and *yūgen*-type literature—from the earliest poetic anthology, the *Manyōshū*, through such later poets as Saigyō and Bashō, a considerable number of the *nō* plays, the lampooning literature of *kyōgen*, the many expression of *ukiyo* art and literature in the Tokugawa era, to the works of such modern writers as Akutagawa Ryūnosuke, Nagai Kafū, Kawabata Yasunari, Dasai Osamu, Yukio Mishima, and others—can be accounted for in these terms. In short, all four ontological orientations, taking different forms and names, are interwoven in the fabric of each of the major historical epochs of Japanese civilization up to the present.

30. See David Hume, *Enquiry Concerning Human Understanding*, sec. 10, pt. 2, par. 101, in *Enquiries Concerning Human Understanding and Concerning the Principles of Morals.*

31. See Thomas Aquinas, *On Being and Essence*, trans. Armand Maurer (Toronto: Pontifical Institute of Medieval Studies, 1949); *Basic Writings of St. Thomas Aquinas*, 2 vols., ed. A. Pegis (New York: Random House, 1945); Frederick Copleston, *A History of Philosophy*, bk. 1, vol. 2, "Augustine to Scotus" (Garden City, N.Y.: Doubleday, Image Books, 1985), pp. 309, 313ff., 423ff.

32. Leibniz, *Discourse on Metaphysics*, secs. 1–6, in *The Rationalists*, trans. George Montgomery (Garden City, N.Y.: Dolphin Books, 1960), pp. 410–15.

33. Alfred North Whitehead, pt. 2, lecture 6, "Civilized Universe," in *Modes of Thought* (New York: Capricorn Books, 1938), p. 142. In *Modes of Thought*, pt. 1, lecture 2, "Expression," Whitehead is referring to Genesis when he writes:

"This lecture is nothing else than a modern rendering of the oldest of civilized reflections on the development of the Universe as seen from the perspective of life on this earth. . . . There is evidence that three thousand years ago there were deep thinkers, enmeshed as to their imaginations in the trivial modes of presentation belonging to their own days" (pp. 55–56). For Whitehead's archic profile, see Watson, *The Architectonics of Meaning*, Index, p. 205, and references.

34. Whitehead, *Process and Reality*, corrected ed., ed. David Ray Griffin and Donald W. Sherburne (New York: Free Press, 1978), pt. 5, chap. 2, "God and the World," pp. 342–352.

35. Ibid., p. 40: "By this recognition of the divine element the general Aristotelian principle is maintained that, apart from things that are actual, there is nothing—nothing either in fact or in efficacy. This is the true general principle which also underlies Descartes' dictum: 'For this reason, when we perceive any attribute, we therefore conclude that some existing thing or substance to which it may be attributed, is necessarily present.'" In Whitehead's text, because of the ingression of eternal objects in degrees of relevance, all actual occasions are essential realities, whose dialectically evolving realizations contribute, both actually and potentially, to the gradated "creative advance" of the universe. Those commentators who strip Whitehead's text of its doctrine of God, or again of eternal objects, transform his ontology into something else.

10. The Architecture of Theories

1. Immanuel Kant, *Critique of Pure Reason*, A:xiii, trans. Norman Kemp Smith (New York: St. Martin's Press, 1965), p. 10.

2. Ibid., B:xiii, p. 20.

3. Kant, *Critique of Pure Reason*, A:831, B:860, trans. F. Max Müller (Garden City: Doubleday and Co., 1966), p. 530.

4. Ibid., A:850–53, B:878–81, pp. 541–43.

5. Ibid., A:831, B:860, p. 530.

6. Peirce regarded his own writings architectonically: "But I seem to myself," he wrote to William James in 1902, "to be the sole depositary of the completely developed system, which all hangs together and cannot receive any proper presentation in fragments." See *Collected Papers of Charles Sanders Peirce*, vol. 7–8, ed. Arthur W. Burks (Cambridge: The Belknap Press of Harvard University Press, 1931, 1958).

7. *Philosophical Writings of Peirce*, selected and ed. with intro. by Justus Buchler (New York: Dover, 1955), p. 315; *Collected Papers*, 6.7–25.

8. The following passage is therefore obliquely autobiographical: "That systems ought to be constructed architectonically has been preached since Kant, but I do not think the full import of the maxim has by any means been apprehended. What I would recommend is that every person who wishes to form an opinion concerning fundamental problems should first of all make a complete

survey of human knowledge, should take note of all the valuable ideas in each branch of science, should observe in just what respect each has been successful and where it has failed, in order that, in the light of the thorough acquaintance so attained of the available materials for a philosophical theory and of the nature and strength of each, he may proceed to the study of what the problems of philosophy consist in, and of the proper way of solving it" (ibid., p. 316).

9. Ibid., p. 72; *Collected Papers,* 1.176–78.

10. Kant, *Critique of Pure Reason,* A:839, B:867, p. 534.

11. Ibid.

12. Building on the work of Richard McKeon, Watson began by taking over McKeon's three categories of principle, method, and interpretation. Watson achieved a more flexible typology that agreed with Aristotle's doctrine of the four causes. In Watson's analysis, McKeon's voluminous career-text proves to be disciplinary in perspective, essentialist in sense of reality, agonistic in method, and reflexive in principle.

13. Walter Watson, *The Architectonics of Meaning: Foundations of the New Pluralism,* pp. 151–70.

14. It would take a separate study to fully compare, for example, the hermeneutical flexibility generated by Watson's archic matrix with that of Stephen Pepper's *World Hypotheses, A Study in Evidence* (Berkeley and Los Angeles: University of California Press, 1957). Pepper distinguishes four (later five) "root metaphors" that underwrite autonomous, mutually exclusive "world hypotheses" in the history of philosophy. Pepper's set is comprised of (1) formism, whose root metaphor is similarity, and whose theory of truth is correspondence (Plato, Aristotle, the Scholastics); (2) mechanism, whose root metaphor is a machine, combining correspondence and operational theories of truth (Lucretius, Hobbes, Locke, Berkeley, Hume, Descartes, Russell); (3) contextualism, whose root metaphor is the historic event, and whose theory of truth is operational or pragmatic (Peirce, James, Dewey, Bergson, Mead); (4) organicism, whose root metaphor is organism, and whose theory of truth is coherence (Hegel, Bradley, Whitehead). (For the wording of this synopsis of Pepper's "metatext" I am indebted to the unpublished work of Edward Marcotte.) Like Watson, Pepper recommends that we do not fall into the dogmatism of neglecting any one of these essential types; but Pepper's more limited set of (four) definitions compresses together textual materials and their first principles which are naturally distinguishable by Watson's set. Pepper also dismisses certain world hypotheses—such as mysticism and skepticism—as inadequate. See n. 22 below.

15. Watson, *The Architectonics of Meaning,* pp. 154–55, 167, and passim.

16. Aristotle *De Anima* 3.2.434a16, trans. J. A. Smith, in *The Basic Works of Aristotle,* ed. Richard McKeon (New York: Random House, 1941).

17. Ibid., 3.6.430b24–25.

18. Ibid., 3.5.430a20–22, 431a1–3.

19. Watson, *The Architectonics of Meaning,* p. 154.

20. Ibid.

21. "For why does a man walk to Megara and not stay at home, when he thinks he ought to be walking there? Why does he not walk early some morning into a well or over a precipice, if one happens to be in the way? Why do we observe him guarding against this, evidently because he does not think that falling in is alike good and not good? . . . Therefore, as it seems, all men make unqualified judgments, if not about all things, still about what is better or worse" (Aristotle *Metaphysics* 4.4.1008b10–25, trans. David Ross in *Basic Works of Aristotle*, ed. Richard McKeon); "Again, however much all things may be 'so and not so', still there is a more or less in the nature of things. . . . If then that which has more of any quality is nearer the norm, there must be some truth to which the more true is nearer. And even if there is not, still there is already something better founded and liker the truth, and we shall have got rid of the unqualified doctrine which would prevent us from determining anything in our thought" (4.4.1009a1–5).

22. Another feature of Watson's archic matrix is that it allows us to overcome the dichotomy between "philosophical" and "metaphilosophical" texts. The latter concept recurs throughout the history of philosophy and generally consists of Sophistic and/or Skeptical elements. Many of the current self-styled postmodern texts insinuate such a dichotomy, while proclaiming the closure of the traditional philosophical enterprise. Examples include the metatexts of Stephen Pepper, Collingwood, Wittgenstein, Thomas Kuhn, Foucault, Derrida, and Lyotard, among others. For a recent example of such a metatext, see Jean-François Lyotard, *The Postmodern Condition: A Report on Knowledge*, trans. Geoff Bennington and Brian Massumi (Minneapolis: University of Minnesota Press, 1984). In our intertextual hermeneutic, however, the semantic factors of all these texts are subject to archic analysis. (Lyotard's discourse, like Foucault's, has three Sophistic elements, with an objective perspective).

23. This notation is employed here as an organizational model in the service of a synoptic ordering of the world-texts. The simple arithmetical ratios (4:0, 3:1, etc.) are not essential to the argument—they can be transposed into any other such comparative set.

24. The simple numerical ratios (4:0, 3:1, and so on) do not bring out the complete picture. The world-texts with a preponderance of Sophistic elements can be judged to be inferior to those with a higher proportion of the other archic elements. Compare for example the 3:1 texts of Kant, Chu Hsi, Locke, and Voltaire. Voltaire's text, which is elementally Sophistic, advises one to cultivate one's own garden. However wise Voltaire's counsel may be, the texts of Kant, Chu Hsi, and Locke articulate more encompassing programs of human thought, behavior, and expression.

25. See Justus Buchler, *Metaphysics of Natural Complexes* (New York: Columbia University Press, 1966), pp. 17–29, and *passim*. Buchler's concept of "natural complexes" is itself a generalization of descriptions of human experience (called "proceptive experience") in such earlier works as *Nature and Judgment* (New

York: Columbia University Press, 1965), and *The Concept of Method* (New York: Columbia University Press, 1961).

26. See Friedrich Nietzsche, *The Birth of Tragedy*, in *The Birth of Tragedy and The Genealogy of Morals*, trans. Francis Golffing (Garden City, N.Y.: Doubleday and Co., 1956), p. 91.

27. See Alfred Einstein, *Mozart: His Character, His Works*, trans. Arthur Mendel and Nathan Broder (London: Grafton Books, 1971), p. 53. For the philosophical quality of Mozart's outlook on life see also Wolfgang Hildesheimer, *Mozart*, trans. Marion Faber (New York: Vintage Books, 1983), and H. C. Robbins Landon, *1791: Mozart's Last Year* (New York: Schirmer Books, 1988), p. 10. Archic analysis has a bright future in establishing the comparative profiles of the artistic texts of higher civilization.

Index